A QUESTION OF SEX?

Hebrew Bible Monographs, 14

Series Editors
David J.A. Clines, J. Cheryl Exum, Keith W. Whitelam

Editorial Board
A. Graeme Auld, Marc Brettler, Francis Landy,
Hugh S. Pyper, Stuart D.E. Weeks

A Question of Sex?

Gender and Difference in the Hebrew Bible and Beyond

edited by
Deborah W. Rooke

SHEFFIELD PHOENIX PRESS

2009

Copyright © 2007, 2009 Sheffield Phoenix Press

First published in hardback 2007
First published in paperback 2009

Published by Sheffield Phoenix Press
Department of Biblical Studies, University of Sheffield
Sheffield S10 2TN

www.sheffieldphoenix.com

All rights reserved.
No part of this publication may be reproduced or transmitted in any form or by any means, electronic or mechanical, including photocopying, recording or any information storage or retrieval system, without the publishers' permission in writing.

A CIP catalogue record for this book
is available from the British Library

Typeset by CA Typesetting Ltd
Printed on acid-free paper by Lightning Source UK Ltd, Milton Keynes

ISBN 978-1-906055-20-2 (hardback)
ISBN 978-1-906055-93-6 (paperback)
ISSN 1747-9614

CONTENTS

Preface — vii
List of Abbreviations — ix
List of Contributors — xi

PART I
METHODOLOGICAL CONSIDERATIONS

GENDER CRITICISM:
A NEW DISCIPLINE IN BIBLICAL STUDIES OR FEMINISM IN DISGUISE?
  Deborah F. Sawyer — 2

PART II
GENDER IN LAW AND RITUAL

THE BARE FACTS: GENDER AND NAKEDNESS IN LEVITICUS 18
  Deborah W. Rooke — 20

GENDER CRITICAL OBSERVATIONS ON TRIPARTITE
BREEDING RELATIONSHIPS IN THE HEBREW BIBLE
  Bernard S. Jackson — 39

THEIR HEART CRIED OUT TO GOD: GENDER AND PRAYER IN THE BOOK
OF LAMENTATIONS
  Amy Kalmanofsky — 53

BATHING, STATUS AND GENDER IN PRIESTLY RITUAL
  Nicole J. Ruane — 66

PART III
ETHNOLOGICAL AND ANTHROPOLOGICAL APPROACHES TO GENDER

CONTESTING THE NOTION OF PATRIARCHY: ANTHROPOLOGY
AND THE THEORIZING OF GENDER IN ANCIENT ISRAEL
  Carol Meyers — 84

THE SILENCED SONGS OF VICTORY: POWER, GENDER
AND MEMORY IN THE CONQUEST NARRATIVE OF JOSHUA (JOSHUA 1–12)
  Ovidiu Creangă — 106

PART IV
GENDER IN POST-BIBLICAL LITERATURE

WOMEN IN THE APOCRYPHA AND THE PSEUDEPIGRAPHA
   Tal Ilan   126

FROM WILD MEN TO WISE AND WICKED WOMEN: AN INVESTIGATION INTO MALE HETEROSEXUALITY IN SECOND TEMPLE INTERPRETATIONS OF THE LADIES WISDOM AND FOLLY
   Andrew Angel   145

GENIZAH MARRIAGE CONTRACTS:
CONTRASTING BIBLICAL LAW AND HALAKHAH WITH MEDIAEVAL PRACTICE
   Rebecca Jefferson   162

Index of References   174
Index of Authors   181

PREFACE

The papers in this volume have emerged from the proceedings of a conference held at King's College London between 31 July and 2 August 2006, with the title 'A Question of Sex? Gender and Difference in the Hebrew Bible'. The conference was arranged in order to meet the perceived need for a UK-based arena in which to explore how an awareness of gender critical issues might impinge upon study of the Hebrew Bible and associated literature. The response of those who attended the conference confirmed that this initial perception was correct; several participants commented that they had been looking for just such a gathering in vain, and expressed the fervent hope that this one would be repeated in some form. In the light of this, and of the number of enquiries received from other interested parties who were unable to attend the conference, it seems entirely appropriate that the academic fruits of the conference should be made available to a wider audience via publication.

Since in the context of biblical study gender criticism is more correctly thought of as an approach to the text rather than as a subject area in itself, the topic areas were selected in order to encourage a broad and inclusive spread of material, thereby demonstrating the exciting range of possibilities for interpretation when gender-critical issues are taken into account. It is hoped that the resulting variety of content will act as an inspiration to others to consider their own particular areas of interest from a gender-critical perspective. Gender is one of the most fundamental, and can be one of the most overlooked, aspects of our existence as human beings, and the influence of gender-based conceptions is all-pervasive. An awareness of how culturally-determined understandings of gender have shaped human societies and artefacts, including textual artefacts such as the Hebrew Bible and associated literature, is therefore vital if we are even to begin to appreciate the multi-layered complexities and fathom some of the depths of meaning inherent in those artefacts. The present collection evidences how a gender-critical approach can indeed uncover new depths of meaning and highlight new dimensions in ostensibly familiar or monochromatic texts and situations.

The structure of the book reproduces the structure of the conference, in which there were three main sections, preceded by a methodological overview. For the overview and for each of the main sections, there was a paper from a keynote speaker in the area. Each of the keynote papers for the three main sections was then followed by several shorter papers. Papers were allocated to the section which seemed most suitable for them, taking into account the authors' views of where their papers fitted and the content and spread of material in each section. The allocations were not intended to be definitive, however, and it is recognized that papers might legitimately have been placed in other sections. Nonetheless the present arrangement seems to make sense, and hopefully will not prevent readers from finding the material in which they are particularly interested.

Finally, some words of thanks. I am extremely grateful to the British Academy, from which a grant was obtained to cover the expenses of the keynote speakers, and to King's College London School of Humanities Research Grant fund, which also offered financial support for the conference. Thanks are also due to Moira Langston and Carys Alder, who took on the administrative burdens of the conference with great efficiency alongside an already-hectic work schedule. Especial thanks are due to the person whose ideas and enthusiasm resulted in the conference being arranged, namely Sandra Jacobs, at the time of the conference a graduate student at King's College London. Sandra not only made suggestions for topics and keynote speakers, but did a huge amount of work in publicizing the conference and getting it mentioned on various international websites, as a result of which a gratifying proportion of the speakers and participants were from abroad. I am personally very grateful to her for everything she did to make the conference a success; indeed, were it not for her the whole thing might never have happened. And if the rapidly developing vision of a regular conference on gender and the Hebrew Bible at King's College London comes to fruition, many more people will be in her debt than just those who attended the 2006 conference.

Deborah W. Rooke
September 2006

ABBREVIATIONS

AB	Anchor Bible
ABD	David Noel Freedman (ed.), *The Anchor Bible Dictionary* (New York: Doubleday, 1992)
ABRL	Anchor Bible Research Library
ALGHJ	Arbeiten zur Literatur und Geschichte des hellenistischen Judentums
AnBib	Analecta biblica
BA	*Biblical Archaeologist*
BAGD	Walter Bauer, *A Greek-English Lexicon of the New Testament and Other Early Christian Literature* (trans. William F. Arndt and F. Wilbur Gingrich; rev. and aug. F. Wilbur Gingrich and Frederick W. Danker; Chicago: University of Chicago Press, 1958).
BASOR	*Bulletin of the American Schools of Oriental Research*
BBB	Bonner biblische Beiträge
BHS	K. Elliger and W. Rudolph (eds.), *Biblia Hebraica Stuttgartensia* (Stuttgart: Deutsche Bibelgesellschaft, 1967–77)
BibInt	*Biblical Interpretation*
BibOr	Biblica et orientalia
BJS	Brown Judaic Studies
BTC	Bible in the Twenty-First Century
BZ	*Biblische Zeitschrift*
BZAW	Beihefte zur *Zeitschrift für die alttestamentliche Wissenschaft*
CBC	Cambridge Bible Commentary
CBQ	*Catholic Biblical Quarterly*
CBQMS	*Catholic Biblical Quarterly* monograph series
CRB	Cahiers de la Revue biblique
CSCO	Corpus scriptorum christianorum orientalium
DJD	Discoveries in the Judaean Desert
EJL	Early Judaism and its Literature
ESHM	European Seminar in Historical Methodology
EJL	Early Judaism and its Literature
FCB	Feminist Companion to the Bible
FCB 2	Feminist Companion to the Bible, Second Series
FOTL	Forms of Old Testament Literature
GCT	Gender, Culture, Theory
HALOT	Ludwig Köhler and Walter Baumgartner, *The Hebrew and Aramaic Lexicon of the Old Testament* (rev. Walter Baumgartner and Johann Jakob Stamm; trans. and ed. M.E.J. Richardson; 5 vols.; Leiden:E.J. Brill, 1994–2000).
HSM	Harvard Semitic Monographs
HTR	*Harvard Theological Review*
HUCA	*Hebrew Union College Annual*
IEJ	*Israel Exploration Journal*

ICC	International CriticalCommentary
JAOS	*Journal of the American Oriental Society*
JBL	*Journal of Biblical Literature*
JJS	*Journal of Jewish Studies*
JNES	*Journal of Near Eastern Studies*
JQR	*Jewish Quarterly Review*
JR	*Journal of Religion*
JSJ	*Journal for the Study of Judaism*
JSNT	*Journal for the Study of the New Testament*
JSOT	*Journal for the Study of the Old Testament*
JSOTSup	*Journal for the Study of the Old Testament*, Supplement Series
JSP	*Journal for the Study of the Pseudepigrapha*
JSPSup	*Journal for the Study of the Pseudepigrapha*, Supplement Series
JSS	*Journal of Semitic Studies*
NCB	New Century Bible
NCBC	New Cambridge Bible Commentary
NIBCOT	New International Biblical Commentary: Old Testament
NICOT	New International Commentary on the Old Testament
NJPS	New Jewish Publication Society translation
NTS	*New Testament Studies*
OBT	Overtures to Biblical Theology
OTL	Old Testament Library
OTS	*Oudtestamentische Studiën*
PAAJR	*Proceedings of the American Academy for Jewish Research*
PEQ	*Palestine Exploration Quarterly*
RevQ	*Revue de Qumran*
RHR	*Revue de l'histoire des religions*
RSV	Revised Standard Version
SBLDS	Society of Biblical Literature Dissertation Series
SBLEJL	Society of Biblical Literature Early Judaism and its Literature
SJLA	Studies in Judaism in Late Antiquity
STJD	Studies on the Texts of the Desert of Judah
SUNT	Studien zur Umwelt des Neuen Testaments
SVTP	Studia in Veteris Testamenti pseudepigrapha
TSAJ	Texte und Studien zum antiken Judentum
TOTC	Tyndale Old Testament Commentaries
SJOT	*Scandinavian Journal of the Old Testament*
VTSup	*Vetus Testamentum*, Supplements
WBC	Word Biblical Commentary
ZAW	*Zeitschrift für die alttestamentliche Wissenschaft*

LIST OF CONTRIBUTORS

Andrew Angel is Biblical Studies tutor at the South East Institute for Theological Education, Kent.

Ovidiu Creangă is a doctoral student in Old Testament at King's College London.

Tal Ilan is a Professor at the Institut für Judaistik, Freie Universität, Berlin.

Bernard S. Jackson is Alliance Professor of Jewish Studies at the University of Manchester.

Rebecca Jefferson is a Research Associate at the Taylor–Schechter Genizah Research Unit, Cambridge University Library.

Amy Kalmanofsky is Assistant Professor of Bible at the Jewish Theological Seminary, New York.

Carol Meyers is Mary Grace Wilson Professor in Religion at Duke University, Durham, North Carolina.

Deborah W. Rooke is Lecturer in Old Testament Studies at King's College London.

Nicole J. Ruane has a PhD from Union Theological Seminary, New York City, and is the author of the forthcoming book *Sacrifice, Purity and Gender* (Cambridge University Press).

Deborah F. Sawyer is Reader in Religion and Gender at the University of Lancaster.

PART I
METHODOLOGICAL CONSIDERATIONS

Gender Criticism: A New Discipline in Biblical Studies or Feminism in Disguise?

Deborah F. Sawyer

In order fully to understand and assess the relationship between gender critique and feminism in the context of biblical studies, it is necessary to begin by briefly mapping the story of feminist critique more broadly as a subject in the academy. A quotation taken from the introduction to the *Woman's Bible* published at the end of the nineteenth century by Elizabeth Cady Stanton neatly sums up the impetus for what is known as first-wave feminism, a phenomenon often identified by its key political aim, the women's suffrage movement. Stanton writes,

> When in the early part of the Nineteenth Century, women began to protest against their civil and political degradation, they were referred to the Bible for an answer. When they protested against their unequal position in the church, they were referred to the Bible for an answer (Stanton 1985: 8).

In this way she explains the reasons that prompted her and her associates to produce the two-volume *Woman's Bible*. For them it was essential to begin with the Bible since its pervading interpretations up to this point had provided justification for treating women as the second sex in social, political and legislative contexts. At this stage there is no observable division between the secular feminist agenda and the aims of feminist biblical scholarship. This reflects the centrality of traditional religion in the social and political spheres of Western Europe and North America at that time in history.

The political and social agenda of Stanton and her co-writers was mirrored by second-wave feminists who first appeared on the Western political scene in the 1960s. However, a divide developed between secular feminists on the one hand, and feminist theologians and biblical scholars on the other, in line with the decline of traditional religion and its influence and the apparent rise of secularization, certainly in the academies of the humanities and social sciences. This divide was evidenced by the relative success of each side. The campaigns of the secular Women's Liberation Movement during the latter part of the twentieth century led to the introduction of legislation prohibiting explicit sexual discrimination in the workplace. In contrast, in the religious domain, although we did witness the ordination of women to new positions of authority in some Christian denominations and in Reform Judaism, religious organisations were exempted from much of this legislation. The exclusively male make-up of the Roman Catholic hierarchy is one clear contemporary illustration of this stasis.

In more general terms, first-wave feminism and its re-birth in the second wave can be identified as elements within the modernity project, or, more accurately, as examples of 'high modernity' where the ascendancy of man naturally evolves into the ascendancy of woman, with both expounding universal agendas. The work of the philosopher and former post-Christian writer Mary Daly is a good illustration of feminism in this context. Daly identifies patriarchy as the key problem for all women; 'woman' is the victim, and the cure is separatism (Daly 1973).

This telescopic vision of women's experience naturally attracted critique. Its diagnosis and subsequent affirmative action for women stemmed from privileged segments of the West, and excluded huge parts of the world, as well as whole sections of societies in more privileged countries. As early as 1979 there is a clear articulated critique of 'universal feminism' in Audre Lorde's letter to Mary Daly:

> The white women with hoods on in Ohio handing out KKK literature on the street may not like you, but they will shoot me on sight (Lorde 1984: 70).

Alice Walker (Walker 1984: xi) named 'womanism' as an alternative to and critique of the concept of a universal feminism, with her definition

Womanist is to feminist as purple to lavender

The impetus for womanism grew from the great unease felt about the tendency to universalize women's experience, and the obvious privileged position of the white, Western women activists, whose ascendancy came via the labour of women who were poor and without privilege, that is to say, via 'this bridge they call my back' (Anzaldúa 1983). Ironically, the exclusion originally suffered by the women who had been at the vanguard of second-wave feminism was inadvertently being dealt out by them to women of difference. Walker's novel *The Color Purple* (Walker 1983) vividly portrays the complexity of Western and colonial patriarchy where, for example, a white woman can be judged to be more culpable than any black male character. Inevitably the sharp dichotomy between men and women drawn by many second-wave feminists seems simplistic when it is set beside Walker's exploration and exposure of the depth and intricacies that make up the stratified relationships between 'master and slave'.

Within the academy the rise of womanism, with its call for feminism to address the experiences of difference, particularly in terms of colour and class, synchronized with the increasing popularity of ways of thinking that can loosely be placed under the umbrella of postmodernity. Here 'meta' categories and truths are constantly being challenged and deconstructed, revealing the relative nature of these values. 'Gender' is one such 'meta' category open to deconstruction, and to deconstruct it involves widening and deepening the critical purview of second-wave feminism. In this way we move from second to third-wave feminism and engage in gender critique.

In the area of biblical hermeneutics, in chronological terms, there is no hard and fast division between second-wave and third-wave (or postmodern) feminism. It is interesting to note that the title of one of the volumes published to mark the centenary of Elizabeth Cady Stanton's *Woman's Bible* was the *Women's Bible Commentary*. The decision to make this subtle but vital change is described by the editors, Carol Newsom and Sharon Ringe, in their introduction:

> But whereas she (Stanton) entitled her work the 'Woman's Bible', we have chosen the plural, 'Women's Bible'. The reason for this is our recognition of the diversity among women who read the Bible and study it. There is no single 'woman's perspective' but a rich variety of insight that comes from the different ways in which women's experience is shaped by culture, class, ethnicity, religious community, and other aspects of social identity (Newsom and Ringe 1992: xv).

If the difference between second-wave and third-wave feminism in relation to biblical studies is measured crudely (but concisely) in terms of essentialism/universalism versus relativism/difference, then the two positions have co-existed since the 1980s and continue to do so at the present time. Not only are they concurrent but they are at times confused. Elisabeth Schüssler Fiorenza, for example, can on the one hand state, 'feminist theologians must no longer articulate wo/men's identity in essentialist universalistic terms' (Schüssler Fiorenza 1995: 188). But at the same time she universalizes the 'struggle for liberation' so that it becomes an abstract rather than a concrete reality. Catherine Keller is particularly critical of Schüssler Fiorenza's positioning, pointing out that her use of imperatives in writing could be construed as one 'kyriarchy' replacing another (Keller 1997: 73). For many women the term 'feminist' is exclusivist and remains the currency of white middle-class Western women.

Phyllis Trible and Elisabeth Schüssler Fiorenza, working on the Hebrew scriptures and Christian scriptures respectively and employing diverse methodologies, are two notable figures who share the hermeneutical stance of feminism in their aim to uncover positive attitudes to women in the Bible. Following in the footsteps of liberation theologians, these feminist biblical scholars allowed pre-eminence to biblical texts that advocate inclusion of the marginalized and liberation for the oppressed, in an era when western culture had at least partially embraced forms of 'political correctness' and aspects of a feminist agenda. Their scholarship is characteristic of second-wave feminism, inspired by the political feminism of that era, which focused on patriarchy as the foundation of western society, culture and politics. Simone de Beauvoir's classic analysis *The Second Sex* (Beauvoir 1970) revealed woman as the 'other' whose existence upholds the authenticity and supremacy of male ascendancy. Trible's 'depatriarchalized' Bible and Schüssler Fiorenza's 'golden age' of female inclusion at the birth of the Jesus movement share the optimism that characterized secular political feminism in its expectation that change will occur if the arguments are objectively convincing. Feminist biblical scholars exposed the many biblical texts that collude with and enable patriarchal systems through the type of relationships depicted between God and human beings, and between men and women. Examples include the Genesis narratives; the legislation in Leviticus; the Household Codes in Colossians, Ephesians and 1 Peter; the silencing of women in the Pastoral Epistles; and also accounts of the victims of patriarchy, including abused women (Judges 19). Reformist feminist scholars identify texts such as these as exceptions to the biblical theme of liberation, and exclude them from the 'feminist canon' (Ruether 1985; Schüssler Fiorenza 1994). Conversely, texts that appear to challenge patriarchy become the new canon, having been processed using feminist hermeneutics. Included in this selection are the account of Tamar in Genesis 38, the book of Ruth, the story of the Samaritan woman in John's Gospel, the women activists in the early urban Christian communities mentioned by Paul, and, *par excellence*, the apparent egalitarian formula found in Gal. 3.28. The tendency to promote 'a canon within the canon' is found consistently throughout the histories of Judaism and Christianity, and is an inevitable feature of traditions that hold such a diverse range of texts as sacred. In modern times feminist biblical scholars are not alone in foregrounding texts that affirm their particular agendas, and in his re-appraisal of the notion of 'canon' George Aichele discusses the continuation of this tendency into a variety of contemporary contexts (Aichele 2001: 96).

It is clear why feminist biblical and theological scholarship has clustered around particular texts, but it should be recognized that this has restricted the vision of contemporary feminist theology and, at times, blinded it from asking more searching questions as to *why* certain texts do in fact challenge the boundaries. Phyllis Trible described a 'depatriarchalized' Bible (Trible 1973) that presumes a metaphysical level of existence for biblical texts—or rather, certain texts. This level of meaning, according to Trible, transcends the culture in which it was produced, and in which it was transmitted. This level is apparent in a space that can only exist, can only be explained, in terms of faith. It is contingent on the reader's particular situation within a community of faith, and in that acknowledged space it can be a reality. For those outside the community of faith there can be no 'depatriarchalized' Bible, however large or small that imagined text might be. In *God, Gender and the Bible* (Sawyer 2002), I have argued that when we stand outside that community of reformist feminist believers and ask why these texts challenge patriarchal boundaries, we may not necessarily conclude with Trible that they are the challenge of a 'depatriarchalized' god, but rather, conversely, we might recognize in them the ultimate finesse of a very patriarchal god. To understand the concepts of power and patriarchy in the Bible more profoundly, a wider lens is needed. The manner in which masculinity is presented is an additional vital issue, and, of course, so is the nature of the deity. Changing to this wider lens takes us into the area of gender critique.

The critical question, then, that needs to be asked is, has the stance of second-wave feminism taken by contemporary feminist biblical scholars and theologians restricted the scope of the hermeneutical project? Or, to put it another way, have the questions demanded of the text by feminist exegetes been sufficiently profound? Their questions posed to the text are asked from the stance of late modernity, and maybe such questions are inappropriate for texts that are pre-modern. Might not postmodernity, with its characteristic of fragmentation, be a more suitable stance from which to begin the interrogation of ancient texts that evolve from the multi-cultural world of antiquity? It could be argued that modernity is the oddity in its aspiration for singularity that is epitomized in its monolithic political, cultural and religious systems.

Feminist critique has uncovered many examples of narratives where biblical writers have employed female characters for pragmatic purposes. Although a 'by-product' is often the emergence of a heroic female displaying initiative, the main purpose underlining the narrative is to demonstrate the omniscient power of the deity. In narratives that allow pre-eminence to particular women, male characters can be denigrated to positions of powerlessness. In the biblical context where male supremacy is assumed, this process of emasculation functions to destabilize the audience's expectations, and allows the author to apply the surprise tactic of a male deity using female vehicles to ensure his plan is accomplished. Narratives employing this tactic include the accounts of Sarah, Hagar and Abraham (Gen. 16.1–18.15; 21); Rebecca and Isaac (Gen. 25.19–27.40); Rachel and Jacob (Genesis 30) ; Tamar and Judah (Genesis 38); and Naomi, Ruth and Boaz (book of Ruth). This theme carries on into the apocryphal literature, which presents us with the supreme example: Judith and Holofernes (book of Judith). It emerges again in early Christian texts, namely the Gospels of Mark and John, where the male disciples are outshone by the faith of the women around Jesus (Sawyer 2002: 99-113). Even, or especially, the account of the first couple in paradise (Genesis 2–3) allows for such a reading.

When contemporary gender theory is applied to these consistent key moments of female empowerment within biblical literature, it becomes evident that *both* masculinity and femininity have been destabilized within the patriarchal framework, and with the intention not to undermine this worldview, but rather to reinforce it. The supreme manifestation of patriarchy, that is, the power of the male God, is triumphant and remains assured. Mere male mortals can be ridiculed in this scheme in the service of this higher purpose.

Gender theorist Judith Butler has argued that the subversion of given gender roles is consistently evident within patriarchy, and she takes these exceptions to demonstrate the fragility of constructed gender:

> If the inner truth of gender is a fabrication and if a true gender is a fantasy instituted and inscribed on the surface of bodies, then it seems that genders can be neither true nor false, but are only produced as the truth effects of a discourse of primary and stable identity (Butler 1990: 136).

Such fragility of the given behaviour patterns is clearly apparent in biblical narrative, whatever theological purpose may be served by it. The biblical law codes reflect an uncompromising construction of prescribed gendered behaviour, and, ironically but deliberately, set beside them are narratives that subvert them. In this alternative scenario, as Butler writes, the reality of plurality can be recognized:

> Cultural configurations of sex and gender might then proliferate or, rather, their present proliferation might then become articulable within the discourses that establish intelligible cultural life, confounding the very binarism of sex, and exposing its fundamental unnaturalness (Butler 1990: 149).

If it is recognised that neither gender nor biological sex reside at two polarities but instead are represented at every point between them, as demonstrated not only by individuals who behave contrary to a given gender role, but also by those who bear characteristics of both sexes, or change from one to another at puberty, then 'gender play' becomes the natural rather than the unnatural order of things. Such 'topsy-turviness' is exactly in line with biblical literary strategies. Thus, although the option put forward by Butler of performative identity—that is, selecting how we perform gendered existence as subjects rather than taking it as a given—has to remain an unreality for the majority who cannot grasp at a vision of life beyond their constructed reality, it is quite another matter for the lives narrated within the biblical world view. Criticism of Butler's abstract presentation of human social reality can be suspended when the scene of the performance is something beyond *human* controlled space. Butler's performative identity theory is the ideal tool to apply to biblical texts where the central characters *can* defy and escape constructed realities. This is obviously true of the main character, God, but it can be detected in female and male characters who behave counter-culturally in the narratives.

Following a different theoretical route, gender theorists whose ideas have developed within the framework of 'new essentialism' both deconstruct and reconstruct the concept of 'woman'. They recognize the identity category 'woman' as the male constructed 'other', but having thus deconstructed it, they go on to present possibilities for *re*constructing woman subjectively (Schor and Weed 1994). This is in contrast to how Butler develops Simone de Beauvoir's famous observation, 'one is not born a woman', and subsequently disposes with the concept of 'woman' since it exists as a male construct. Luce Irigaray's use of 'mimesis' (*mimétisme*) in exploring female subjectivity is one example of new essentialism. She explores where authenticity might lie more in the *parody* of objectified womanhood than in the male constructed model. Here there is a resonance with the gender games apparent in biblical narratives. Woman can become woman through and of herself, as opposed to being what is 'other' to male identity.

Through her application of the concept of mimesis, Irigaray attempts to transform the notion of 'woman' by deconstructing the patriarchal construct of woman as 'other' to man and allowing for the possibility of woman to emerge from within that difference, to be 'herself' for the first time:

> One must assume the feminine role deliberately. Which means already to convert a form of subordination into an affirmation, and thus to begin to thwart it (Irigaray 1985: 76).

Irigaray's parody of the constructed notion of woman allows for the appropriation of femininity with the female as subject:

> To play with mimesis is thus, for a woman, to try to recover the place of her exploitation by discourse, without allowing herself to be simply reduced to it (Irigaray 1985: 76).

Irigaray works with the notion of difference, and proposes a new essentialism that is both individual and independent of the masculine 'other'. In the 'normal' biblical world, maleness and masculinity is constructed as the 'other' to God, that is, except when the authors allow for the exceptional. Applying Irigaray's notion of mimesis to biblical manhood and womanhood could suggest new ways of reading biblical texts that impact on both male and female images, and allow these exceptions to be foregrounded. For example, Eve can be seen as taking the initiative on behalf of her partner, rather than playing out her given and expected role as the passive helpmate; Abraham can be seen as taking his role as a man to mean that he *can* stand up to God, and argue justice with the deity in an attempt to save innocent victims being destroyed in Sodom and Gomorrah. The gender games apparent in biblical literature apply as much to constructed masculinity as to femininity. However, through focusing primarily on female characters in biblical literature feminist critique has often overlooked the implications of constructed masculinity.

The analysis of gender construction is vital to understanding the way in which the themes of biblical texts often interact between one another within the canon, where the given gender behavioural patterns in one text are challenged in another. But gender roles are enacted by the secondary characters in the major plot. God, the one main character, remains in place throughout the biblical narrative; sometimes this deity is quite hidden, often wearing different guises within or outside gendered boundaries, even cross-dressing, but always steering the plot and being served by the supporting cast. While it is important to analyse human biblical characters, the minor players, in order to understand the plot, and to gain insights into the main character, to over-invest in their significance is to lose sight of the grand narrative. In biblical literature these secondary characters with their stories always remain shadows, reflecting a diminished form of the divine glory.

Walter Brueggemann has foregrounded the tension that exists between many biblical themes and values. Rather than attempt to harmonize this tension and thereby dilute it, he encourages biblical readers to confront this challenge because it is an essential characteristic of biblical theology:

> A careful understanding of the literature shows that we are *not free to resolve* the tension. The Old Testament both partakes of the common theology and struggles to be free from it. The Old Testament both enters the fray of ambiguity and seeks distance from the fray to find something certain and sure. The God of Israel is thus presented variously as the God above the fray who appears like other Near Eastern gods and as a God who is exposed in the fray, who appears unlike the gods of common theology, a God peculiarly available for Israel's historical experiences (Brueggemann 1992: 5).

In terms of gender critique it is possible to identify texts that are in harmony with a hierarchical and patriarchal society, but there are also texts which challenge, subvert and infer the reformation of such a society, and furthermore, there are texts that are anarchic in turning upside down expected patterns of behaviour.

Bearing in mind the socio-political contexts that produced the biblical texts, it is unsurprising that the dominant characterization of God encountered in the texts is one that is clearly pre-Enlightenment. The Bible consistently represents a power structure that cannot be compromised, whether God is conveyed as the benign figure heading a form of love patriarchalism, or an all-demanding father who desires the ultimate sign of obedience from his offspring. Any notion of egalitarianism or democracy is inappropriate in the context of divine will, and absolute trust in the rightness of that will is the only appropriate response. Does this observation mean that these texts should be rejected, and are relevant only for those who wish to abandon autonomy?

An alternative approach for those of us with subversive tendencies who wish to engage with these texts would be to accept their limitations for addressing our own world, but at the same time to explore the examples they contain for challenging boundaries and for anarchic behaviour in relation to power structures. Within these subversive paradigms, it is possible to find a striking anticipation of our postmodern world. As mentioned earlier, in articulating her concept of performative gender Judith Butler shifts her lens from the normative, that which conforms, to that which destabilizes expectation:

> The abiding gendered self will then be shown to be structured by repeated acts that seek to approximate the ideal of a substantial ground of identity, but which in their occasional *dis*continuity, reveal the temporal and contingent groundlessness of this 'ground' (Butler 1990: 141).

If this process is translated to the biblical worldview, alternative notions of being human emerge that are in antithesis to the given divine/human relationship, but subsist within it. As such they work as parody within the text.

By means of applying to sacred literature and symbols contemporary philosophical and psychoanalytical ideas which inform current gender theory, it is possible to discover ways of both deconstructing and reconstructing the archetypes that lie at the core of Western and Colonial culture. In the case of the

Christian concept of the virgin mother, both Julia Kristeva (Kristeva 1986b) and Luce Irigaray (Irigaray 2002, 2004) have deconstructed the traditional interpretations of the person and motherhood of Mary, and both reconfigure the concept in ways that allow for the possibility of a positive, if not divine, figure of the maternal that stands in critique of traditional psychoanalytical readings of the mother, and, in particular, the Oedipal reading of the relationship between mother and daughter. Both Kristeva and Irigaray were born into the context of Catholicism and can make easy recourse to the traditions and symbols associated with the Madonna.

While the virgin mother symbol is culturally central, the figure of Eve could be argued to be more critical since it is her traditional role as the first woman that laid the foundations for the concept of the 'second sex'. In revisiting the site of the first human couple of Western imagination, we discover the embedded sacred identities of both men and women clearly recounted. Adam and Eve are made sacred through their imaging of the divine, and their relationships—to the divine and to one another—are also sacred. Female submission goes beyond simply being the normative cultural practice of societies throughout history and becomes the sacred will of God. In the context of the Christian theological world-view, Mary, who becomes identified from the second century CE onwards as the new Eve, is simply a corrective commentary on the first Eve, as Jesus is to Adam. The figure of Eve, and her relationship to God and Adam, deserves both critical scrutiny from the stance of contemporary psychoanalytical thought and the attention of gender theorists. Western society's Christian heritage has marked women as daughters of Eve, and not as daughters of the virgin mother.

Such an approach to the story of the Garden of Eden can draw on the subversive element in Luce Irigaray's use of 'mimesis', which was discussed above, where parody can function within deconstructive and reconstructive strategies. Irigaray uses mimesis to evolve an alternative notion of 'becoming' woman, distinct from the masculine realm of discourse that names 'her' as the other, but that distinction begins with engaging with the given category 'woman', so that through its parody woman—as subject, not object—creates herself.

In order to illustrate more clearly the points discussed above I shall take a closer look at that most familiar biblical text, the Eden narrative, and examine it more closely alongside some of the thinking that has emerged from contemporary gender theorists. The imagery of Eden has become embedded in and has informed Western and colonial cultures for more than two millennia, and the power of the archetypes it represents never seems to diminish.

Through the lens of gender critique it is possible to analyse the narrative's construction of gender roles and the events that led up to the couple's expulsion from Eden, and by using this means I shall attempt to show that the option for autonomy taken by Eve in the form of the forbidden fruit allows for a form of 'becoming' human that is immanent rather than transcendent, from 'within' rather than from 'without'. Whilst gendered sacred identity in the biblical mould has been understood historically as inevitably hierarchical, with Eve as the first of the second sex, alternative readings offer striking parallels with postmodern understandings of gender construction.

Michel Foucault's theory of power and its relation to the body and sexuality has been a significant influence on third-wave feminists and gender theorists, and his ideas resound with biblical concepts of power, both human and divine, and constructions and reconstructions of gender roles that one can discover in the text:

> Discourse transmits and produces power; it reinforces it, but also undermines and exposes it, renders it fragile and makes it possible to thwart it (Foucault 1984: 100).

For centuries the biblical creation story has furnished and influenced Western and colonial culture with archetypal imagery through philosophy, art and literature, and it continues to inform perceptions of what it is to be male and female. As Hélène Cixous comments, 'Every entrance to life finds itself *before the apple*' (Cixous 1991: 150).

The opening narrative of Genesis presents us with four key characters: God, Adam, Eve, and the Serpent. It explains that God, the main character in the narrative, created the heavens and the earth and all that is in them, and arranged things in order, with the human species in control but subjugated to divine power and will, a relationship that is mirrored in the sexual hierarchy embedded in the narrative. The text continues with an account of how the primordial couple act out ways of being human in relation to the divine within the utopian setting of the Garden of Eden. Two options are laid before them, one voiced by God, and the other by the Serpent. The first promises nurture and protection so long as they remain subject to the divine will. The second offers apotheosis and autonomy so long as they disobey that will. This scene encapsulates the tension between submission and autonomy that lay at the heart of Enlightenment religious critique, and that characterized the feminist agenda from its inception.

'... [A]nd your desire shall be for your husband, and he shall rule over you' (Gen. 3.16). This compact phrase from the beginning of Genesis not only tells us that according to biblical theology desire, the key to human identity formation, is God-given, constructed and controlled, but also that its object within the primary relationship for the woman is characterized by dominance and power. For women, identity, and with it desire, is constructed outside and beyond any notion of self as subject:

> ... female identity always comes down to empirical parameters that prevent a woman, and the world of women, from getting them*selves* together as a unit. The sexual-familial dimension remains one of these parameters, 'Are you a virgin?' 'Are you married?' 'Who is your husband?' 'Do you have any children?' these are the questions always asked, which allow us to place a woman. She is constituted from outside in relation to a social function, instead of to a female identity and autonomy (Irigaray 2002: 47-48).

The creation of Eve described in the Bible and presented to us in art and literature down the centuries depicts woman being taken from man, derived from, and always in relation to, her source, her 'other'.

Within the creation narrative it is possible to see newly created humanity develop into a relationship of contestation with the divine, and as such represent a parody of divine intentionality. Adam and Eve are created according to a blueprint that excludes autonomy, but they subvert the divine pattern by deliberately opting for an alternative. They remain recognizable as the created 'other' to the divine, but exist as a parody, or mimesis, of the humanity intended by God. Eve, the instigator of the subversion, presents the greatest parody of all. Created as an afterthought to Adam, as his helper in the process of procreation, she emerges as the initiator. The object, the 'other' not only to God but also to man, becomes the subject who acts and allows the emergence of an alternative type of humanity.

When Kristeva discusses Eve she interprets her as a figure entirely subject to the male symbolic order, servicing the relationship between man and his God through her essential role of reproduction. She reads the Genesis narrative in terms of Eve's materialism, despite her key role in the continuance of community and with it 'man's very dialogue with his God':

> But woman's knowledge is corporal, aspiring to pleasure rather than tribal unity (the forbidden fruit seduces Eve's senses of *sight* and *taste*) (Kristeva 1986: 140).

Kristeva reads Eve's action as a sensual one by focusing on her physical attraction to and her taking of the fruit, which is the normative depiction of her and her action down the centuries of theological interpretation and artistic portrayal.

Kristeva makes the point that Eve has 'no direct relation with the law of the community and its political and religious unity: God generally speaks only to men' (Kristeva 1986: 104). In biblical narrative this is not strictly true; for example, God's words to Rebecca in the Genesis narrative enable a union between the divine will and the dreams of a mother for her favourite son, and brings about an outcome where mutual desires are satisfied (Gen. 25.19-28). Although Eve quotes God's words that were delivered to Adam before she was created, prohibiting him to eat the forbidden fruit, implying that she has only indirect access to the divine 'law' (Gen. 3.2-3; cf. 2.16-17), she does own it for herself in her speech in dialogue with the Serpent. And this is what Kristeva's comment ignores, the fact that, rather than presenting Eve as merely subject to her senses, the narrative rehearses a dialogue between Eve and the Serpent.

This stands in contrast to the monological relationship that exists between God and Adam. It is only after the couple have eaten the forbidden fruit that any form of dialogical relationship develops between God and humanity, in recognition, perhaps, of humanity's coming of age. In the scene with the Serpent, Eve anticipates the gift of discernment between good and evil, symbolized by the forbidden fruit, by exercising her own judgment. Discernment between good and evil is the fruit of dialogue, reflecting that becoming human is a process, or negotiation, between the self and another, in contrast to the static monologic relationship between God and Adam. In the light of the Serpent's argument that they will not die if they eat this fruit, but rather receive discernment, like God, Eve is described as making a decision that is both sensual and cognitive:

> So when the woman saw that the tree was good for food, and that it was a delight to the eyes, and that the tree was to be desired to make one wise, she took of its fruit ... (Gen. 3.6).

When the focus is switched to Adam in this scene, he appears as a figure that is more readily identifiable with the figure of Eve that Kristeva describes. He is without dialogue, mute, despite having been the direct recipient of the divine prohibition. He personifies passivity, before God and before Eve. Without speaking, he takes and he eats. His action is presented as corporal, an instinctive response to his bodily senses.

In Hélène Cixous' discussion of the Eden myth in her essay, 'The Author in Truth' (Cixous 1991), there is a more conscious Eve figure than the one that is encountered in many interpretations. Cixous plays with the homophony that exists in French between the nouns *scène* (scene) and *cène* (meal). Through this word-play the primordial scene of the Eden narrative becomes the primordial meal. The focus is placed on Eve's consumption of the fruit, on her pleasure in opening up to the 'other' which is represented by the fruit. Cixous makes a sharp contrast between the fruit (named as an apple, as tradition dictates) and the 'absolute discourse', that is, the prohibition against eating the fruit made by God:

> We are told that knowledge could begin with the mouth, the discovery of the taste of something. Knowledge and taste go together. Yet the mystery of the stroke of the law is also staged here, absolute, verbal, invisible, negative. A symbolic *coup de force*. Its power lies in its invisibility, its non-existence, its force of denial, its 'not'. And facing the law, there is the apple which is, is, is (Cixous 1991: 151).

In recognizing that knowledge and taste go together Cixous allows Eve an element of subjectivity that goes beyond the mere senses of sight and taste. She comprehends that the 'apple' is 'invested with every kind of power'. Her action of taking the forbidden fruit exposes a level of subjectivity that had been hidden within her, disguised by her identity as the 'other' and the very mode of her creation. Her autonomy, her subjectivity, displays a way of being human that parodies the feminine role that had been prescribed for her and, in Irigaray's terms, she becomes woman by and of herself.

Carefully hidden by centuries of misogynist interpretation, the secret of Eve's wisdom can be revealed, and through her initiative it is possible to discover a blueprint for autonomous humanity. Such autonomy is clearly recognized by previous generations of Christian theologians, but its dangerous implications both social and political, particularly in relation to its manifestation in female form, ensured that it was declared devil's work and consigned to be the antithesis of perfect humanity, or worse, as the Devil's Gateway for the sons of Adam. Eve is a clear example of '*dis*continuity' in the accounts of human identity in relation to the divine in biblical discourse. While her existence has stood to depict the consequences of disobedience to the divine will, it also, paradoxically, presents a competing and subversive counter-discourse. And this counter-discourse is rehearsed throughout the biblical narratives as other female, and male, characters act out their roles at the boundaries of what is lawful, even crossing over those boundaries, and often with the active collusion of the divine.

The narrative of the Garden of Eden presents two expressions of desire and power. One is suggested by Eve. Her desire is directed at the fruit of the tree that the Serpent has told her will give her the knowledge to discern between good and evil. With this knowledge the eyes of humanity will be opened and they 'will be like gods'. Divinity, then, will no longer be a transcendent 'other', but instead an immanence, emanating from within the person. This immanence is a relationship with the interior subjective self, in opposition to the external given self. Cixous recognises that

> ... Eve is not afraid of the inside, neither of her own nor of the other's. The relationship to the interior, to penetration, to the touching of the inside, is positive. Obviously Eve is punished for it, but that is a different matter, the matter of the jealousy of god and society (Cixous 1991: 152).

This knowledge, objectified as the fruit of the tree, Eve shares with her partner. Their true humanity, their 'becoming', as Irigaray would describe it, or even their divinity, does not have to be hierarchical, based on ignorance and submission. The figure of Eve is truly symbolic of sacred identity. At once both created by God, in the image of God, and created through and by herself, she manifests the tension of experiencing the divine without and within: submission versus autonomy.

Returning to the text, the second expression of desire is voiced by the transcendent God, who is presented in terms of the angry parent, coming home to discover that his naughty children have been disobedient, rebelling against his clear instructions. He deals with them by explicitly denying them the parent/child relationship. They are confronted with the harsh realities of the grown-up world. For Eve this is the pain associated with childbirth, that is, her own role of becoming a parent, rather than remaining a child. The hierarchical relationship between God and humanity will be mirrored in her relationship with her husband to whom she will be subject and whom she will desire. For Adam hard labour in the fields replaces the parental provision of food and plenty offered in the pre-lapsarian paradise. Desire is constructed within the male/female relationship. It is imposed from without rather than realised from within. It is inseparable from the power structure that has been constructed for humanity.

Eve's initiative ensures that humanity does come of age, but, in biblical terms, this maturation represents an act of rebellion. Dependent and obedient pre-lapsarian Adam and Eve remain the ideal, often presented in eschatological terms, and encapsulated by the concept of the obedient new Adam and new Eve that evolved in early Christian theology. On the other hand, when it is understood as a positive initiative, Eve's action presents a biblical paradigm for human behaviour that does not resist autonomy, and allows an engagement between the text and the myriad ways of being human that are manifest in the modern world. On the theological level such a reading of Eve allows for a deity that dares to risk the liberation of his creation, rather than one who knowingly creates a defective, or potentially defective, humanity.

The patterns of identity that suspend human maturity are difficult to reconcile with our post-Enlightenment expectations of autonomy, those biblical ideals, for example, expressed within the image of the child-like, pre-lapsarian Adam and Eve, or the apostle Paul's concept of the children of God. But whilst for many individuals such images mean that the biblical text must be rejected as an irrelevance in the modern world, we should recognize that this is not a monolithic discourse. Rather, the Bible comprises multiple, contesting discourses which contradict and parody one another in a constant state of tension. Moreover, within biblical discourses subversions of normative power paradigms clearly exist. They are the jokers in the pack. They provide the clues for deconstruction, or, more positively, the tools for a myriad reconstructions.

This is why reading the Bible from the standpoint of gender critique broadens the lens that was first introduced by feminist interpreters, allows us to engage with ideas that are perhaps more in sympathy with the pre-modern writers who produced them, and perhaps might even allow us to gain clearer insights into the character of the God who inspired them to write.

BIBLIOGRAPHY

Aichele, George
    2001   *The Control of Biblical Meaning: Canon as Semiotic Mechanism* (Harrisburg, PA: Trinity Press International).

Anzaldúa, Gloria
    1983   *This Bridge Called my Back: Writings by Radical Women of Color* (New York: Kitchen Table Press).

Beauvoir, Simone de
    1970   *The Second Sex* (trans. H.M. Parshley; New York: Knopf).

Brueggmann, Walter
    1997   *Theology of the Old Testament: Testimony, Dispute, Advocacy* (Minneapolis: Fortress Press).

Butler, Judith
    1990   *Gender Trouble: Feminism and the Subversion of Identity* (Thinking Gender; London: Routledge).

Cixous, Hélène
    1991   'The Author in Truth', in Deborah Jenson (ed.), *'Coming to Writing' and other Essays* (trans. Sarah Cornell; Cambridge, MA: Harvard University Press): 136-81.

Daly, Mary
    1973   *Beyond God the Father: Toward a Philosophy of Women's Liberation* (Boston: Beacon Press).

Foucault, Michel
    1984   *The History of Sexuality: An Introduction* (London: Penguin Books).

Irigaray, Luce
    1985   *This Sex Which is Not One* (trans. Catherine Porter with Carolyn Burke; Ithaca, NY: Cornell University Press).
    2002   'Divine Women', in Morny Joy, Kathleen O'Grady and Judith L. Poxon (eds.), *French Feminists on Religion* (London: Routledge): 41-48.
    2004   'The Redemption of Women', in *Luce Irigaray: Key Writings* (London: Continuum): 150-64.

Keller, Catherine
    1997   'Seeking and Sucking: On Relation and Essence in Feminist Theology', in Rebecca S. Chopp and Sheila Greeve Davaney (eds.), *Horizons in Feminist Theology: Identity, Traditions, and Norms* (Minneapolis: Fortress Press): 54-78.

Kristeva, Julia
    1986a   'About Chinese Women', in Moi 1986: 139-59.
    1986b   'Stabat Mater', in Moi 1986: 161-86.

Lorde, Audre
    1984   *Sister Outsider: Essays and Speeches* (Ithaca, NY: Crossing Press).

Moi, Toril (ed.)
    1986   *The Kristeva Reader* (Oxford: Blackwell).

Newsom, Carol A., and Sharon H. Ringe (eds.)
    1992   *The Women's Bible Commentary* (London: SPCK).

Ruether, Rosemary Radford
    1985   *Womanguides: Readings Toward a Feminist Theology* (Boston: Beacon Press).

Sawyer, Deborah F.
    1996   *Women and Religion in the First Christian Centuries* (Religion in the First Christian Centuries, 1; London: Routledge).
    2002   *God, Gender and the Bible* (London: Routledge).
    2006   'Gender', in John F.A. Sawyer (ed.), *The Blackwell Companion to the Bible and Culture* (Oxford: Blackwell): 464-79.

Schor, Naomi, and Elizabeth Weed (eds.)
    1994   *The Essential Difference* (Books from Differences; Bloomington: Indiana University Press).

Schüssler Fiorenza, Elisabeth (ed.)
    1994   *Searching the Scriptures* (2 vols.; New York: Crossroad).

Schüssler Fiorenza, Elisabeth
    1995   *Jesus: Miriam's Child, Sophia's Prophet: Critical Issues in Feminist Christology* (London: SCM Press).

Stanton, Elizabeth Cady
    1985   *The Woman's Bible* (Edinburgh: Polygon, abridged edn).

Trible, Phyllis
    1973   'Depatriarchalizing in the Biblical Tradition', *Journal of the American Academy of Religion* 41: 30-48.

Walker, Alice
    1983   *The Color Purple* (London: Women's Press).
    1984   *In Search of our Mothers' Gardens: Womanist Prose* (London: Women's Press).

Weir, Allison
    1996   *Sacrificial Logics: Feminist Theory and the Critique of Identity* (Thinking Gender; London: Routledge).

Part II
Gender in Law and Ritual

THE BARE FACTS: GENDER AND NAKEDNESS IN LEVITICUS 18

Deborah W. Rooke

Although in recent years there has been a good deal of interest in the legal and ritual texts of the Hebrew Bible, and a renewed appreciation of them as expressing a distinctive, cohesive and meaningful world view, to date relatively little attention has been paid to their gendered characteristics. That is not to say that they have received no attention at all, but rather that less sustained attention has been paid to them than to other areas of the Hebrew Bible which have perhaps seemed more easily approachable. Inasmuch as legal and ritual texts have received attention from scholars interested in gender issues, most attention seems to have been focused on material in Exodus and Deuteronomy. Works dealing with Exodus and Deuteronomy from a gendered perspective include Carolyn Pressler's seminal volume *The View of Women Found in the Deuteronomic Family Laws* (Pressler 1993), followed by the edited collection *Gender and Law in the Hebrew Bible and the Ancient Near East* by Victor Matthews, Bernard Levinson and Tikva Frymer-Kensky.[1] More recently Cheryl Anderson's *Women, Ideology, and Violence* deals with gender constructions in the Book of the Covenant and Deuteronomy (Anderson 2004); and Hagith Sivan's *Between Woman, Man, and God* offers a re-reading of the Ten Commandments (Sivan 2004). However, it is less easy to find comparable extended studies of the Priestly material. Jione Havea's *Elusions of Control* addresses biblical law on women's vows (Numbers 30) (Havea 2003), and there have been a number of articles and essays on topics from Priestly law, including blood discharge and female (im)purity in P,[2] the suspected adulteress ritual of Numbers 5 (Bach 1993), and the childbirth regulations in Leviticus 12.[3] But

---

1. Matthews, Levinson and Frymer-Kensky 1998. Although this collection is not confined to material from Deuteronomy and the Book of the Covenant, or indeed from the Hebrew Bible, the articles that discuss legal material from the Hebrew Bible focus almost exclusively on Deuteronomy and the Book of the Covenant. The one exception to this is a discussion of honour and shame in gender-related legal situations (Matthews 1998), in which six pages are devoted to discussing the case of the suspected adulteress (Num. 5.11-31) (Matthews 1998: 102-108), alongside discussions of the unwilling levir (Deut. 25.5-10) and the suspect virgin (Deut. 22.13-21).
2. Be'er 1994; Philip 2006: 44-57
3. Schearing 2003; Philip 2006: 111-25. For a survey of Leviticus from a feminist perspective,

there is still plenty of scope for investigation of the Priestly legislation from a gender-sensitive perspective; and this is the area to which the present study aims to make a contribution, by means of a study of the theme of nakedness as it appears in the incest regulations of Leviticus 18.

Incest Laws in the Ancient Near East

The lists of forbidden sexual partnerships in Leviticus 18 and 20 are some of the most comprehensive to have survived from the ancient Near Eastern context. Other legal material in the Hebrew Bible outside the P/H tradition shows little or no interest in the topic of incest: it does not occur at all in the Book of the Covenant (Exodus 20–23),[4] and Deuteronomy, for all its concern with female sexual purity and continence,[5] has only one actual law against incest, prohibiting males from having sex with their father's wife (Deut. 23.1 [ET 22.30]).[6] It also curses those who lie with their father's wife, with a beast, with one of their sisters, or with their mother-in-law (Deut. 27.20-23), although these curses are not part of the central law code. Other surviving ancient Near Eastern law codes are similarly low-key about incest.[7] Hammurabi (c. 1750 BCE) inveighs against the man who has sex with his daughter (LH 154), the man who sleeps with his daughter-in-law (LH 155) and his daughter-in-law-to-be (LH 156), and the man who sleeps with his mother (LH 157) or his father's principal wife (LH 158), but no other liaisons between kin by blood or marriage are mentioned. The Middle Assyrian Laws (c. 1076 BCE) have a large number of provisions on Tablet A concerning issues of marriage and fornication, but apparently nothing on incest (although, of course, it is possible that there were such provisions but they have not survived; several of the tablets are in a fragmentary condition). The law code with the most elaborate extant provisions on unlawful sexual couplings is the Hittite Laws (c. 1650–1500 BCE).[8] The incestuous liaisons it

---

see Wegner (1992). Wassen's (2005) study examines how a variety of biblical laws concerning women are adapted in the Damascus Document, including the laws concerning childbirth and menstruation (Leviticus 12, 15), the suspected adulteress (Numbers 5), and rules for women's vows (Numbers 30). My thanks to Professor Michael Knibb for drawing this study to my attention.

4. Bestiality, however, is condemned in Exod. 22.18 (ET 22.19).

5. For discussion of the themes of sexual purity and continence in Deuteronomy, see Rooke (2000: 18-20, 25-31).

6. Phillips (1980) argues that this is in fact two different prohibitions, one against incest with the mother and one against incest with the father.

7. For translations of all the major surviving ancient Near Eastern law codes, see Roth (1995).

8. In the Hittite code there is a much greater emphasis on types of bestiality than there is in the Hebrew material. According to the code, bestiality with cows, sheep, pigs and dogs is a capital offence (187, 188, 199), but bestiality with horses and mules is (merely) defiling (200), and necrophilia is apparently permissible (190).

prohibits are a man with his own mother, daughter or son (189), a man with his stepmother during the lifetime of his father (190), a free man with free sisters and their mother if he knows the women are related to each other (191), a man with his brother's wife during his brother's lifetime (195a), and a man with his living wife's daughter, mother or sister (195b-c). However, not even this can match the wide-ranging prohibitions on sexual relationships with kin by blood or marriage that appear in Leviticus. This implies that the compilers of Leviticus had particular views of human sexuality that can presumably be teased out by an examination of what they chose to include in their laws, and of the form that those laws took.[9]

It is now generally accepted among scholars who are sensitive to gender concerns that the material in the Hebrew Bible reflects a patriarchal, androcentric world-view, whereby power, privilege and authority are held by males and male concerns are primary, while females occupy a secondary position of perpetual dependence upon males, in which they have few legal or social rights and their concerns are rarely if ever addressed. This attitude is certainly evidenced in Leviticus 18, and has been noted by commentators.[10] However, there is more to be said about the gendered nature of the chapter than just noting the patriarchal character of the legislation, and so the present study will explore the presentation of gender models in Leviticus 18 with a particular focus on the incest regulations and the terminology they employ.

Leviticus 18

Leviticus 18 in its present form is a self-contained unit that formally speaking stands apart from what precedes and what follows it; it begins with the introductory formula וידבר יהוה אל־משה לאמר (18.1) and ends with the concluding formulaic assertion אני יהוה אלהיכם (18.30), after which chapter 19 begins again with the introductory formula וידבר יהוה אל־משה לאמר (19.1). Leviticus 18 consists of four main sections: an exhortatory prologue (vv. 1-5); laws restricting sexual relationships between people related by blood and marriage (vv. 6-18); laws forbidding menstrual intercourse, adultery, child sacrifice, male-male intercourse and bestiality (vv. 19-23); and closing exhortations (vv. 24-30). The opening and closing exhortations are quite revealing

---

9. Whether or not the law was ever enforced, and to what extent, is not the issue here, but rather what its compilation betrays about how masculinity and femininity were understood by those who compiled these laws. Sexual practice and sexuality is a highly significant component of gender constructions in every culture, both ancient and modern, no doubt because it directly concerns the external genitalia and their associated reproductive functions, and it is from these organs and functions that the fundamental distinction between men and women is assumed to stem. As such, the appropriate use of one's genitalia is thus a highly emotive issue that is often determinative for acceptance or non-acceptance within a given community.

10. So, for example, Gerstenberger (1996: 249).

from the point of view of their gender ideology, and so these will be considered first before an examination of the laws themselves.

a. *Exhortatory prologue and epilogue*
The first point worthy of note is the addressees of the chapter. In Lev. 18.2 Moses is told to speak to 'the sons of Israel', who will thus be the recipients of the legal stipulations that follow. Although this could be regarded as simply reflecting the paucity of the Hebrew language in not having a direct equivalent to the English gender-neutral term 'children', that fact in itself indicates a mindset that regards 'sons' as the default concept of all children. However, there may be more than mere paucity of language at stake here, in that the subsequent laws are clearly addressed specifically to men and not to women.[11] Thus, from early on in the prologue the reader (or hearer) is primed to understand what follows as an expression or definition of masculinity—an expectation that is not disappointed. Secondly, Moses' initial words to the 'sons of Israel' consist of a statement of Yahweh's claim over the Israelites (Lev. 18.2), and an exhortation not to do as they do in Egypt whence the Israelites have come, nor to do as they do in Canaan whither the Israelites are going at Yahweh's behest (Lev. 18.3), but to follow Yahweh's commands because Yahweh is the Israelites' god (Lev. 18.4). In other words, again as might be expected from the initial mention of the 'sons of *Israel*', this is not about being just any sort of man but about being an Israelite man. Whether or not the Egyptians and Canaanites (whoever they were) did indulge to a significant extent in the practices that are forbidden to the Israelites is largely immaterial;[12] what does matter is the lawgiver's perception that such practices should not be a part of what makes an Israelite man an Israelite man. It is notable that in Leviticus 18 there are no judicial punishments prescribed

---

11. Joosten (1996) discusses the use of the phrase בני ישראל in the Holiness Code, of which Leviticus 18 is usually thought to be a part. Using the example of Lev. 18.2, he concludes that the expression in principle includes only men, but that this does not mean that women are excluded from the laws; rather, they are subsumed under the men in whose households they live, and who are responsible for ensuring that the women keep the laws (30-32). It is difficult to see how this applies to the vast majority of Leviticus 18, which so clearly conceptualizes sexual activity as male-initiated and which in terms of its content is so clearly addressed to men.

12. Gerstenberger (1996: 256-57) claims that the vast weight of evidence indicates that they did not. Milgrom (2000) claims that 'Egypt was reputed for its licentiousness' (1518), but admits, '[T]here is no extrabiblical evidence that the Canaanites were steeped in sexual immorality' (1520), and also suggests that the text may be exaggerating the sexual sins of both Egypt and Canaan for polemical purposes (1520). Levine (1989: 118) comments that there is no clear evidence that incest was widespread in Egypt or Canaan apart from the tendency among Egyptian royalty at certain periods to encourage brother-sister marriage, although he thinks that homosexuality and bestiality were quite common in Canaanite culture. He does not, however, offer any evidence to support this latter opinion. Hartley (1992: 293) interprets the prohibition literalistically, taking it to refer to 'cultic practices rooted in fertility rites and alternative patterns of family relationships' (293)—again, a position that is unsupported by any evidence.

for those who break these laws, just the general threat that whoever does these things shall be cut off from their people (Lev. 18.29);[13] in other words, it is not possible to be an Israelite man and to behave in this manner, because the two things are mutually exclusive.[14] This shows that the laws reflect a *construction* of masculine sexuality, in that breaching them results in forfeiting one's identity as part of the community that is promulgating them. Equally notable is the comment in 18.27 that all the things prohibited for the 'sons of Israel' were done by 'the *men* of the land' (אנשי־הארץ) who were there before the Israelites, with the result that the land became defiled. Here there is a clear distinction between what apparently constitutes acceptable masculine sexual behaviour among the Canaanites, and what constitutes the same for the Israelites.

It is also quite noticeable that sexual immorality is the only sin that is linked directly and specifically with potential pollution of the land and a resultant threat of expulsion from it. Certainly, there are threats elsewhere of dreadful consequences, including expulsion, if the Israelites fail to keep Yahweh's 'statutes and commandments' in general; Leviticus 26 is a good example of such threats. There, however, expulsion is the climax of a series of punishments designed to produce repentance, and it only occurs after four other punishments have been inflicted without success: plagues and defeat by enemies (26.16-17); famine and drought (26.18-20); more plagues and attacks by wild animals (26.21-22); and pestilence, famine and subjection (26.23-26). This contrasts strikingly with Leviticus 18, where expulsion is the direct result of

---

13. The penalty of being 'cut off' is thought by some commentators to refer to a direct act of God, whether in striking the offender dead either instantaneously or prematurely, or in depriving him of descendants or an afterlife. See Levine (1989: 241-42); Milgrom (1991: 457-60); Budd (1996: 122-23, 245); Lipka (2006: 56-58). Such divine punishment would be particularly appropriate for offences such as incest, which take place in private and may well be difficult to prove on a human level. Clearly, a man who is 'cut off' in this way has his membership of Israel terminated, so the penalty indicates that sexual immorality as defined in the foregoing laws is incompatible with identity as an Israelite man.

14. Joosten (1996) observes that the law in Leviticus 18 applies to both native Israelite and resident alien (cf. Lev. 18.26), and infers from this that being 'cut off from their people' (Lev. 18.29) refers to being cut off from one's circle of kinsmen rather than from the nation as a whole (82). However, for an Israelite man this would of necessity involve being cut off from membership of the people of Israel, so the point made here still stands. The statement that the incest laws also apply to resident aliens does not undermine the idea that the laws are setting out a construction of Israelite masculinity, since resident aliens are to all intents and purposes Israelites for the time that they reside within the boundaries of Israel, and are bound by other laws within the corpus that are presented as distinctively Israelite, including the Sabbath (Exod. 20.10), the prohibition against leaven during the feast of Unleavened Bread (Exod. 12.19), the Day of Atonement (Lev. 16.29) and the prohibition against eating blood (Lev. 17.12-13). Mohrmann (2004) makes a similar point, commenting that Lev. 18.1-5, 24–30 is speaking of the external boundaries around Israel's culture, boundaries which are embodied in the incest laws, and which also encompass resident aliens (62).

sexual immorality (18.26-28), and there is no 'intermediate state' of punishment within the land to allow time for repentance. Such a direct link between act and serious consequences makes sexual behaviour something that is of absolutely fundamental importance. Indeed, judging from the text of Leviticus, correct sexual behaviour is of even more fundamental importance than not sacrificing to satyrs, an act which is not said to lead to general defilement of and expulsion from the land, only the cutting off of the person who does it (Lev. 17.8-9). Even more interesting than this, however, is the observation that only in the context of the incest laws is the land itself said to vomit out its inhabitants, rather than Yahweh driving them out. Leviticus 26 shows expulsion from the land as the action of Yahweh (26.33), a premeditated, controlled punishment for accumulated sins; by contrast, Leviticus 18 speaks of the land vomiting out the sinful inhabitants (18.25, 28; cf. 20.22),[15] implying that the very land will rebel against something that is so contrary to nature, and in the process challenging the masculinity of those who are vomited out. After all, land (ארץ) is conceptualized as feminine, as reflected in its feminine grammatical gender, and in the beginning humans are given the command to 'subdue the earth' (הארץ, Gen. 1.28), which underlines its feminine conceptualization inasmuch as femininity is associated with passivity and subjection to mastery. Hence, for the very land (הארץ) in Leviticus 18 to rebel by vomiting out those who are supposed to be able to subdue it is a reversal of the natural created gendered order, since the (feminine) subdued is subduing the (masculine) subduer.

The ideological weight that is attached to sexual practices is therefore enormous, implying a strong desire on the part of the legislator to control them tightly. And since sexual practice is such an important element of gender constructions, it is arguable that what is really at stake in this chapter are gender constructions, which have an integral relationship to family structures as envisaged by the sociological analyses of these verses. Men must be men, and women women, in the way that is prescribed by the laws, because if not the

---

15. Leviticus 20 also contains a series of prohibitions against incest and other sexual misdemeanours (20.10-21), preceded by laws against giving one's children to Molech (20.1-5) and wizardry (20.6), and like Leviticus 18 it follows these prohibitions with the exhortation to keep 'all my statutes and my ordinances ... so that the land will not vomit you out' (20.22). It is clear that Leviticus 18 and 20 are related, although the precise nature of that relationship is obscure. As well as the fact that the various prohibitions appear in a different order in each chapter, in Leviticus 20 the various types of sexual misdemeanour are interspersed with each other, whereas in Leviticus 18 all the incest-type offences are presented together, followed by prohibitions against menstrual intercourse, adultery, offering children to Molech, male-male intercourse and bestiality. Additionally, in Leviticus 20 each offence is given its own punishment, rather than the single generalized punishment of being cut off that Lev 18.29 prescribes for all the offences it lists. Although the content of Leviticus 20 bears strong similarities to that of Leviticus 18, its presentation points to a different conceptualization of that content from the conceptualization in Leviticus 18. Given that the focus of the present study is on Leviticus 18 as a self-contained unit rather than on the incest laws in Leviticus more generally, Leviticus 20 will not be discussed here.

whole structure of the society is threatened. This is perhaps what is implied in 18.5, where the text urges its addressees to observe Yahweh's statutes and commandments, אשר יעשה אתם האדם וחי, 'by doing which *ha-adam* shall live'. The RSV renders this as, 'by doing which a man shall live', and the NRSV as, 'by doing so one shall live'; however, the use of the term אדם instead of the more gender-specific איש at this point is intriguing. Either the laws are being presented as a universal human law, and as the only correct way for humans of any race to live;[16] or their male purview is being widened to include women, if only in the sense of urging that women too should keep to the models being promulgated by the statutes, even though they are not addressed directly by those statutes.

b. *'Incest' laws (Leviticus 18.6-18)*
What kind of gender models, then, are discernible in these laws, and in the incest laws in particular? It was remarked earlier that the laws are addressed to men, as is the case for all the laws in the Hebrew Bible, where despite the fact that some laws specifically concern women, no laws are actually addressed to women. This fact is often noted by commentators, and has implications for the construction and perception of both manhood and womanhood envisaged by the laws. Here in the list of incest prohibitions, as elsewhere, the overwhelmingly male-centred conception of the laws is evident. The sequence in Lev. 18.6 begins with the generic exhortation 'No *man* of you shall approach anyone who is closely related to *him*', using the idiomatic phrase איש איש to define the addressees of the exhortation; the laws that then follow are all framed in the masculine singular, as second-person apodeictic prohibitions; and they all describe the (inappropriate) sexual actions of males towards females rather than of females towards males, in a way that pictures sex as something normally done by males to females without consideration of the female's wishes. Indeed, the only independent sexual action countenanced for a woman in these verses is bestiality (18.23), and whereas this (like its masculine counterpart in the same verse) is officially condemned on the grounds that it is 'confusion' or 'mixing' (תבל), one cannot but wonder if part of what was so frowned upon was the rejection of male authority over both women and beasts that was implied by a woman making such a sexual choice. As Fewell and Gunn rather cynically remark, 'Men have better use for their male animal's seed than to waste it on a woman' (Fewell and Gunn 1993: 106). Be that as it may, even in this situation the woman is not addressed directly by the law, but is spoken of to the male addressee in the third person: 'You (m.s.) shall not have sex with a beast, nor shall a woman'. Men are thus presented in these laws as both legal and sexual agents, or subjects: just as it is the man who approaches the woman, rather

---

16. So Joosten (1996: 77).

than vice-versa, so it is the man to whom the instructions are given, and upon whom the primary responsibility for maintaining these laws falls. Male legal authority is reflected in male sexual authority, and both are characteristic of a construction of masculinity that associates males with power. It is this male power that the incest laws set out to regulate by means of their characteristic formulation, as I hope to show.

Uncovering Nakedness

a. *The Right to Uncover Nakedness*

One of the most interesting features of the incest laws in Leviticus 18 is the use of the phrase 'uncover the nakedness', which appears throughout these laws as a euphemism for incestuous sexual contact. This formulation has some interesting ramifications from the gender point of view. In other places where the expression 'uncover the nakedness' (גלה ערוה) appears, it is invariably negative, denoting shameful exposure; and it almost always refers to female or feminine objects. Thus, it appears in Isa. 47.3 to describe the conquered Babylon, metaphorized as a woman, who is told, 'Your nakedness shall be uncovered (תגל ערותך), and your shame shall be seen'. Ezek. 16.36-37 uses the phrase to speak of Jerusalem, similarly metaphorized as a promiscuous woman: 'Because your shame was laid bare and your nakedness uncovered (ותגלה ערותך) in your harlotries with your lovers, ... behold, I will gather all your lovers ... against you from every side, and will uncover your nakedness (וגליתי ערותך) to them, that they may see all your nakedness'. The same picture appears in Ezekiel 23, where both Samaria and Jerusalem are metaphorized as promiscuous women. First, Samaria is condemned for her 'harlotries', in punishment for which God delivers her into the hands of the Assyrians: 'These uncovered her nakedness (גלו ערותה); they seized her sons and her daughters; and her they slew with the sword' (Ezek. 23.10). Then Jerusalem is condemned along the same lines, as God declares, 'When she carried on her harlotry so openly and flaunted her nakedness (ותגל את־ערותה), I turned in disgust from her, as I had turned from her sister' (Ezek. 23.18). The punishment for this is for Jerusalem to be delivered into the hands of her enemies (Ezek. 23.28), 'and they shall deal with you in hatred, and take away all the fruit of your labour, and leave you naked and bare, and the nakedness of your harlotry shall be uncovered (ונגלה ערות זנוניך)' (Ezek. 23.29). As a counter to the language of uncovering nakedness, there are also examples of men covering women's nakedness, in contexts that imply marriage. Thus, Ezek. 16.8 shows God speaking about the beginning of 'his' relationship with the pubescent Jerusalem to whom 'he' is attracted: 'When I passed by you again and looked upon you, behold, you were at the age for love. I spread the edge of my cloak over you, and covered your nakedness (ואכסה ערותך); yes, I pledged myself to you and entered into a covenant with you, says the Lord GOD, and you became mine'.¹⁷ And Hos. 2.11-12 (ET 2.9-10) combines the motifs of covering and uncovering to describe the establishing and the breaking down of a marriage relationship: God, in the role of jilted husband, threatens to take away from unfaithful Israel 'my wool and my flax, which were to cover her nakedness (לכסות את־ערותה)' (Hos. 2.11 [ET 2.9]), and then declares, 'Now I will uncover her lewdness (אגלה את־נבלתה) in the sight of her lovers, and no one shall rescue her out of my hand' (Hos. 2.12 [ET 2.10]). The word 'lewdness' here, נבלת, is a hapax legomenon which can be glossed as (female) genitals,¹⁸ a meaning which is often also the force of the term 'nakedness'. These examples, then, portray the uncovering of female nakedness as a punishment for sexual immorality that was inflicted upon women by the men who claimed ownership of the women's sexuality, and indicate that men expressed such ownership by the provision of materials to cover the woman's nakedness (presumably a way of speaking of a husband's duty to provide for his wife, as reflected in Exod. 21.10).¹⁹ Hence, only the one who covered the woman was entitled to uncover her sexually. Not even the woman herself was allowed to uncover her nakedness in other sexual relations, and should she do so she was liable to involuntary exposure, whether at the hands of her husband, or at the hands of those to whom he surrendered her.

If, then, these comments are applied to the use of the phrase 'expose or uncover nakedness' (גלה ערוה) in Leviticus 18, it is possible to suggest a more specific interpretation of it there. On the assumption that exposure of a woman's nakedness is a way of claiming or expressing control over her sexuality, the prohibition against uncovering nakedness is a way of invalidating a given male's claim to sexual control of a given woman, by presenting his uncovering of her as a violation. In the light of this, it is significant that the phrase is only used of incestuous relationships, and is used neither to denote common adultery (Lev. 18.20) nor to denote male–male intercourse (Lev. 18.22). This would suggest that the incest laws are addressing a situation where kinship links might lead men to think that they were entitled to sexual rights over particular women, and so the function of the 'nakedness' language in the prohibitions is both to acknowledge this mistaken perception and to dispel it

17. A similar idea is often thought to be present in Ruth 3.9, where Ruth asks Boaz to spread his skirt over her, although in this instance the vocabulary of covering nakedness is absent. See, for example, Kruger (1984: 83-85); Bush (1996: 164-65); Nielsen (1997: 73).

18. This, however, should not be taken to exhaust the meaning of the term. See Olyan (1992) for a discussion of the range of meanings that may be attributed to it in the context of Hosea 2.

19. According to Kruger (1984: 80-83), in the light of the Old Babylonian divorce procedure in which a man cuts off the hem of the woman's garment, the references in Ezekiel and Hosea suggest that a man would symbolically clothe his wife-to-be in the presence of witnesses in order to guarantee that he would support her materially, and would symbolically strip her if he was divorcing her, in order to indicate that his maintenance responsibilities for her were at an end.

once and for all. However, the same sexual rights would not automatically be assumed over those outside the family group, and so in forbidding certain sexual relationships in this sphere the 'nakedness' language is not employed. There would be no pre-existing grounds for claiming sexual control over an unrelated woman who was married to a man from another family group, nor in a patriarchally-constructed society such as that envisaged by the laws was there anything automatic to induce a man either to claim or to submit to sexual control in relation to another man. Hence, in these instances it was sufficient simply to use forms of prohibition that did not address any pre-existing potential for such a control claim.[20]

b. *The Bodily Nature of Nakedness*

Speaking in terms of 'uncovering nakedness' can thus be seen as a way of emphasizing to males that females who belong to their immediate kinship circle are not accessible to them sexually, since this is a situation potentially open to misinterpretation. However, there is another aspect of the 'nakedness' language that is worthy of investigation, and that is the physicality of the imagery. As noted, prohibitions against uncovering nakedness are only used of relationships that are deemed incestuous (with one exception—that of intercourse with a menstruant, which will be discussed below); and the definition of an incestuous relationship is one in which a man copulates with someone who is 'near of kin to him' (Lev. 18.6). The Hebrew idiom behind this phrase 'near of kin to him' is equally physical: it is שאר בשרו, 'meat of his flesh'.[21] Thus, the whole prohibition in Lev. 18.6, which in Hebrew reads, איש איש אל־כל־שאר בשרו לא תקרבו לגלות ערוה, may be literally translated, 'no man of you shall approach any flesh of his (own) flesh to uncover nakedness'. This emphasis on the bodily nature of both the kin relationship and the forbidden act which is described as exposing the genitals is extremely interesting, given that ideas about the body and how it is constructed by social and cultural forces into an appropriately gendered entity are an important and revealing aspect of gender studies.[22] The use of 'body' language in the incest prohibitions suggests that in offering its construction of Israelite masculinity, Leviticus 18 also presents a distinctive view of gendered human bodies, and it is this view that provides the basis for the prohibitions.

---

20. Levine (1989: 117) glosses the meaning of ערוה as 'exclusive sexual access'. This is certainly an important part of its significance in the context of Leviticus 18, but it does not explain why in Leviticus 18 such language should only be applied to liaisons that are perceived as incestuous, rather than to adulterous liaisons more generally, for which it would seem equally appropriate if it really does signify no more than 'exclusive sexual access'.

21. According to Hartley (1992: 293), שאר denotes the inner flesh with the blood, while בשר denotes the outer flesh.

22. Perhaps the best-known gender theorist in this area is Judith Butler. See particularly her work, *Bodies That Matter* (Butler 1993).

Sociologically speaking, what the incest prohibitions reflect is a societal structure based on male kinship links, as a number of commentators have remarked.[23] This is most clearly seen in the prohibitions against taking women who are already married to other males in the kin group (e.g. father's wife, Lev. 18.8; daughter-in-law, Lev. 18.15; sister-in-law, Lev. 18.16), and suggests that part of what it means to be an Israelite man is to observe sexual loyalty towards one's own male kinship group, giving a communal character to the construction of masculinity. The comment made earlier about male sexuality being constructed to reflect a masculinity of male power becomes relevant here: while it is apparently an appropriate exercise of power for males to 'take' certain females, it is an abuse of that power for males to use it against their own male paternal kin. Hence, what might be construed as an individualistic construction of male power is modified into a more socially orientated one. To that extent, therefore, the incest laws are an exercise in male bonding, that is, in protecting the kinship bonds between men by making sure that they are not in competition with each other for the same women.[24] A further important sociological function of the prohibitions, once again reflecting their male perspective, is protecting the male lines of descent that are so important in a patriarchal community such as that evidenced in the materials of the Hebrew Bible,[25] and this would certainly be achieved by prohibiting sexual relationships with female relatives (that is, by constructing masculinity to encompass male kinship loyalty so that a male does not trespass on his relatives' women).

However, what is of interest here is not so much who is prohibited to whom, but the construction of gender that is used to enforce the prohibitions, and this is where the bodily imagery that is used to describe incestuous relationships becomes significant. In the Hebrew Bible, and indeed, in the Priestly stratum of the Pentateuch to which Leviticus belongs, human bodies are constructed as male (זכר) and female (נקבה), as the well-known statement in Gen. 1.27-28 declares: 'So God created man in his own image; in the image of God he created him; male and female (זכר ונקבה) he created them. And God blessed them, and God said to them, Be fruitful and multiply'. Unlike the more pictorial account of human creation in the following chapter of Genesis, this version of human creation has no sense that these two types of body are variations of each other; there is no אשה who is taken from איש or bone of bone and flesh of flesh as there is in Gen. 2.23. Instead, in a classic example of the phenomenon known as gender dimorphism,[26] there are two (and only

---

23. See, for example, Bigger (1979: 194); Rattray (1987: 540); Levine (1989: 117).

24. Mohrmann (2004: 70) makes a similar comment, although he does not draw any inferences from the text about gender constructions.

25. Brenner (1994b: 131) sees this as the major function of the incest laws.

26. For a discussion of dimorphic conceptions of sex and gender, see Wharton (2005: 17-40, 47-49). See also Bem (1993: 80-81, 138-49) for a discussion of gender polarization, that is, the

two) contrasting types with separate roles and functions: the male type (זכר) whose name denotes its association with memory, identity and continuity, as evidenced in the male-focused genealogies through which individuals find their own place in the community, and the female type (נקבה) whose name denotes its association with passivity, with being pierced or penetrated, a hollow into which the material of male memory is poured (Brenner 1997: 11-12). Male and female are thus constructed by divine fiat as 'others' in relation to each other, and it is via this otherness that multiplication is to take place, as women become the vessels for men's procreative designs to which female sexuality is subordinated. In Genesis 1 no other type of body is envisaged, nor is any limit envisaged on male-female relationships: all males can apparently mate with all females, and every female body is available to every male body. However, by the time of Leviticus 18 the situation has changed, and the physical idiom used to express close family relationships points to the construction of a third category of body, a third gender, as it were, namely, that of שאר or kin. Bodies that are constructed as belonging to this category cannot be treated in the same way as other bodies, because the construction as 'kin' means that the difference that is necessary for normal sexual relationships to take place is undermined. The bodies that are viewed as belonging in this category are a kind of 'intersex' body from the perspective of the Israelite male. Physically female, they are nevertheless of the same flesh (שאר בשרו, 18.6) as the male; these bodies therefore destabilize the normal male/female divide, threatening the binary categorization of human bodies, because they participate in both genders.[27] As a result they are forbidden to the male sexually in the same way that another male would be, because they do not fall simply and unproblematically into the category 'woman'. Many studies of the Priestly writings of which this chapter

---

social process via which males and females are defined as mutually exclusive opposites and those who exhibit traits of the opposite gender are problematized.

27. For a discussion of the phenomenon of intersexuality, and the complex gendered political and social issues surrounding the condition, see Fausto-Sterling (2000: 30-114). Fausto-Sterling argues that the high incidence of intersex births, estimated at a rate of 1.7% of all births (by comparison, albinism occurs only once in every 20,000 births) challenges the idea that everyone is naturally either male or female (51-4), and she advocates the acceptance and recognition of 'gender multiplicity and ambiguity' (114). As an illustration of what is at stake in defining intersexuals as male or female, she cites the case of an Australian XX intersexual whose body was surgically corrected to male norms but whose marriage was subsequently annulled on the grounds that 'in a legal system that requires a person to be either one or the other, for the purpose of marriage, he could be neither male nor female' (112). Just as with the Leviticus legislation, the identity of the 'nakedness', that is, the genitalia, of the intersex person is a major issue, and surgery to make the genitalia conform to either male or female norms is often undertaken at a very early stage, because assigning the child to one or other gender category is seen as an essential step to enable 'proper' social and psychological development, and social gender must correlate with genital gender, even though genitals are normally hidden. The point is, of course, that Western society as it is currently arranged cannot tolerate more than two gender-types.

forms a part have emphasized the importance of categorization in Priestly thinking and suggested interpretative schemas whereby impurity is associated with people and things that cannot be fitted neatly into one category;[28] so such a reading of gender models in Leviticus 18 is entirely in keeping with the Priestly mindset in general.

Although all of these bodies are threatening to gender dimorphism and the male/female divide, some are more threatening than others. Just as the physical phenomenon of intersexuality has various manifestations, so too here various degrees of intersexuality are recognized. The bodies that are most threatening to normal gender categories are those female bodies which are constructed entirely as male bodies: the body of the father's wife (18.7-8), of the father's brother's wife (18.14), and of the brother's wife (18.16), and the bodies of one's granddaughters (18.10).[29] All of these women are constructed as the nakedness of a man; the first three as the nakedness of the man to whom they are married, and the others as the nakedness of their grandfather, who is the addressee of the laws. Less threatening, but still forbidden, are those female bodies that are constructed as participating in male bodies: the sister (18.9, 11), who participates in the addressee's body ('she is *your* sister', 18.11); the daughter-in-law (18.15), who participates in the son's body ('she is *your son's* wife', 18.15); the paternal aunt (18.12), who participates in the father's body ('she is the שְׁאֵר of your father', 18.12); and the step-(grand)daughter (18.17), who participates in the addressee's body ('they are שַׁאֲרָה',[30] 18.17). Probably the least threatening (though still forbidden) are those that are constructed as participating in other female bodies which themselves participate in male bodies: the maternal aunt (18.13), who is שְׁאֵר to the woman who is termed the nakedness of the addressee's father (18.7, 13); and the wife's sister

---

28. See, for example, Gorman (1990: 39-60); Jenson (1992).

29. Bigger (1979: 200) comments that the 'nakedness' motive clause in the granddaughter prohibition is secondary and indicates confusion over the concept of the man's nakedness. However, the present schema can incorporate the prohibition without needing to dismiss it as secondary.

30. The RSV and NRSV translations both understand the term שַׁאֲרָה here to mean that the women are viewed as kin to the addressee of the law, an interpretation that appears in the LXX (οἰκεῖαι γάρ σού εἰσιν). However, other interpretations are possible. BHS suggests that the word be pointed שְׁאֵרָה, which would indicate clearly that the daughter and granddaughters are viewed as the wife's kin rather than the addressee's kin, and this is followed by Hartley (1992. 281, 283). Milgrom (2000: 1547) also understands the phrase to mean that the women are kin to each other rather than to the addressee, although he sees no need to change the pointing, viewing שַׁאֲרָה as an abstract collective noun. However, it seems that although the word is ambiguous, the point of the terminology of 'kin' is to associate all the women with the addressee. The forbidden women are prohibited to the addressee not just because all the women are kin to each other, but because one of the women has become 'kin' to the addressee via marriage, thus making them all effectively kin to him.

(18.18),[31] who is a sister to the woman who participates in the addressee's own body. When these constructions are viewed in the light of the hierarchical male kinship structure by which the family is organized, it becomes clear that the most dangerous bodies are those which relate to paternal male relatives whose social status is either equal to or higher than that of the addressee, in other words, men of his own or the previous generation; and this is where the particular overtones of the 'nakedness' formulation come out most clearly. Given that the women in question are not blood relatives of the addressee (except for his mother), the question arises as to why liaisons between a man and his equal or senior female marital kin are not simply treated as adultery, and conversely, why adultery is not described using the nakedness terminology that is so characteristic of the incest provisions. One answer that suggests itself is that by using the nakedness terminology, and constructing the forbidden women not only as males but as the males to whom they belong, incest is constructed not just as an offence or insult against another male but as an actual physical violation of his person. As such incest is a worse crime than (mere) adultery (which is effectively wrongful sex) because it threatens the basic family structures and disrupts the social hierarchy in a more fundamental way than adultery does.[32] Gender construction is thus made to serve social ends, by being used to protect and preserve the male hierarchy of authority. This would also explain the fact that a prohibition using 'nakedness' language is applied to the addressee's daughter-in-law, but her nakedness is not said to be the son's nakedness. The father is his son's social superior, with authority over his son, and although it is possible to abuse that authority, such abuse does not threaten the social hierarchy or the relative status of father and son.[33] However, it may well threaten the coherence of the family unit, which again makes it rather more serious than 'mere' adultery in the eyes of the legislator.

---

31. The cultural relativity of these prohibitions can be seen from the fact that the prohibited liaisons are quite acceptable in other societies. A case study of Navajo Indians in the 1960s found that where polygyny occurred, the most common type was sororal polygyny, whereby the same man married two or more sisters. The study also found cases of 'stepdaughter marriage', whereby a man married both a woman and the woman's daughter; the rationale for this type of union was that the woman became too old to be a wife to the man, so she gave him his daughter. Another study reported cases where a man married a woman with the understanding that he should also marry her daughter when the daughter came of age. See Stone (1997: 128) for details.

32. Schenker (2003: 166, 181) comments that incestuous relationships make it impossible for individuals to play their appropriate social part relative to each other in the family group because it confuses the relationships between the members. This in turn makes it impossible for the members to situate themselves in the wider community.

33. Bigger (1979: 197) makes a similar observation about the relative status of father and son as accounting for the lack of the 'male nakedness' clause in this instance. However, he does not comment on the significance of nakedness language in general in these laws, apparently regarding it as simply characteristic of a particular redactor instead of having any positive significance for the meaning of the laws (202).

Hence, adultery with one's daughter-in-law is constructed as intercourse with a woman who participates in a blood-related male and is therefore an 'intersex'; in other words, it is viewed as the joining of two bodies that are insufficiently different from each other to satisfy the demand that males join with females.

The message of this gender-bending construction is thus that 'real Israelite men don't sleep with their female relatives, because female relatives don't count as real women, but as pseudo-men'. From this perspective, it is little wonder that such abominations lead to ejection from the land, because they are a distortion of the most fundamental principle of continued existence, namely, that men sleep with women. Once one aspect of the natural order has been so disturbed, there is a knock-on effect to other aspects, and the failure to distinguish properly between male and female principles is just such a disturbance that is bound to have far-reaching consequences.

There is still one prohibition that needs to be examined, though, and that is the prohibition against sleeping with a menstruant (Lev. 18.19). Although this too is phrased using 'nakedness' language—'you shall not approach a woman to uncover her nakedness during her menstrual impurity' (ואל־אשה בנדת טמאתה לא תקרב לגלות ערותה)—it seems to have little or nothing to do with the incest provisions, and indeed commentators usually regard it as belonging with the remaining few prohibitions against adultery, bestiality and male-male sexual activity, with the 'nakedness' language merely borrowed from the incest prohibitions by a later redactor.[34] However, the interpretative model that has been offered for the nakedness language suggests the possibility of an alternative view. The status and identity of the woman are not defined, but if the interpretation of the 'nakedness' language already offered holds good in this case too, its use here indicates that she is someone over whom the male addressee might legitimately expect to exercise sexual control, and this is most naturally interpreted as the man's wife.[35] The point of the idiom is that normally the man would exercise sexual control over her, but this is not to be the case when she is menstruating, and indeed, in a previous chapter the law has already said that a man who has sex with a woman and is touched by her menstrual fluid is unclean for seven days (Lev. 15.24)—the same length of time as the woman is unclean when she is menstruating. Contrast this with male ejaculation of semen, which causes only a day's uncleanness (15.16-18) for both partners. The male who is touched by menstrual fluid is therefore feminized inasmuch as for the seven days of his impurity he is effectively cut off from the rest of

---

34. Bigger (1979: 202) views the 'nakedness' language as a redactional rewriting of an older prohibition. All of the commentators reviewed for this essay take Lev. 18.19 with the following prohibitions (Lev. 18.20-23) rather than with the preceding ones (Lev. 18.6-18).

35. Levine (1989: 122) comments that the prohibition regulates a man's sexual relationship with his own wife, although he gives no reason for saying so.

male society; he is unclean, so he cannot go near the Temple or participate in the ritual observances such as sacrifices that other men would carry out, and his uncleanness is at least partially transferable, as is indicated by its polluting effect on every bed that he lies on (Lev. 15.24). So once again it can be argued that the 'nakedness' formulation is linked with a distortion or blurring of the normal patterns of gender construction, although this time it is the male who is feminized because of contact with female blood rather than the female who is masculinized because of participation in male flesh.[36]

Conclusion

In conclusion, then, positioned as they are in a patriarchal society that is characterized by androcentrism and strict gender dimorphism, the incest laws of Leviticus 18 use the bodily terminology of relatedness and nakedness to categorize certain forbidden females as conceptually 'intersexed' in relation to the males to whom they are forbidden, thus effectively characterizing the women as pseudo-males. Such women are seen as dangerous because they blur the category boundaries of male and female. This is a way of protecting the social boundaries and keeping the lines of descent clean within the patriarchal family.

BIBLIOGRAPHY

Anderson, Cheryl B.
    2004   *Women, Ideology, and Violence: Critical Theory and the Construction of Gender in the Book of the Covenant and the Deuteronomic Law* (JSOTSup, 394; London: T. & T. Clark International).

Bach, Alice
    1993   'Good to the Last Drop: Viewing the Sotah (Numbers 5.11-31) as the Glass Half Empty and Wondering How to View it Half Full', in J. Cheryl Exum and David J.A. Clines (eds.), *The New Literary Criticism and the Hebrew Bible* (JSOTSup, 143; Sheffield: JSOT Press): 26-54.

Be'er, Ilana
    1994   'Blood Discharge: On Female Im/purity in the Priestly Code and in Biblical Literature', in Brenner 1994a: 152-64.

Bem, Sandra Lipsitz
    1993   *The Lenses of Gender: Transforming the Debate on Sexual Inequality* (New Haven: Yale University Press).

Bigger, Stephen F.
    1979   'The Family Laws of Leviticus 18 in their Setting', *JBL* 98: 187-203.

Brenner, Athalya
    1994a   (ed.) *A Feminist Companion to Exodus to Deuteronomy* (Sheffield: Sheffield Academic Press).

---

36. For further discussion of the laws pertaining to menstrual impurity and how they affect both men and women, see the essay by Nicole Ruane in the present volume.

    1994b   'On Incest', in Brenner 1994a: 113-38.
    1997   *The Intercourse of Knowledge: On Gendering Desire and 'Sexuality' in the Hebrew Bible* (Biblical Interpretation series, 26; Leiden: E.J. Brill).

Budd, Philip J.
    1996   *Leviticus* (NCB; London: Marshall Pickering).

Bush, Frederic W.
    1996   *Ruth, Esther* (WBC, 9; Dallas, TX: Word).

Butler, Judith
    1993   *Bodies That Matter: On the Discursive Limits of Sex* (New York: Routledge).

Fausto-Sterling, Anne
    2000   *Sexing the Body: Gender Politics and the Construction of Sexuality* (New York: Basic Books).

Fewell, Danna Nolan, and David M. Gunn
    1993   *Gender, Power, and Promise: The Subject of the Bible's First Story* (Nashville, TN: Abingdon Press).

Gerstenberger, Erhard S.
    1996   *Leviticus* (trans. Douglas W. Stott; OTL; Louisville, KY: Westminster/John Knox Press).

Gorman, Frank H.
    1990   *The Ideology of Ritual: Space, Time and Status in the Priestly Theology* (JSOTSup, 91; Sheffield: JSOT Press).

Hartley, John E.
    1992   *Leviticus* (WBC, 4; Dallas, TX: Word).

Havea, Jione
    2003   *Elusions of Control: Biblical Law on the Words of Women* (Semeia Studies, 41; Atlanta: Society of Biblical Literature).

Jenson, Philip Peter
    1992   *Graded Holiness: A Key to the Priestly Conception of the World* (JSOTSup, 106; Sheffield: JSOT Press).

Joosten, J.
    1996   *People and Land in the Holiness Code: An Exegetical Study of the Ideational Framework of the Law in Leviticus 17–26* (VTSup, 67; Leiden: E.J. Brill).

Kruger, Paul A.
    1984   'The Hem of the Garment in Marriage: The Meaning of the Symbolic Gesture in Ruth 3.9 and Ezek. 16.8', *JNSL* 12: 79-86.

Levine, Baruch A.
    1989   *Leviticus* (JPS Torah Commentary; Philadelphia: Jewish Publication Society).

Lipka, Hilary B.
    2006   *Sexual Transgression in the Hebrew Bible* (Hebrew Bible Monographs, 7; Sheffield: Sheffield Phoenix Press).

Matthews, Victor H.
    1998   'Honor and Shame in Gender-Related Legal Situations in the Hebrew Bible', in Matthews, Levinson and Frymer-Kensky 1998: 97-112.

Matthews, Victor H., Bernard M. Levinson and Tikva Frymer-Kensky (eds.)
    1998   *Gender and Law in the Hebrew Bible and the Ancient Near East* (JSOTSup, 262; Sheffield: Sheffield Academic Press).

Milgrom, Jacob
    1991   *Leviticus 1–16* (AB, 3; New York: Doubleday).

2000   *Leviticus 17–22* (AB, 3A; New York: Doubleday).
Mohrmann, Douglas C.
    2004   'Making Sense of Sex: A Study of Leviticus 18', *JSOT* 29:57-79.
Nielsen, Kirsten
    1997   *Ruth* (trans. Edward Broadbridge; OTL; Louisville, KY: Westminster/John Knox Press).
Olyan, Saul M.
    1992   '"In the sight of her lovers": On the Interpretation of *nablūt* in Hos. 2.12', *BZ* 36: 255-61.
Philip, Tarja S.
    2006   *Menstruation and Childbirth in the Bible: Fertility and Impurity* (Studies in Biblical Literature, 88; New York: Peter Lang).
Phillips, Anthony
    1980   'Uncovering the Father's Skirt', *VT* 30: 38-43.
Pressler, Carolyn
    1993   *The View of Women Found in the Deuteronomic Family Laws* (BZAW, 216; Berlin: W. de Gruyter).
Rattray, Susan
    1987   'Marriage Rules, Kinship Terms and Family Structure in the Bible', in Kent H. Richards (ed.), *Society of Biblical Literature 1987 Seminar Papers: One Hundred Twenty-Third Annual Meeting December 5-8, 1987, Boston Marriott Copley Place, Sheraton Boston Hotel & Towers, Boston, Massachusetts* (Atlanta: Scholars Press): 537-44.
Rendtorff, Rolf, and Robert A. Kugler (eds.)
    2003   *The Book of Leviticus: Composition and Reception* (VTSup, 93; Leiden: E.J. Brill).
Rooke, Deborah W.
    2000   'Wayward Women and Broken Promises: Marriage, Adultery and Mercy in Old and New Testaments', in Larry J. Kreitzer and Deborah W. Rooke (eds.), *Ciphers in the Sand: Interpretations of the Woman Taken in Adultery* (Biblical Seminar, 74: Sheffield: Sheffield Academic Press): 17-52.
Roth, Martha T.
    1995   *Law Collections from Mesopotamia and Asia Minor* (SBL Writings from the Ancient World, 6; Atlanta: Scholars Press).
Schearing, Linda
    2003   'Double Time ... Double Trouble? Gender, Sin, and Leviticus 12', in Rendtorff and Kugler 2003: 429-50.
Schenker, Adrian
    2003   'What Connects the Incest Prohibitions with the Other Prohibitions Listed in Leviticus 18 and 20?', in Rendtorff and Kugler 2003: 162-85.
Sivan, Hagith
    2004   *Between Woman, Man and God: A New Interpretation of the Ten Commandments* (JSOTSup, 401; BTC, 4; London: T. & T. Clark International).
Stone, Linda
    1997   *Kinship and Gender: An Introduction* (Boulder, CO: Westview Press).
Wassen, Cecilia
    2005   *Women in the Damascus Document* (Society of Biblical Literature Academia Biblica, 21; Atlanta: Society of Biblical Literature).

Wegner, Judith Romney
    1992   'Leviticus', in Carol A. Newsom and Sharon H. Ringe (eds.), *The Women's Bible Commentary* (London: SPCK; Louisville, KY: Westminster/John Knox Press): 36-44.

Wharton, Amy S.
    2005   *The Sociology of Gender: An Introduction to Theory and Research* (Key Themes in Sociology; Oxford: Blackwell).

GENDER CRITICAL OBSERVATIONS ON TRIPARTITE
BREEDING RELATIONSHIPS IN THE HEBREW BIBLE

Bernard S. Jackson

1. *Introduction*

A 'tripartite breeding relationship' may be defined as an arrangement to use the reproductive capacities of two members of a household for the benefit of a third member. In this paper, I shall juxtapose a number of legal and narrative texts which manifest such relationships either explicitly or implicitly. They involve use of the reproductive capacities of both males and females, free and slave. In order to compare them, the following four 'systematic' questions may be posed:

(a) Who may be used for breeding?
(b) What is the effect of this on the dependency relationship within the household, between master (or mistress) and dependant? This may be termed the vertical relationship.
(c) What status between the breeding partners results from this relationship? Is it a marriage, and if so what kind of marriage? This may be termed the horizontal relationship.
(d) What is the status of the children so produced?

The biblical texts are not comprehensive in providing answers to these questions; none of the texts explicitly answers all four questions. Nevertheless, I shall attempt to elucidate what is implicit in some texts from what is explicit in others. I shall also pose to the texts a gender critical question: is there a difference in the terms on which the reproductive capacities of males and females (both free and dependent) may be deployed? Finally, I shall suggest that the answers to (c), in particular, reflect the fact that marriage as seen in the Hebrew Bible is weakly institutionalized.

2. *The Male Hebrew Debt-Slave (Exod. 21.2-6)*

Exod. 21.2-6 deals with the position of the male Hebrew debt-slave[1] whom you 'acquire'.[2] The law is addressed to the creditor, and the paragraph as a whole

---

1. On the interpretation of עבד עברי, and the argument, generally but not universally accepted, that the context here is that of debt-slavery, see Jackson (2006: 80-83).
2. On the use of the verb קנה to include distraint as well as voluntary sale into debt-slavery, see Jackson (2006: 82).

may be taken to reflect this interest as much as those of the debt-slave. This is particularly important when considering the implications of Exod. 21.4:

אם אדניו יתן לו אשה וילדה לו בנים או בנות האשה וילדיה תהיה לאדניה והוא יצא בגפו

> If his master gives him a woman[3] and she bears him sons or daughters, the woman and her children shall be her master's and he shall go out alone.

If we ask, *cui bono?*, the answer is that this is clearly for the benefit of the master, who may use his debt-slave for reproductive as for any other kind of labour during the six years of his service. Unless the debt-slave exercises the option given to him in vv. 5-6 to remain as a permanent slave in his master's household, such familial ties as may have been created in this context are severed when the debt-slave goes free; the children he produced during his service remain the property of his master. It is difficult, realistically, to view them as incidental benefits of the master's humanitarian concern in providing a companion for his debt-slave. Rather, this was the whole object of giving him a 'woman'. The Hebrew debt-slave may be used, quite simply, for breeding. (We are not told whether he may refuse.)

The status of the 'woman' given to the debt-slave is not mentioned here. She is generally regarded as a gentile permanent slave[4] whose status derives originally from capture (as in Deut. 21.10-14), though the present owner may have acquired her by purchase on the slave market, or she may have been bred from a slave so acquired (perhaps even in just the circumstances to which she herself is now subjected).

I would therefore suggest the following answers to the four 'systematic' questions, as they relate to the male Hebrew debt-slave:

(a) A Hebrew male debt-slave may be used for breeding purposes, within the maximum six years of his service. Before he became a debt-slave, he was free, and he reverts to his free status at the end of his service (unless he opts otherwise). The fact that he has been used for breeding has no impact on this.

(b) What matters to the writer are the vertical relationships between owner and female slave (and her children) on the one hand, and between owner and debt-slave on the other.

(c) Conversely, there is no concern with the horizontal relationship, that is, with the status of the relationship between the debt-slave and the woman. Certainly, it is not a marriage;[5] it is temporary and terminates automatically on the debt-slave's departure.

---

3. RSV and many other translations render אשה here as 'wife'. But see further n. 5 below.

4. Though unlikely, it is not impossible that she may be a Hebrew אמה as in Exod. 21.7-11, despite the fact that only a relationship with the purchaser and his son is contemplated in that text. See further Jackson (2006: 88-89 n. 52, 91).

5. See further Jackson (2006: 95-96 n. 97).

(d) As for the status of the children, the implication is that they follow the status of their mother; thus they are permanent slaves if she is.[6]

The Priestly writer presents a radically different approach to the position of the male Hebrew debt-slave in Lev. 25.39-46. Service here is reconceptualized as, or analogized to, that of a 'hired servant and a sojourner' (v. 40), and the slave's children go out with him (v. 41). However, this is in the context of a period of service that is not terminable after six years but rather extends until the next Jubilee. We are not told here whether the debt-slave was married when he commenced service or was given a breeding partner by the master. The greater length of service, combined with the fact that no mention is made of the release of the woman along with the debt-slave and his children, suggests at least the possibility that the debt-slave, here as in Exod. 21.4, is given a breeding partner while in service. If so, the children here follow the status of the father, in going free in the year of the Jubilee. Nevertheless, the master will have had the benefit of their service for a potentially extended period.

3. *The Female Hebrew Debt-Slave (Exod. 21.7-11)*

Immediately following the paragraph of the עבד עברי in the *Mishpatim* is that of the female Hebrew debt-slave,[7] sold לאמה. It is clear that she is sold for sexual services, and that this entails the creation of a permanent relationship, with no *ex lege* release after six years. There is in fact evidence that debt-slavery terminable after six years did apply to women as well as men,[8] and that the status of אמה was a distinct form of dependence.[9] Indeed, the documentary evidence from the ancient Near East indicates that women were actually taken as debt-slaves (for general, not sexual, services) more often than were men.[10] In the Bible, Jeremiah refers to the דרור[11] under King Zedekiah[12]

---

6. If she is in fact a Hebrew אמה (see n. 4 above), the answer would be that given below in section 3 question (d).

7. As indicated by the fact that she is sold by her father, and by the explicit cross-reference to the preceding paragraph. Cf. Isa. 50.1, where מכר is used and where the object of sale, in context at least, includes daughters. For daughters as debt-slaves, see also Jeremiah 34 and Nehemiah 5, cited in the discussion below. See also n. 21 below.

8. For primary sources, see below. For the secondary literature, see Jackson (2006: 87 n. 42).

9. Cf. Mendelsohn 1935: 195; Cardellini 1981: 252-53.

10. Jackson and Watkins (1984: 418), in relation to distraint. Crüsemann (1996: 157) observes that 'daughters are usually the first to be sold when situations of need arise'.

11. Both in the Bible and the ancient Near East, it was common for an incoming king to proclaim a form of economic amnesty, an immediate measure of debt-relief. In the Bible, it is termed דרור, in the ancient Near East *andurârum*. See Hudson (1993), Weinfeld (1995: 75-96), Jackson (1998a: 229-32; 2006: 444-45).

12. Chavel (1997: 74-75) comments, 'Zedekiah makes no reference to the pentateuchal

as involving the setting free of both male and female debt-slaves,[13] the latter here being referred to not by the term אמה, but rather שפחה (Jer. 34.9); the same appears from the complaint made to Nehemiah (5.2, 5).[14] The existence of a social institution of debt-slavery for women, distinct from the form mentioned in the אמה paragraph, thus appears certain. Indeed, it is clear from Deut. 15.12 that a female Hebrew debt-slave (עבריה) does go out free after six years, along with the male Hebrew debt-slave, if she is used for purely domestic services: 'If your brother, a Hebrew man, or a Hebrew woman, is sold to you, he shall serve you six years, and in the seventh year you shall let him go free from you'.[15] The very omission of this (perhaps more common) case from the juxtaposed paragraphs of the *Mishpatim* serves to convey an important message: the creditor may use the reproductive capacities of the Hebrew male debt-slave without altering his long-term status, but he may use the reproductive capacities of the Hebrew female debt-slave only if he does alter her long-term status.[16] It

---

codes. He simply declares דרור, similar more to the ancient Near Eastern *andurârum* acts than to the law in Leviticus 25'. But the background here may well have been military more than economic, that is, the need to recruit personnel for the army, in order to defend Jerusalem against the Babylonians. See David (1948: 63); Kessler (1971) (the release, though, not to be understood as a purely practical measure—affecting both male and female slaves—but as 'a solemn and sacred act' involving a 'touch of mimetic magic' to induce God to free the Judaeans from the siege); Westbrook (1991: 16-17 n. 4, 37-38); Weinfeld (1995: 155 n. 1). See also Jackson (1998a: 238-42).

13. This, however, is a simultaneous release of all slaves, rather than release fixed in terms of the service of the particular slave, despite the invocation of Deut. 15.12 in Jer. 34.14. David (1948) sees a similar tension within Deuteronomy 15 (general release of debts in the שמטה year, Deut. 15.1; individual release of debt-slaves after six years' service, Deut. 15.12), and writes, 'So evidently in the days of Jeremiah the development had come to pass which should have taken place in Deuteronomical times if the legislator had not taken an older regulation as his starting-point: from the individual manumission after six years of labour a general one had come into being in a fixed year in which, at least in theory, all slaves had to be set free simultaneously' (75). Indeed, without such an 'older regulation' (Exod. 21.2), it is difficult to make sense of Deuteronomy 15.

14. See further Weinfeld (1995: 168-74); Jackson (1998a: 242-44).

15. Deut. 15.17b reinterprets the אמה status of Exod. 21.7-11 as the result of a voluntary decision of the woman, parallel to the option of the male Hebrew slave to remain (Exod. 21.5-6).

16. See further Jackson (2006: 87-89, 92-93). The argument was first advanced in Jackson (1988a: 93-94; 1988b: 235-36). Cf. Chirichigno (1993: 246); Pressler (1998: 170 n. 52).

According to the interpretation offered by Westbrook (1988: 101-109), Lev. 19.20-22 provides a near-explicit confirmation of this. He takes it to mean: 'If a man has sexual intercourse with a married woman, she being a slave pledged to the man and not redeemed or given her freedom, an action lies for her return. They may not be put to death because she was not freed. He shall bring his guilt-offering' (1988: 108). Without entering into the details of the argument, we may note that there is no other evidence in the Hebrew Bible of wives being taken as debt-slaves (although there is elsewhere in the ancient Near East). Interestingly, the Laws of Lipit-Ishtar also recognise that a woman (here a street prostitute) used for breeding purposes must be given an assured status

is true that breeding is not mentioned in Exod. 21.7-11; there is no reference to any children which may be born to the אמה. But this is hardly significant: even if the primary object here is the sexual relationship itself, the likelihood of reproduction is obvious, and must have been in contemplation.

The text is subject to a number of difficulties, particularly in the phrase אשר לא יעדה in v. 8. I take the *qere* rather than the *kethib,* and interpret the verb euphemistically: the text tells us what the master may and may not do if he is displeased with her after he has had relations with her.[17] The concern of the present study, however, is with the basic relationship rather than with what ought to happen should it go wrong. In this context, the answers to the systematic questions are as follows:

(a) A Hebrew female debt-slave may be used for breeding. This is the implication of the juxtaposition of the אמה paragraph with the עבד עברי paragraph, even though children are not here mentioned explicitly.

(b) A tripartite relationship is contemplated here too, if the purchaser designates her for his son (Exod. 21.9). But as before, what matters, even without that, is the vertical (dependency) relationship between owner and slave (and her children), rather than the horizontal relationship between the debt-slave and her partner. Although the 'woman' was originally a free Israelite woman, she clearly has an inferior status as אמה while in the household,[18] but because she was originally a free Hebrew woman who has been purchased for sexual/reproductive services, both her rights and (by implication) those of her children are superior to those of an ordinary אמה[19]

(in the form of the three-fold maintenance clause): 'If a man's wife does not bear him a child but a prostitute from the street square does bear him a child, he shall provide grain, oil and clothing rations for the prostitute, and the child whom the prostitute bore shall be his heir; as long as his wife is alive, the prostitute will not reside in the house with his first-ranking wife' (Roth 1995: 31).

17. See further Jackson (2006: 90-91). The explanation בבגדו־בה makes sense only if we both adopt the *qere* and take the verb יעד euphemistically, comparable to ידע (as Budde [1891:102-103]; see, however, Driver [1911: 214]; Neufeld [1944: 69]; David [1948: 68 n. 18]): the 'deceit' consists in the fact that though the purchaser has acquired the woman for sexual purposes, and has indeed had the benefit of that contract, he then seeks to dispose of her on the slave market.

18. The woman's position here differs from that of Hagar, Bilhah and Zilpah in that both aspects of her 'split personality' (marriage and servitude) relate to the same person. *Pace* the argument of Fleishman (2000: 47-64), discussed in Jackson (2006: 117-19) (Appendix B), one cannot totally neutralize לאמה in v. 7, nor the implications of the comparison in that verse with עבדים.

19. It is difficult to understand the basis of Levine's understanding of the term אמה when he writes (1999: 137), 'Since this girl has been acquired not with the juridical status of servant (Heb. *siphah*) but as a free lass (Heb. *'amah*), she has to be treated like any free-born woman ('*kemispat habbanot*', v. 9)'.

(whom the owner would be free to dispose of 'abroad', and to whom he would have no duties of support).

(c) Despite the fact that rabbinic sources incorporate to this very day the threefold rights of Exod. 21.10 into the traditional marriage contract, there is debate as to whether the horizontal relationship here is indeed a marriage, and if so what is its form (or status).[20] Although from its very inception it is not a temporary relationship like that of the male debt-slave in Exod. 21.4, it terminates on redemption or failure to maintain, rather than on divorce.[21] The law gives the woman a status somewhat akin to that of a secondary wife,[22] but the context of debt-slavery continues to inform her situation: ultimately she will be released and the debtor retains a residual[23] right to redeem her.[24]

(d) What is the status of the children? This question is not often asked, because children are not mentioned in the text, but if they follow the status of their mother (as in Exod. 21.4), they will also be debt-slaves who are not themselves disposable on the market but who gain their freedom on the death of the purchaser. Thus they too will ultimately become free, and return to their mother's original household.

4. *The Foreign Female Captive (Deut. 21.10-14)*

Thematically, the law of the foreign female captive in Deut. 21.10-14 has much in common with the law of the Hebrew אמה in Exod. 21.7-11, and may well have been conceived as a humanitarian extension of the latter. If the captor, after

---

20. See further Jackson (2006: 93-94, 99-102), which concludes, 'It is not inappropriate to use here language which would fail the standards of precision of a modern lawyer: she has a "quasi-servile" status and a relationship "somewhat akin" to marriage' (102).

21. *Pace* Levine (1999: 160), there is no use of divorce terminology in this paragraph in relation to the cessation of the relationship. Westbrook (1998: 218-19) sees the references to sale, manumission and redemption as markers of her debt-slave status.

22. Avigad (1953: 143-44) argues that אמה on a pre-exilic Hebrew tombstone inscription, which says that the bones of the man and his אמה must not be disturbed, must refer to a second-wife: 'Legally, the *amah* was a bondswoman, but in practice her rank in the household depended entirely upon the position her master wished to give her'. See also Avigad (1946) and Sarna (1991: 120) on the seal of Alyah the אמה of Hananel. Others compare her status to that of a (free) concubine. See Jackson (2006: 100 n. 128).

23. There is some parallel here with the position of the 'surrogate' אמה of the patriarchal narratives (discussed below), over whom, in the words of Westbrook (1998), her mistress retains 'residual' rights (228).

24. For other views as to who may redeem her, see Fleishman (2000: 52 n. 24). If it is someone other than the debtor/father who originally sold her, questions arise as to her subsequent status, particularly if she is redeemed by a stranger to the family. Underlying the issue is the question for whose benefit these regulations are made.

having relations with the captive woman, loses sexual interest in her, protection is afforded to her, in that she may not be traded on the slave market but may be released for nothing. Indeed, the main difference between the two laws resides in the circumstances of the original enslavement, namely, internal debt-slavery on the one hand and external capture in warfare on the other, corresponding to the original status of the woman as an insider on the one hand and an outsider on the other. This latter distinction informs the ultimate disposition of the slave (and any children she may produce): it is assumed that she has no right (or prospect) of returning home, and thus will remain in the captor's family as an inheritance.[25] Against this background, the four systematic questions may be addressed as follows:

(a) Foreign female captives may be used for breeding (again, by implication; children are not here mentioned explicitly).

(b) No tripartite relationship is mentioned here, in that no designation for someone else is contemplated. But surely it must have been possible here, if it was possible in the case of the Hebrew אמה? In any event, the issue of the vertical relationship still arises: what matters more, the captor's relationship with her as owner or as 'husband'? There is no suggestion that any 'marital' relationship with her captor renders her free, either during the relationship or even after its termination.

(c) Here too there is uncertainty as to the nature of the horizontal relationship indicated by והיתה לך לאשה in v. 13.[26] It can hardly be a primary marriage (what might the captor's primary wife think?). However, here again it is (in principle) a permanent relationship. Sale on the market is excluded by law; redemption is not mentioned (unlikely in the circumstances) but may not be excluded. Termination without payment is contemplated if the captor gets fed up with her, and terminology *akin* to divorce, ושלחתה לנפשה, is used.[27] Probably, her status is that of slave concubine.[28] The important thing,

---

25. Cf. Lev. 25.44-46.

26. Despite the RSV rendering of ולקחת לך לאשה in v. 11 as 'and would take her for yourself as wife', this refers purely to the warrior's initial 'taking' (rape) of the captive (cf. Van Seters [2003: 93]; *aliter*, and more commonly, Fleishman [2000: 60-61]). The captor is here exercising his ('vertical') rights, as slave-owner, over the woman. Cf. Tosato (1982: 16-17, 36-37, 40-41).

27. Westbrook (1998: 235) argues that termination of the relationship is by divorce, and interprets ושלחתה לנפשה as meaning that he divorces her 'to herself'. But it is more likely that he sends her 'to be by herself' within the household, i.e. that she is no longer his concubine. Neufeld (1944: 72-73) agrees that there is no divorce here, on the grounds that the captive is only a 'de facto wife', and divorce is inapplicable if there is no 'strict marriage' in existence. See also Tosato (1982: 128-29).

28. See further Jackson (2006: 116), against the view of Tosato (1982: 42) that she is a *pilegesh* (understood as a free woman who is a secondary wife) and Westbrook (1998), who states, 'There is no question of slave concubinage here' (235).

however, is that she may not be traded on the slave market (v.14). Here, too, the sexual/reproductive relationship has altered the terms of slavery. There can be no doubt that a foreign captive woman not used for sexual services could be traded on the slave market.

(d) What is the status of the children? This question is not often asked, because children are not mentioned here, but if they follow the status of their mother, presumably they are permanent slaves and probably *may* be sold on the market, in that the captor has committed no offence against them.[29]

5. *The Foreign Slave Used as Surrogate*

The narratives of Hagar, Bilhah and Zilpah provide perhaps our clearest example of a 'tripartite breeding relationship'. They differ from the other cases of women used for breeding in the circumstances in which the relationship arises: these women come into the household as the permanent, foreign[30] domestic slaves of a primary wife. But because of the infertility of the primary wife, the foreign אמה is given to the husband as a surrogate, to produce children who will have the status of children of the primary wife.[31] That creates a tension between the 'vertical' and 'horizontal' relationships, in that the אמה here enjoys what Westbrook has aptly termed a 'split legal personality'.[32] In other circumstances, where the 'split' is not so manifest (the Hebrew אמה and the foreign captive woman), we have seen that the 'horizontal' (sexual/reproductive) relationship has an effect on the vertical (the terms of slavery). Here, however, it appears that the 'vertical' relationship is clearly more important than the 'horizontal'. The systematic questions may thus be answered as follows:

---

29. The verb used in the concluding motive clause in v. 14 (תחת אשר עניתה) is the same as that which provides the motivation for the Deuteronomic rape law (תחת אשר ענה [Deut. 22.29]), where the rapist has an obligation to marry his victim. Both laws contemplate the same sequence of events: rape, followed by regularization of the relationship, followed by contemplation of its possible termination. Just as, in the case of the free woman, reversion by divorce to her original (unmarried) status is prohibited, so too here the woman is not to revert to the status of a captive slave, available for disposal on the slave market.

30. Hagar is Egyptian (Gen. 16.1). Zilpah and Bilhah were given to Leah (Gen. 29.24) and Rachel (Gen. 29.29) respectively by Laban on their marriages (presumably as part of their dowries). Though Jacob is sent to Laban in order to marry within the kin, there is no suggestion that Zilpah and Bilhah were family members; by implication, they were permanent slaves of Laban.

31. Gen. 16.2: אבנה ממנה. Cf. Gen. 30.3.

32. Westbrook 1998: 215. Westbrook also notes an explicit formula found in Old Babylonian marriage contracts: 'To H, W2 is a wife; to W1, she is a slave' (1998: 228). We may note that the עבד עברי too has both a vertical (to the master) and a horizontal (to the אשה) relationship within the household; but the latter is so weak, as argued above, that the term 'split legal personality' would hardly seem appropriate for him.

(a) Foreign slaves of the primary wife may be used for breeding: Gen. 16.2 (Hagar), Gen. 30.3-4 (Bilhah), 9 (Zilpah).

(b) As for the vertical relationship, the woman remains a slave of her mistress. There is no suggestion that any 'marital' relationship with her mistress's husband renders her free. Indeed, when it comes to a conflict between the vertical and horizontal relationships, the former clearly prevails. When in Gen. 16.5-6 Sarai complains to Abram that Hagar, having conceived, no longer respects her, Abram replies, 'Behold, your maid (שפחתך) is in your power (בידך); do to her as you please'.

(c) Here too, the nature of the horizontal relationship is left unclear and generates debate in the modern literature: is this is a primary marriage, a secondary marriage or concubinage? Arguing from LH 146-47,[33] Westbrook maintains that it must have been a full marriage, to explain the legitimacy of the offspring: 'the offspring of a free concubine had no better right to inherit than the offspring of a slave concubine', unless explicitly adopted (as in LH 170-71).[34] Against this, he acknowledges that Hagar is referred to subsequently as אמתך (Gen. 21.12), and Zilpah and Bilhah are referred to as the שפחתיו of Jacob (Gen. 32.23).[35] Westbrook tries to avoid the implication of this terminology by attributing it, 'albeit reluctantly', to 'an inconsistent narrative': 'Either there was some confusion in the tradition as to whether they had been given as concubines or wives, or the author of these passages was concerned to maximise the status of the primary wives at the expense of the secondary wives'.[36] I do not think, however, that an external model should be so readily imposed upon the biblical text. The status of Hagar clearly appears inferior to that of the primary wife, Sarah. Moreover, even in LH 146-47, the surrogate achieves equality of status only by bearing children; she does not have a full marital status before then, and even when she has borne children the man may treat her merely as a maidservant rather than as a full wife.

(d) Overall, what appears to matter here is (i) the relationship between the primary wife and the אמה, and (ii) the relationship between the

---

33. 'If a man take a wife and she give this man a maid-servant as wife and she bear him children, and then this maid assume equality with the wife: because she has borne him children her master shall not sell her for money, but he may keep her as a slave, reckoning her among the maid-servants. If she have not borne him children, then her mistress may sell her for money'. Translation of L.W. King, http://www.yale.edu/lawweb/avalon/medieval/hamframe.htm. Compare, however, Roth (1995: 109).

34. Westbrook 1998: 222. See also Houtman (2000: 124-25), who cites in addition LI 25-26.

35. Westbrook 1998: 232.

36. Westbrook 1998: 233.

'husband' and the children of the אמה; there is little concern with the status of the relationship between the 'husband' and the אמה.[37]

(e) What is the status of the children? Here, clearly, the whole object of the 'surrogacy' relationship is to produce children who would have the same status as those of the primary wife (Gen. 16.2, 30.3, 9). Indeed, the children of Zilpah and Bilhah are fully legitimate, and constitute four of the twelve tribes of Israel. It is also clear that without the expulsion of Hagar and Ishmael, the latter would have been an heir alongside Isaac (Gen. 21.10). The same appears to apply to the children of Keturah (described as a פילגש), who are sent away with a payoff, in order not to share the inheritance with Isaac (Gen. 25.6). Nevertheless, there does seem to have been a social ranking between the sons of primary wives and the sons of surrogates (even though theoretically these are the sons of the wives who 'own' those surrogates). In Deut. 27.12-13, the six tribes associated with 'blessing' (located on Mount Gerizim) are all children of primary wives; those associated with curses (on Mount Ebal) are (i) the four children of the surrogates, (ii) Reuven, who had blotted his copybook and been deprived of the birthright;[38] and (iii) Zebulun, the youngest of the sons of Leah (Gen. 30.20).[39]

There is also some evidence of the use of male foreign slaves as surrogates.[40] Explicit evidence for this is found in a little-noted genealogical observation in 1 Chron. 2.34-35: 'And Sheshan had no sons, but only daughters, and Sheshan had an Egyptian slave (עבד מצרי), and his name was Jarha. And Sheshan gave his daughter to his slave Jarha as a wife (לאשה), and she bore him Attai'. (A good job this was not suggested to the daughters of Zelophehad!) Whether in fact a marital relationship was created here may be doubted, not least if we follow the plausible argument of Pirson, that this is precisely the role assigned to Joseph by (the eunuch) Potiphar (Genesis 39).[41] Here too the vertical relationship is more important than the horizontal: there is clearly (even on this interpretation)

---

37. See further Jackson (2006: 100-101).
38. Gen. 48.3-19, 49.3-4 (referring to Gen. 35.22); 1 Chron. 5.1. In Num. 26.5, however, Reuven is still described as בכור ישראל and is mentioned first in the census.
39. Similarly, the sons of Bilhah and Zilpah are listed after those of Leah and Rachel in Gen. 35.23-26. On the other hand, the list of Jacob's family which went down to Egypt notes that Zilpah had been given to Leah by Laban, and lists her descendants immediately after those of Leah (Gen. 46.8-19, cf. the presentation of the descendants of Rachel and Bilhah in vv. 19-24).
40. I am indebted to Diana Lipton for drawing to my attention both 1 Chron. 2.34-35 and Pirson's interpretation of the Joseph narrative.
41. Pirson 2004. A similar argument was advanced by Diana Lipton in a Cambridge OT seminar in March 2006, and will appear in Diana Lipton, *Longing for Egypt: The Virtue of Complexity in Biblical Interpretation* (Sheffield Phoenix Press, forthcoming).

no marital relationship between Joseph and Potiphar's wife, nor is Joseph given thereby any permanent status within the household. When, in fact, he declines to perform the breeding (or sexual fulfilment) task, he is simply assigned different duties.[42] We may note the very strong association with Egypt which emerges from these sources: Hagar, Jarha and the household of Potiphar.

6. *The Patriarch*

There is a sense in which the patriarch is himself used for breeding purposes in the narratives of Hagar, Bilhah and Zilpah. In the first case, Sarai uses the language of request to persuade Abram to fulfil this role (בא נא, Gen. 16.2); the language used by Rachel (בא, Gen. 30.3) is less petitionary,[43] but there is no implication that she had a right to demand this, or that the patriarch's compliance was involuntary. On the other hand, the story in Gen. 30.14-16 of Leah's one-night 'hire' of Jacob's reproductive services from Rachel does conclude with the language of command: when Jacob came from the field in the evening, Leah went out to meet him, and said, 'You must come in to me (אלי תבוא); for I have hired you (שכר שכרתיך) with my son's mandrakes' (RSV). Just as in the case of the עבד עברי, where the reproductive capacities of the debt-slave may be used by his master to produce children for him without affecting the slave's status within the household, so here Leah 'hires' Jacob for a night from Rachel, and Issachar (note the name) is born.[44] However, it is clear that neither this one-night stand, nor the surrogacy relationships, had any effect on the patriarch's vertical relationships within the household.

7. *Conclusions*

Comparison of these different forms of breeding relationships yields the following conclusions:

(a) Hebrew males (slave and free) and both Hebrew and foreign female slaves are used for breeding.
(b) Whereas this has no fundamental effect on the status of the male, it has a fundamental effect on the status of the female (with the exception of the surrogate, whose 'mistress' is still present in the

---

42. Pirson (2004: 258) argues that Joseph was not sent to prison as a punishment (inappropriate for either adultery or rape), but rather was assigned work in the prison, for which Potiphar was responsible.

43. No request is attributed to Leah at all; she simply gives Zilpah to Jacob לאשה.

44. Rabbinic sources later debate whether the ענה of Exod. 21.10 is a monetary right, subject to contractual negotiation (between husband and wife!) or not. Whether ענתה there did originally mean 'her conjugal rights' has been disputed; see Jackson (2006: 92). The narrative in Genesis hardly assists us in deciding that question: Rachel might appear to treat her sexual rights as a commodity, but would Leah have so readily bought them had she had them already by law?

household). However, the status which is affected is not the 'horizontal' relationship of marriage but rather the 'vertical' relationship of slavery.
(c) The horizontal ('marital') relationship so produced is in all cases less clear, and apparently of less concern.
(d) Of greater concern is the status of the children (itself a vertical relationship), whether they will be permanent slaves who will remain in the household or be disposable on the slave market, or will be debt-slaves like the mother, or will be legitimate heirs (albeit of lower social status).

I would suggest that the main reason for (c) is not the liminal character of the particular marital relationships here involved, but rather the weak level of institutionalization of marriage as a whole in much of the Hebrew Bible.[45] Marriage, like inheritance, is a 'social' rather than a legal institution: certain facts on the ground are socially recognized, namely, love and retention on the one hand, hatred and expulsion on the other. It is not surprising that the same applies to inheritance. As the story of Hagar and Ishmael indicates, expulsion and disinheritance often go together,[46] and, as the story of Jephthah indicates, they share a common terminology.[47]

BIBLIOGRAPHY

Avigad, Nahman
    1946   'A Seal of a Slave-Wife (Amah)', *PEQ* 78: 125-32.
    1953   'The Epitaph of a Royal Steward from Siloam Village', *IEJ* 3: 137-52.
Budde, Karl
    1891   'Bemerkungen zum Bundesbuch', *ZAW* 11: 99-114.
Cardellini, Innocenzo
    1981   *Die biblischen 'Sklaven'-Gesetze im Lichte des keilschriftlichen Sklavenrechts: ein Beitrag zur Tradition, Überlieferung und Redaktion der alttestamentlichen Rechtstexte* (BBB, 55; Königstein/Taunus: Hanstein).

---

45. See further Jackson (2007), forthcoming.
46. Gen. 21.10: 'Cast out this slave (גרש האמה הזאת) and her son; for the son of this slave shall not be heir (לא יירש) with my son, with Isaac'.
47. Judg. 11.1-7: 'Now Jephthah the Gileadite was a mighty warrior, but he was the son of a harlot (בן אשה זונה). Gilead was the father of Jephthah. And Gilead's wife also bore him sons; and when his wife's sons grew up, they thrust Jephthah out (ויגרשו את יפתח), and said to him, "You shall not inherit in our father's house; for you are the son of another woman". Then Jephthah fled from his brothers, and dwelt in the land of Tob; and worthless fellows collected round Jephthah, and went raiding with him. After a time the Ammonites made war against Israel. And when the Ammonites made war against Israel, the elders of Gilead went to bring Jephthah from the land of Tob; and they said to Jephthah, "Come and be our leader, that we may fight with the Ammonites". But Jephthah said to the elders of Gilead, "Did you not hate (שנאתם) me, and drive me out (ותגרשוני) of my father's house? Why have you come to me now when you are in trouble?"'

Chavel, Simeon
    1997   '"Let my people go!": Emancipation, Revelation, and Scribal Activity in Jeremiah 34.8-14', *JSOT* 76: 71-95.

Chirichigno, Gregory C.
    1993   *Debt-Slavery in Israel and the Ancient Near East* (JSOTSup, 141; Sheffield: JSOT Press).

Crüsemann, Frank
    1996   *The Torah: Theology and Social History of Old Testament Law* (trans. Allan W. Mahnke; Edinburgh: T. & T. Clark).

David, Martin
    1948   'The Manumission of Slaves under Zedekiah', *OTS* 5: 63-79.

Driver, S.R.
    1911   *The Book of Exodus in the Revised Version* (Cambridge Bible for Schools and Colleges; Cambridge: Cambridge University Press).

Fleishman, Joseph
    2000   'Does the Law of Exodus 21:7-11 Permit a Father to Sell his Daughter to be a Slave?', *The Jewish Law Annual* 13: 47-64.

Houtman, C.
    2000   *Exodus Volume III: chapters 20–40* (trans. Sierd Woudstra; Historical commentary on the Old Testament; Leuven: Peeters).

Hudson, Michael
    1993   *The Lost Tradition of Biblical Debt Cancellations* (New York: Social Science Forum, Henry George School of Social Science).

Jackson, Bernard S.
    1988a   'Biblical Laws of Slavery: A Comparative Approach', in Léonie J. Archer (ed.), *Slavery and other Forms of Unfree Labour* (History workshop series; London: Routledge): 86-101.
    1988b   'Some Literary Features of the Mishpatim', in Matthias Augustin and Klaus-Dietrich Schunck (eds.), *Wünschet Jerusalem Frieden: Collected Communications to the XIIth Congress of the International Organization for the Study of the Old Testament, Jerusalem 1986* (Beiträge zur Erforschung des Alten Testaments und des antiken Judentums, 13; Frankfurt: Peter Lang): 235-42.
    1998a   'Justice and Righteousness in the Bible: Rule of Law or Royal Paternalism?', *Zeitschrift für altorientalische und biblische Rechtsgeschichte* 4: 218-62.
    1998b   '"Law" and "Justice" in the Bible', *JJS* 44: 218-29.
    2006   *Wisdom-Laws: A Study of the Mishpatim of Exodus 21:1-22:16* (Oxford: Oxford University Press).
    2007   'The "Institutions" of Marriage and Divorce in the Hebrew Bible', in G. Brooke and C. Nihan (eds.), *Studies in Biblical Law and its Reception* (JSS Supplementary Series; Oxford: Oxford University Press).

Jackson, Bernard S. and Trevor F. Watkins
    1984   'Distraint in the Laws of Eshnunna and Hammurabi', *Studi in onore di Cesare Sanfilippo* (Rome: Giuffrè): V, 411-19.

Kessler, Martin
    1971   'The Law of Manumission in Jer 34', *BZ* 15: 105-108.

Levine, Etan
    1999   'On Exodus 21,10 *'Onah* and Biblical Marriage', *Zeitschrift für altorientalische und biblische Rechtsgeschichte* 5: 133-64.

Matthews, Victor H., Bernard M. Levinson and Tikva Frymer-Kensky (eds.)
    1998   *Gender and Law in the Hebrew Bible and the Ancient Near East* (JSOTSup, 262; Sheffield: Sheffield Academic Press).

Mendelsohn, Isaac
    1935   'The Conditional Sale into Slavery of Free-Born Daughters in Nuzi and the Law of Ex. 21.7-11', *JAOS* 55: 190-95.

Neufeld, E.
    1944   *Ancient Hebrew Marriage Laws: with Special References to General Semitic Laws and Customs* (London: Longman, Green and Co.).

Pirson, Ron
    2004   'The Twofold Message of Potiphar's Wife', *SJOT* 18: 248-59.

Pressler, Carolyn
    1998   'Wives and Daughters, Bond and Free: Views of Women in the Slave Laws of Exodus 21.2-11', in Matthews, Levinson and Frymer-Kensky 1998: 147-72.

Roth, Martha T.
    1995   *Law Collections from Mesopotamia and Asia Minor* (Writings from the Ancient World, 6; Atlanta: Scholars Press).

Sarna, Nahum M.
    1991   *Exodus* (JPS Torah commentary; Philadelphia: Jewish Publication Society).

Tosato, Angelo
    1982   *Il matrimonio israelitico: una teoria generale* (AnBib, 100; Rome: Biblical Institute Press).

Van Seters, John
    2003   *A Law Book for the Diaspora. Revision in the Study of the Covenant Code* (Oxford: Oxford University Press).

Weinfeld, Moshe
    1995   *Social Justice in Ancient Israel and in the Ancient Near East* (Jerusalem: Magnes Press; Minneapolis, MN: Fortress Press).

Westbrook, Raymond
    1988   *Studies in Biblical and Cuneiform Law* (CRB, 26; Paris: Gabalda).
    1991   *Property and the Family in Biblical Law* (JSOTSup, 113; Sheffield: JSOT Press).
    1998   'The Female Slave', in Matthews, Levinson and Frymer-Kensky 1988: 214-38.

THEIR HEART CRIED OUT TO GOD: GENDER
AND PRAYER IN THE BOOK OF LAMENTATIONS

Amy Kalmanofsky

Biblical women pray. When the matriarch Rebecca suffers during pregnancy she prays to God and receives the prophecy that she will bear twin sons who will become twin nations.¹ When Leah, the lesser-loved wife of Jacob, gives birth to her fourth son she names him Judah, declaring, 'This time I will praise the Lord'.² Barren Hannah prays silently and bargains with God that if granted a child she will dedicate him to God as a Nazir.³ In the book of Ruth, Naomi offers blessings.⁴ The prophetesses Miriam and Deborah offer prayerful songs of triumph and thanksgiving.⁵

If one may extrapolate from actions of biblical characters, these examples suggest that women in biblical Israel prayed. But they do not reveal much about the place and nature of women's prayer within the Israelite cult. Were women's prayers welcome in and a regular part of the official cult?⁶ Did women have access to the Psalter? Do the psalms reflect and relate to women's religious experience?⁷

1. Gen. 25.22-23.
2. Gen. 29.35. Biblical quotations are taken from *JPS Hebrew-English Tanakh: The Traditional Hebrew Text and the New JPS Translation* (Philadelphia: Jewish Publication Society, 2000).
3. 1 Samuel 1–2.
4. Ruth 2.19-20.
5. Exod. 15.20-21; Judges 5.
6. Scholars continue to study the place of prayer within the Temple cult. Knohl (1996) maintains that prayer had a peripheral place in biblical Israel and that the priests performed their cultic duties within the Temple in silence. Only the High Priest recites a prayer within the Temple on the Day of Atonement. Yet, Knohl notes, he prays once he has left the Holy of Holies *after* the sacrifice is made. In contrast, the Temple courtyard was noisy with the prayers of the people. In effect, prayer is a folk tradition of biblical Israel, as Knohl observes: 'It is worth noting the distinction between the circle of the priestly cult (and similar to it that of the song of the Levites), which is entirely fixed and obligatory, and that of prayer, which was more on the order of a goodly custom and an act of piety, but did not carry the stamp of fixity and was not understood as an obligation imposed on every person in Israel' (Knohl 1996: 23).
7. Brettler (1998) considers the relationship between women and the psalms. Although he

Naturally, and sadly, these questions remain unanswerable. Women's place within the cult of ancient Israel cannot be understood through biblical Israel's official and singular testimony. Even widening the lens to include material artifacts from ancient Israel and other ancient Near Eastern neighbours does not provide clarity.[8] In her call for a reconstruction of the history of Israelite religion based on a new, gender-inclusive interpretative model, Phyllis Bird admits to the particular limitations of understanding biblical women's devotional participation in the cult. She writes:

> Of possible greater significance for an understanding of women's religious participation and the total religious life of the community is the hidden realm of women's rituals and devotions that take place entirely within the domestic sphere and/or in the company of other women. Cross-cultural studies show that these often constitute the emotional center of women's religious life as well as the bulk of their religious activity, especially where their participation in the central cultus is limited. For such practices, however, we have little or no direct testimony, as this order of religious practice is generally seen as unworthy of note unless it challenges or undermines the central cultus (Bird 1999: 12-13).

Although the real form and function of the prayers of women in ancient Israel may be forever beyond our grasp, I will address the nature of women's prayer as reflected in one particular biblical text. I will compare the prayers in response to the destruction of Jerusalem of Daughter Zion in the book of Lamentations with those of the גבר, the unnamed man who prays in the book's third chapter. As I interpret these two pray-ers, I am fully aware that Daughter Zion is a female character constructed by a presumably male author. She is also the personified city of Jerusalem.[9] For these reasons, I have no expectation that this figure reveals the religious lives of real religious women. The book of Lamentations presents two distinct and gendered *characters*. My

---

recognizes the androcentric nature of the psalms which were composed by 'male elites' and reflect 'male ideologies', Brettler does not believe this excludes women from reciting the psalms, the character of Hannah providing a nice example of a woman who recites a highly formulaic prayer. Still, Brettler considers prose prayer, which can be recited by any individual and tailored to any situation, or perhaps the unofficial and lost prayers of popular religion, to be the more likely domain of women's particular prayers.

8. Both Carol Meyers and William Dever combine the study of archaeology and the Hebrew Bible to illuminate the rites of folk religion and, in particular, the roles of women in Israelite religion. See Dever (2005), Meyers (1996), and Meyers (2003).

9. Lanahan (1974: 41) defines persona as 'the mask or characterization assumed by the poet as the medium through which he perceives and gives expression to his world ... The most obvious example of the existence of a *persona* in the Book of Lamentations appears in the first two chapters, in those verses (1:9c, 11c-22; 2:20-22) during which Jerusalem speaks in her own voice. Obviously, the city of Jerusalem cannot speak except in some figurative sense, but it is precisely this personification of the city which expresses the anguish of these verses'. The personification of cities as female was common in the ancient Near East. For a comprehensive discussion, see Dobbs-Allsopp (1993: 75-91).

goal is to see if and how gender defines these figures in the context of their prayers.

Desolate and distressed, Daughter Zion is the focus of the first two chapters of Lamentations. Scholars consistently consider her presence in these chapters to be a rhetorical device intended to heighten the emotional intensity and impact of the poem. In her commentary on Lamentations, Adele Berlin writes:

> The author personifies Jerusalem as a woman because this is commonplace in his world of thought. He chooses particular female images precisely because they are shocking and do not represent normative behavior. The imagery is meant to evoke a strong feeling of horror and outrage, immorality and shame, suffering and pity, because this mixture of reactions is a crucial part of the poet's message (Berlin 2002: 9).

Similarly, Kathleen O'Connor notes:

> By making Jerusalem a woman, the poetry gives her personality and human characteristics that evoke pity or disdain from readers. Her female body is the object of disgrace and shaming, and her infidelities become shocking, intimate betrayal.[10]

Emotional Daughter Zion is often seen in contrast to the more typical,[11] more theological, and less emotional[12] male characters of the narrator and the גבר. Again, scholars consider the inclusion of these two distinct voices to be a rhetorical strategy. For Adele Berlin, it is a way for the poem to communicate the full experience of human suffering, male and female.[13] For Alan Mintz, it is a necessary strategy for the poem to address the theological implications of the destruction of Jerusalem. Due to the 'cultural code of Lamentations', believes Mintz, Daughter Zion's voice is the most effective means for communicating

---

10. O'Connor 2002: 14. In her broader study of the image of Daughter Zion, Kaiser (1987: 166) observes: 'In each case the poet begins with a third-person narrator but changes to the female persona at the point of greatest tension; that is the poet chooses the female persona to express the intensity of his grief'.

11. Berlin (2002: 9) writes: 'The men suffer in a typically masculine way—they lose power and physical prowess... Chapter 3 is especially vivid in this regard, with its military imagery and its physical brutality'. Heim (1999: 155) also uses the adjective 'typical' to describe the male voice of the *gever*; he writes, 'Consequently, the speaker of Lamentations 3 may be modeled on Job as the paradigmatic sufferer ... Thus he may indeed be intended to represent a 'typical' sufferer'.

12. O'Connor (2002) describes the difference between the voice of the narrator and the voice of Zion. She writes, 'From the outside, the narrator focuses repeatedly on her losses and reversals of circumstance... His feelings are not there; he does not expose himself, even as he describes unutterable horrors. Daughter Zion speaks from within the trauma. Her first-person statements carry the power of experience and the cascading confusion of the survivor. She is immersed in emotions, overwhelmed by horror' (28).

13. Berlin (2002) writes, 'The poet wants to make God participate in the national experience. The suffering that is put before God is the suffering of all people, as a whole and in its component parts. It is the suffering of the men and women, the old and young, the rich and poor, the elite and common' (9-10).

the misery of the moment. Yet, in order to handle the theological implications of the destruction of Jerusalem, the poet employs the male voice of the גבר.[14]

However one accounts for the differences between the male and female voices of Lamentations, it seems reasonable to assume that gender is a factor. Since both Daughter Zion and the גבר respond to the same catastrophe, one must ask what is gained by including the perspectives of both a male and a female sufferer. Does Daughter Zion suffer like a woman and the גבר like a man? While expressing their pain, Daughter Zion and the גבר pray to God. These prayers occur in the midst of longer descriptions and expressions of misery. The texts I consider prayers, Lam. 1.9c, 11c, 18-22;[15] 2.20-22; 3.40-66,[16] are first-person, direct addresses to God.[17] In these prayers, do the characters of Daughter Zion and the גבר pray differently? Is Daughter Zion more emotional? Is the גבר more theological? Do they use different language and images? Can gender account for differences in their prayer style and strategy?

In this paper I contend that Daughter Zion and the גבר employ similar prayer strategies designed to confront more than to appease God. Both describe their suffering in gruesome detail and leave little room for repentant confessions. Yet the content of their prayers reveals a difference. Whereas Daughter Zion suffers because others suffer, the גבר laments his personal situation. Gender helps explain this difference. Enmeshed in her social network, the female figure suffers for and with her community. Unlike the גבר, she cannot stand independent of her family and therefore prays for their wellbeing. As a man, however, the גבר is an autonomous, individual entity. Though he may represent all of Israel, as a character he is able to pray for himself.

Before addressing the differences between the prayers of Daughter Zion and the גבר, I will begin with the similarities. The prayers share common elements. Both include an admission of guilt (Lam. 1.18, 20, 22; 3.42), an accusation

---

14. Mintz (1982) writes, 'To deal with this threatened loss of meaning—what amounts to a threat of caprice, gratuitousness, absurdity—Zion as a figure is simply not sufficient; a woman's voice, according to the cultural code of Lamentations, can achieve expressivity but not reflection. And now acts of reasoning and cognition are the necessary equipment for undertaking the desperate project of understanding the meaning of what has happened. The solution is the invention of a new, male figure, the speaker of Chapter Three' (9).

15. Though vv. 18-19 do not appear to address God directly, I consider them part of the prayer. These verses, in which Daughter Zion speaks in the first person, follow the narrator's description of Zion's outstretched hands, a gesture that can indicate prayer. See Ps. 143.6; Isa. 1.15; Jer. 4.31.

16. Though the prayer begins in the first person plural voice, I identify the speaker as the *gever* speaking for the people. In the following discussion, I will consider the rhetorical impact of his adoption of the first person plural voice.

17. I define prayer as a human being's one-sided, direct address to God. Unlike the exchange between God and Abraham in Genesis 18 over the fate of Sodom and Gomorrah, prayer is not a *conversation* between a human and God. There is no give and take. For general discussion on the nature of prayer in the Bible see Balentine (1993), Greenberg (1983), Newman (1999), Blank (1961), and Werline (1998).

against God (Lam. 2.21; 3.42, 43), description of suffering (Lam. 1.18-20; 2.20-22; 3.43-54) and the mention of enemies (Lam. 1.9, 21, 22; 3.46, 52, 60). These shared elements indicate a similar mindset among the pray-ers.[18] Both Daughter Zion and the גבר take some responsibility for their fate, yet they also share a feeling of outrage against God. Their language of confession is similar. In Lam. 1.18 Daughter Zion admits, 'The Lord is in the right, for I have disobeyed Him (כי פיהו מריתי)'. In Lam. 1.20 she confesses, 'See, O Lord, the distress I am in! My heart is in anguish, I know how wrong I was to disobey (כי מרו מריתי)'. In Lam. 1.22 she says, 'Let all their wrongdoing come before You, and deal with them as you have dealt with me for all my transgressions (על כל פּשׁעי). In Lam. 3.42, the גבר echoes the words of Daughter Zion and confesses, 'We have transgressed and rebelled (נחנו פשׁענו ומרינו)'.

Similarly, their accusations against God share common language. In Lam. 2.21 Daughter Zion accuses God, 'You slew them on Your day of wrath, You slaughtered without pity (טבחת לא חמלת)'. In 3.42-43 the גבר says:

> We have transgressed and rebelled,
> And you have not forgiven.
> You have clothed Yourself in anger and pursued us,
> You have slain us without pity (הרגת לא חמלת).

Besides the similarity of language, what is striking about both the confession and the accusation is the relatively limited space they occupy in the prayers. Though this may suggest an element of insincerity, as if Daughter Zion and the גבר perfunctorily admit their guilt, it may also reveal a common strategy.

Descriptions of their suffering and the particular role the enemies play in their suffering fill the bulk of their prayers. Perhaps Daughter Zion and the גבר believe this will be more effective than confession for activating God's mercy. Daughter Zion's first words in Lam. 1.9 are the prayer, 'See (ראה), O Lord, my misery (עניי)'. Again in Lam. 1.11 she pleads, 'See (ראה), O Lord, and behold!' The גבר echoes Daughter Zion's prayer in his opening statement, 'I am the man who has known affliction (ראה עני) under the rod of his wrath' (Lam. 3.1). Daughter Zion and the גבר want God to witness their affliction. By describing their suffering, they are calling God's attention to their agony. Perhaps if God will see how they suffer, God will respond with mercy, as the גבר makes clear in his prayer. He declares, 'My eyes shall flow without cease,

---

18. It may also introduce a conversational element, suggesting that the *gever* may be shaping his prayer in response to Daughter Zion. Noticing similarities in language between the narrator and Daughter Zion, Miller (2001) suggests that there is an implicit dialogue, what he calls 'double-voiced discourse,' between the two in chapter one. He writes, 'Jerusalem's speech actively affects both the content and the structure of the narrator's speech although it remains outside it. The narrator does not explicitly acknowledge her speech, but the emphatic repetition of his accusations against Jerusalem and the further illustrations of her guilty behavior reveal the narrator's attempt to vindicate his position in the face of Jerusalem's challenge' (399-400).

without respite, until the Lord looks down and beholds in heaven' (Lam. 3.49-50). And towards the end of the prayer he pleads, 'You have seen, O Lord, the wrong done me; Oh, vindicate my right!' (Lam. 3.59).

Mention of their enemies is another strategy employed by both Daughter Zion and the גבר. Both include descriptions of the harm caused by the sadistic enemies as well as a prayer that their fate will be overturned and their enemies will suffer as they do (Lam. 1.21-22; 3.59-66). Similar mention of enemies appears throughout the psalms.[19] Like the descriptions of suffering, the inclusion of the enemies may be an effort to provoke God's mercy. God will want to save helpless Daughter Zion and the גבר from these evil enemies. Yet God may also want to intervene in order to save face. In Lam. 1.9 Daughter Zion declares, 'How the enemy jeers!' In Lam. 1.21, she describes the enemy rejoicing over her suffering. Elsewhere in the Bible, God is assuaged by an appeal to God's reputation. In the aftermath of the golden calf, when God threatens to destroy Israel and start over again with the descendants of Moses, Moses appeases God by saying, 'Let not the Egyptians say, "It was with evil intent that He delivered them, only to kill them off in the mountains and annihilate them from the face of the earth"' (Exod. 32.12).

It is unclear why Daughter Zion's and the גבר's justly deserved suffering should compromise God's reputation. Given the context of Lamentations, they deserve no less and certainly a great deal more. However, in Lamentations mention of enemies is complicated. Although in their prayers Daughter Zion and the גבר seem to refer to external, flesh-and-blood enemies, elsewhere in Lamentations God is described either explicitly or implicitly as an enemy, as Lam. 2.4-5 illustrates:

> He bent His bow like an enemy,
> Poised His right hand like a foe;
> He slew all who delighted the eye.
> He poured out His wrath like fire
> In the Tent of Fair Zion.
> The Lord has acted like a foe,
> He has laid waste Israel,
> Laid waste all her citadels,
> Destroyed her strongholds.
> He has increased within Fair Judah
> Mourning and moaning.

If God behaves like an enemy, then Daughter Zion's and the גבר's prayers to invert the fate of the enemy have interesting implications. Could Daughter Zion and the גבר be offering a veiled threat against God? They accuse God of showing no mercy, of standing by and watching them suffer, in essence, of behaving like an enemy who laughs as they suffer. Perhaps Daughter Zion and the גבר would like the tables turned so that God feels the pain God inflicts on others. Or perhaps

---

19. For examples, see Pss. 6.11, 9.4, 27.12, 28.3-4, 30.1 and 31.9.

Daughter Zion and the גבר simply want God to hear how God's actions are experienced and perceived.[20] Either way, mention of the enemies allows Daughter Zion and the גבר to confront God in an indirect, safe way.

Thus far we have seen common elements and language in the prayers of Daughter Zion and the גבר that suggest a shared prayer strategy. Although I think it is important to recognize these similarities, it is equally important to address the differences in their prayers. If differences did not exist, why include both the prayers of Daughter Zion and the גבר? In order to address these differences, I want to begin with the common assumption among commentators that Daughter Zion is the more emotional and that the גבר is the more theological character.[21]

Certainly, Daughter Zion is an emotional character. Her tears flow freely in the first two chapters.[22] She mourns, despairs, shouts, and moans. Scholars interpret Daughter Zion's physical displays of emotion in light of similar displays exhibited by the weeping goddesses found throughout Mesopotamian lament literature.[23] Like the goddess Ningal who laments over the destruction of her city Ur and her temple, Daughter Zion weeps over her destroyed city and Temple. The comparison between Daughter Zion and the weeping goddess provides an insight into the power and purpose of her tears. Goddesses weep in order to appeal to, accuse, and perhaps appease the god responsible for the destruction. Thus their tears are not a spontaneous expression of emotional weakness and vulnerability, but are part of a calculated strategy of intervention.

Yet Daughter Zion is not the only figure to cry in Lamentations. The גבר also weeps copiously, as in Lam. 3.48-51:

> My eyes shed streams of water
> Over the ruin of my poor people.
> My eyes shall flow without cease,
> Without respite,
> Until the Lord looks down
> And beholds from heaven.
> My eyes have brought me grief
> Over all the maidens of my city.

---

20. Sheppard (1991) discusses the role the enemies play in the psalms. He suggests that prayers were spoken in public and that often the 'enemies' were present. Thus he considers the rhetorical impact of publicly referring to enemies. He writes, 'Finally, there is some protection in the hope that the prayer itself might lead the enemy to repent and stop the wrongdoing. Although the address of prayer to God explains why the enemies do not need to be named, it also provides an opportunity for the enemies to save face, alter their actions, or perhaps even to seek face to face reconciliation and reparation' (75).

21. Introducing the third chapter of Lamentations, Berlin (2002) comments, 'This chapter, more than all the others in the book, combines descriptions of suffering with theological inquiry into that suffering' (86).

22. Lam. 1.2, 16; 2.11, 18.

23. See Dobbs-Allsopp (1993: 75-91) and Kramer (1983).

Unlike Daughter Zion, the גבר's tears are part of his prayer and his intent is explicit. He will cry until God looks down and takes note. The expression 'over all the maidens of my city' is problematic and scholars suggest emendation.²⁴ It is possible to read the phrase as a comparison.²⁵ If read in this way, then the גבר boasts that his suffering, his tears, have brought him more grief 'than all the daughters of my city'. In other words, he has cried more tears than the women of Jerusalem. He will not be emotionally outdone by a woman!

Despite the גבר's expressions of emotion, the argument that his perspective is more theological rests on his adept use of familiar, theologically inflected language and images. In Lam. 3.40-44 he opens his prayer,

> Let us search and examine our ways,
> And turn back to the Lord;
> Let us lift up our hearts with our hands
> To God in heaven:
> We have transgressed and rebelled,
> And you have not forgiven.
> You have clothed Yourself in anger and pursued us,
> You have slain without pity.
> You have screened Yourself off with a cloud,
> That no prayer may pass through.

In this passage, he uses language familiar from wisdom literature²⁶ and images that resonate with other passages in the Bible to offer a powerful critique of God. Elsewhere, the verb סכך, 'to cover, veil, shield, screen', and the image of the cloud have positive connotations. Often סכך indicates protection from danger, usually in the context of the wings of the cherubs and the covering on the ark, both of which protect the ark.²⁷ The cloud appears in moments of theophany. It guides the Israelites through the wilderness and rests upon Sinai and within the tabernacle to indicate divine immanence. Yet in this passage, the cloud is a dangerous obstacle between God and the people that prevents Israel's prayers from reaching God. Thus, even though the people have admitted their sins, they are not forgiven.²⁸ By inverting traditional language and images, the גבר makes it clear that God has not behaved properly.

---

24. See Renkema (1998: 443).

25. This is how Berlin translates it. See Berlin (2002: 97).

26. The words 'search' and 'examine' are common in wisdom literature. See Prov. 2.4, 20.27; Job 5.27, 28.3, 27; Ps. 139.1, 23. These words serve as admonitions, urging individuals to examine and redirect themselves toward God. See Westermann (1994: 179).

27. See Exod. 25.20, 37.9; 1 Kgs. 8.7.

28. Berlin (2002) comments, 'This is a devastating negation of a fundamental religious concept inscribed in traditional sources. It is a fierce indictment of God. Nowhere in Lamentations, and perhaps in the entire Bible, is God's refusal to be present more strongly expressed. This is the climax of the poem's theodicy for at this point the poet reaches a theological impasse' (96).

Although Daughter Zion uses language in her prayers that resonates with other passages in the Bible,[29] her objective does not appear to be to demonstrate how God has failed to uphold traditional expectations. Instead, her language and methods seem more straightforward. She depicts a disturbing reality in an effort to draw attention to her suffering and the suffering of her children. 'Look at me', she cries. 'Look at my suffering, my wounds, my dead children'. In contrast, the גבר opens his prayer in the first person plural voice as if he speaks for all of Israel. This broader perspective may suggest a radical difference between the two figures: Daughter Zion is self-centred while the גבר is concerned with others. At first glance there might be some support for this assumption. Throughout her prayers, Daughter Zion draws attention to herself. 'See, O Lord, my misery!' (Lam. 1.9). 'See, O Lord, and behold, how abject I have become!' (Lam. 1.11). 'Hear, all you people, and behold my agony!' (Lam. 1.18). 'See, O Lord, the distress I am in!' (Lam. 1.20). '*My* priests and *my* elders have perished in the city' (Lam. 1.19). '*My* maidens and youths are fallen by the sword' (Lam. 2.21).

Yet closer examination of their prayers reveals a different reality. Though the גבר begins speaking for all of Israel, at the onset of his tears he switches to the first person singular voice. His lament is a noticeably personal lament. The cloud may be blocking all of Israel's prayers, but it is the failure of his own prayer that the גבר laments: 'Hear *my* plea! Do not shut Your ear to *my* groan, to *my* cry!' (Lam. 3.56). Although it appears that both the גבר and Daughter Zion are equally focused on their own personal suffering, the content of their laments suggests that the גבר is more self-focused than Daughter Zion. To illustrate his agony, the גבר uses images that convey the feeling of being trapped. He is trapped like a bird, cast into a pit, covered with water (Lam. 3.52-54). Like the language and images found in the opening of his prayer, these images are conventional. Feeling trapped in a pit and desiring release is a common theme in the psalms.[30] The גבר's lament does not mention the suffering of others. Once he reverts to the first person singular voice in Lam. 3.48, the rest of his prayer sounds like a personal, generic lament.[31] He wants his prayer heard, his life redeemed and his enemies punished.

Although Daughter Zion never abandons her first person singular perspective and refers constantly to her own pain, she also draws attention to the suffering of others:

---

29. For example, 'looking upon affliction' (Lam. 1.9, 11) is found in Pss. 9.14, 25.18, 31.8 and 119.153. The expression 'for I have disobeyed Him' in Lam. 1:18 occurs in Num. 20.24, 27.14, Deut. 1.26, 43, 9.23, Josh. 1.18 and 1 Kgs. 13.21, 26. The mention of Daughter Zion's lovers (Lam. 1.19) echoes Jer. 22.20-22, 30.14, Ezek. 16.33, 36 and Ezek. 23.5, 9, 22.

30. Pss. 28.1; 30.4; 69.2-3, 15-16; 88.5-6, 18; 143.7.

31. Berlin (2002) notes the formal components: the plea for God to hear the lamenter, forensic language, the plots and taunts of the enemies, and the hope for punishing the enemy (97).

> Hear, all you peoples,
> And behold my agony:
> My maidens and my youths
> Have gone into captivity!
> I cried out to my friends,
> But they played me false.
> My priests and my elders
> Have perished in the city
> As they searched for food
> To keep themselves alive (Lam. 1.18b-19).

In Lam. 2.20, Daughter Zion prays:

> See, O Lord, and behold,
> To whom You have done this!
> Alas, women eat their own fruit,
> Their new born babes!
> Alas, priest and prophet are slain
> In the sanctuary of the Lord!

The shocking and gruesome nature of this image intensifies its effect. Whereas the גבר's cloud image demonstrates how God's behaviour defies expectations, Daughter Zion's cannibalistic mothers demonstrate how human behaviour defies expectation. In contrast to the גבר, Daughter Zion remains focused on the human pain and tragedy. Her own pain is intimately connected with the pain of others. She uses her pain to draw attention to the suffering of others. Daughter Zion suffers because her children are held captive and her priests lie dead in the street.

Having observed both similarities and differences in the prayers of Daughter Zion and the גבר, I will draw some conclusions about how the gender of the prayers affects their prayers. First, common elements among the prayers of Daughter Zion and the גבר reflect a shared prayer strategy. Both Daughter Zion and the גבר spend little time confessing their crime and more time describing their suffering. Their prayers are designed to effect change. Through graphic images of suffering, they appeal to God's mercy. By praying for the demise of their enemies, Daughter Zion and the גבר invite God to save God's reputation and indirectly to feel the pain God inflicts on others. This shared strategy suggests that men and women addressed God similarly—that women prayed with the same purpose and power as men.[32] Both men and women are emotional pray-ers who use emotion to

---

32. This conclusion supports the work of Tikva Frymer-Kensky who argues that though the Bible is a product of a patriarchal society, women are not presented as 'other' in the Bible. She writes, 'The role of woman is clearly subordinate, but the Hebrew Bible does not "explain" or justify this subordination by portraying women as different or inferior. The stories do not reflect any differences in goals and desires between men and women. Nor do they point out any strategies or methods used by women that are different from those used by men who are not in positions of authority' (Frymer-Kensky 2002: xv).

appeal to God. The גבר prays that his tears will attract God's attention. Daughter Zion hopes that God will notice her anguished heart (Lam. 1.20).³³

Despite these structural similarities, there is one striking difference between the prayers of Daughter Zion and the גבר. The גבר opens his prayer in the first person plural voice, speaking for all of Israel. Yet he switches to the first person singular to offer a personal lament that is filled with images of his own anguished suffering apart from the community. He stands alone in the pit awaiting release. In contrast, Daughter Zion's personal lament is intimately connected to her suffering community. Her children, young and old, lie dead in the street. Gender provides one explanation for this difference. Daughter Zion's prayer as the mourning mother and the גבר's prayer as captured prey may reflect typical roles within ancient Israelite society.³⁴ Yet what is interesting to note is not the obvious division in labour—the woman takes care of the children while the man hunts—but rather the effect these roles have on the consciousness of those who experience them. The גבר feels free to speak to and for all of Israel, urging Israel to redirect itself toward God, and confessing Israel's sins. Yet the גבר also feels free to express his own suffering apart from the community. Perhaps as a male, he represents and suffers for the community, but is also able to stand apart from the community as an autonomous individual. By contrast, like the גבר, Daughter Zion suffers as an individual, yet her suffering is in response to the suffering of others. Her emotional life is bound up with the lives of her dependants. Her release will come through the release of her children.

Why does the book of Lamentations include both the prayers of Daughter Zion and the גבר? Because though they pray similarly, their prayers are different and reflect different perspectives. The independent גבר seeks his own salvation. He wants to be saved from the pit. Enmeshed Daughter Zion wants her children to live. Together, their prayers offer a fuller appeal to God to cease God's rage and to return the people to God's presence.

BIBLIOGRAPHY

Balentine, Samuel E.
    1993   *Prayer in the Hebrew Bible: The Drama of Divine-Human Dialogue* (OBT; Minneapolis: Fortress Press).
Berlin, Adele
    2002   *Lamentations* (OTL; Louisville, KY: Westminster/John Knox Press).

---

33. The expression translated 'my heart is in anguish' literally means 'my bowels burn/churn', and indicates severe emotional distress. For a discussion of the relationship between physical and emotional discomfort see Smith (1998: 427-36).

34. While comparing the imagery of Lamentations 3 to Lamentations 1, Berlin (2002) notes, 'Just as the imagery in chapter 1 was feminine—the widow, the unfaithful wife, the raped woman—so here the imagery seems more masculine, invoking the physical violence against the male body associated with war and exile' (84).

Bird, Phyllis
    1999   'The Place of Women in the Israelite Cultus', in A. Bach (ed.), *Women in the Hebrew Bible: A Reader* (London: Routledge): 3-20.

Blank, Sheldon H.
    1961   'Some Observations Concerning Biblical Prayer', *HUCA* 32: 75-90.

Brettler, Marc Zvi
    1998   'Women and Psalms: Toward an Understanding of the Role of Women's Prayer in the Israelite Cult', in Victor H. Matthews, Bernard M. Levinson and Tikva Frymer-Kensky (eds.), *Gender and Law in the Hebrew Bible and the Ancient Near East* (JSOTSup, 262; Sheffield: Sheffield Academic Press): 25-56.

Dever, William G.
    2005   *Did God Have a Wife? Archaeology and Folk Religion in Ancient Israel* (Grand Rapids: Eerdmans).

Dobbs-Allsopp, F.W.
    1993   *Weep, O Daughter Zion: A Study of the City-Lament Genre in the Hebrew Bible* (BibOr, 44; Rome: Pontifical Biblical Institute).

Frymer-Kensky, Tikva
    2002   *Reading the Women of the Bible: A New Interpretation of their Stories* (New York: Schocken Books).

Greenberg, Moshe
    1983   *Biblical Prose Prayer: As a Window to the Popular Religion of Ancient Israel* (Berkeley: University of California Press).

Heim, Knut M.
    1999   'The Personification of Jerusalem and the Drama of her Bereavement in Lamentations', in Richard S. Hess and Gordon J. Wenham (eds.), *Zion, City of Our God* (Grand Rapids: Eerdmans): 129-69.

Kaiser, Barbara Bakke
    1987   'Poet as "Female Impersonator": The Image of Daughter Zion as Speaker in Biblical Poems of Suffering', *JR* 67: 164-82.

Knohl, Israel
    1996   'Between Voice and Silence: The Relationship between Prayer and Temple Cult', *JBL* 115: 17-30.

Kramer, Samuel Noah
    1983   'Weeping Goddess: Sumerian Prototypes of the *Mater Dolorosa*', *BA* 46: 69-79.

Lanahan, William F.
    1974   'The Speaking Voice in the Book of Lamentations', *JBL* 93: 41-49.

Meyers, Carol
    1996   'The Hannah Narrative in Feminist Perspective', in Joseph E. Coleson and Victor H. Matthews (eds.), *'Go to the Land I Will Show You': Studies in Honor of Dwight W. Young* (Winona Lake, IN: Eisenbrauns): 117-26.
    2003   'Everyday Life in Biblical Israel: Women's Social Networks', in Richard E. Averbeck, Mark W. Chavalas and David B. Weisberg (eds.), *Life and Culture in the Ancient Near East* (Bethesda, MD: CDL Press): 185-204.

Miller, Charles William
    2001   'Reading Voices: Personification, Dialogism, and the Reader of Lamentations 1', *BibInt* 9: 393-408.

Mintz, Alan
    1982   'The Rhetoric of Lamentations and the Representation of Catastrophe', *Prooftexts* 2: 1-17.

Newman, Judith H.
    1999   *Praying by the Book: Scripturalization of Prayer in Second Temple Judaism* (SBLEJL, 14; Atlanta: Scholars Press).

O'Connor, Kathleen M.
    2002   *Lamentations and the Tears of the World* (Maryknoll, NY: Orbis Books).

Renkema, Johan
    1998   *Lamentations* (Historical Commentary on the Old Testament; Leuven: Peeters).

Sheppard, Gerald T.
    1991   '"Enemies" and the Politics of Prayer in the Book of Psalms', in David Jobling, Peggy L. Day, Gerald T. Sheppard (eds.), *The Bible and the Politics of Exegesis: Essays in Honor of Norman K. Gottwald on his Sixty-Fifth Birthday* (Cleveland, OH: Pilgrim Press): 61-82.

Smith, Mark S.
    1998   'The Heart and Innards in Israelite Emotional Expressions: Notes from Anthropology and Psychobiology', *JBL* 117: 427-36.

Werline, Rodney Alan
    1998   *Penitential Prayer in Second Temple Judaism: The Development of a Religious Institution* (SBLEJL, 13; Atlanta: Scholars Press).

Westermann, Claus
    1994   *Lamentations: Issues and Interpretation* (trans. Charles Muenchow; Minneapolis: Fortress Press).

Bathing, Status and Gender in Priestly Ritual

Nicole J. Ruane

In both Judaism and Christianity, some of the most powerful ritual expression occurs in the form of ritual bathing. The water rite of baptism is the definitive Christian ritual; the various uses of a ritual bath or *miqveh* in Judaism form an important part of religious experience and practice. In these religions, as well as others, bathing rituals can enact religious devotion and personal spiritual transformation. The rites are also means of establishing and exhibiting membership in a practising community: by the act of baptism one assumes a Christian identity; by bathing in a *miqveh*, among other things, one expresses membership in a Jewish community. While these bathing rites foster community and religiosity, they are also a means of establishing and articulating difference; difference between the religious community and outsiders, and difference among members of the same religious community. For instance, the rite of baptism not only distinguishes the Christian from the non-Christian, but because it is usually carried out by a member of the clergy, it enacts the hierarchy of clergy and laity: the ordained clergy person has the power to manipulate the baptismal water and imbue it with cultic efficacy, while the baptized takes a passive role in the act.

The practices of baptism and *miqveh*-immersion, though quite distinct, share a common heritage in biblical ritual, especially in the cultic prescriptions for ablutions by the priestly writer in the books of Exodus and Leviticus (Wegner 1992: 39). As in these contemporary religions, many of the dynamics of community construction and hierarchical relationships occur in biblical bathing rituals too. The rites of bathing (רחץ) and laundering (כבס) are integral aspects of most priestly ritual practice, yet they occur in different contexts and with various effects.[1] Bathing and laundering often take place along with other rituals such as anointing with oil, sacrifice, and elimination rites, and like them, ritual bathing helps to define a religious community and the relative status of its members. As in Judaism and Christianity, bathing in priestly texts is a means of showing cultic participation and privilege, but also differences and hierarchy.

---

1. For a general introduction to the meaning and occurrence of ablutions in P and in general, see Milgrom (1991: 957-68). Milgrom emphasizes that P always uses these neutral terms for ablutions while non-P writers employ piel and hithpael forms of the verb קדש (1991: 967).

The intent of this essay is to begin an examination of how priestly bathing rites foster community and hierarchy and how in some cases these processes also effect the social construct of gender. In general, priestly ritual coordinates the acts of bathing and laundering with increased cultic privilege and responsibility. As a person becomes hierarchically superior in the priestly cult, the quantity and complexity of his or her ritual action increases as well. As one kind of ritual behaviour, the frequency of bathing can become a means of expressing this rise in status. The priestly texts create gender disparities by portraying bathing as almost exclusively a male cultic activity. Leviticus 12 and 15, which specify purificatory rituals according to sex, reinforce gender distinctions by emphasizing bathing rites for men and yet omitting such rites for women, especially in parallel circumstances, such as that of the זב and זבה in Leviticus 15.

Bathing and Meaning

The acts of bathing and laundering, which I will here treat as one with bathing, can obviously act as a literal means of cleansing.[2] The fundamental notion of being clean is certainly tied to the acts of bathing and washing clothes. Thus the common act of washing is easily adapted for ritual meaning, especially to express ideas of purification and the changing of a physical condition. In fact, in some rites of purification people wash after doing things that would quite literally make them dirty, such as wearing the ashes of the red heifer for seven days (Numbers 19). However, the bathing described in the priestly rituals is not an antidote to dirt but to ritual impurity (טמאה). As ritual acts, bathing rites take on an importance far beyond that of general cleanliness, though it is difficult to discern their precise meaning. Many interpretations of specific priestly rites of bathing, like those of all priestly ritual acts, have attempted to

---

2. Laundering is often performed together with bathing (e.g. Exod. 19.11, 14; Lev. 11.25, 28, 40; 13.6, 34; 14. 8, 9, 47; 15.5, 6, 7, 8, 10, 11, 13, 21, 22, 27; 16.26, 28; 17.15-16; Num. 19.7, 8, 10, 19, 21). A ritual changing of clothes can also accompany bathing (Exod. 29.4-6; 40.12-13; Lev. 8.6-9; 16.4, 24), perhaps implying that laundering is a counterpart to changing into special clothes, or vice versa. Bathing also occurs as a rite on its own, for example, in Lev. 8.6; 15.16, 18; and 22.6, as does laundering (e.g. Num. 19.21). Whether or not laundering is required along with bathing may depend on the type of act that defiles. For instance, Milgrom (1991: 668), following the rabbis, suggests that the reason laundering is required along with bathing in Lev. 11.25 is because the act of carrying a dead animal is a more intense activity than merely touching it. The intensity of the contact requires a more intense antidote, a principle called 'pressure' (מדרס) by the rabbis. Alternatively, as proposed by the Ramban, it may be because the act of carrying a carcass would necessarily mean that the carrier's clothes had been touched by the animal's body (Milgrom 1991: 668). In any event, the acts of bathing and laundering are closely related and are often performed together; for the purposes of this paper they will be treated as the same, though they may have more distinct functions.

ascertain the singular literal meaning of a particular rite.[3] For instance, Jacob Milgrom argues that when the high priest bathes after conducting the Yom Kippur חטאת rites (Lev. 16.24), the rite is part of his process of 'de-sanctification' from being in the holy of holies. He must in effect wash off his holiness (Milgrom 1991: 1051). Other commentators suggest that the priest must bathe because he has absorbed some of the impurity and sinfulness that has been transferred to the Azazel goat during the rites[4]—in other words, the priest must wash as a result of impurity, not holiness. These contradictions show that it is difficult to know precisely how the bathing is functioning. As Hyam Maccoby says, 'Sometimes it is hard to say whether a washing procedure is intended to wash away impurity, lest it should contaminate, or to wash away holiness, lest it sanctify' (Maccoby 1999: 116). The text does not tell us why the priest must bathe, or what he washes off, but only that he must do it, so that the meaning of the priest's bathing cannot be definitively ascertained.

David P. Wright offers an important description of the purpose of bathing in biblical ritual; ritual acts of bathing or washing 'establish the purity of persons or objects so that they may perform or be employed in cultic service' (Wright 1992: 732). This description is most useful because it coordinates the ritual with the privilege of cultic viability: the act of bathing creates and exhibits a positive cultic status (purity). However, even this description ties bathing to a specific meaning (purity) when that meaning is not unambiguous; again, the bathing of the high priest may be expressing something beyond purity per se, such as uncommon ritual fitness. Theorists of ritual have emphasized that all ritual is multivalent; it does not have a single meaning or purpose.[5] Even if a reason or meaning for the bathing rite were specified, this does not mean that it would pertain to every performance of that rite or that it would have the same meaning for all participants. Instead, the power of ritual is most readily ascertained not in the meaning of a ritual act, but in the way its performance enacts relationships and power dynamics among its various participants (Bell 1992: 198-222). Hence a more tangible, if less satisfying, significance of the high priest's bathing may be found in the effect of the action. That is, regardless of what he is washing off, the high priest's unusual act of bathing here contributes to the overall unusual and cultically charged nature of the Yom Kippur complex of rites which only the high priest can perform. His bathing upon leaving the adytum, which only he may enter and then only once a year, helps to enact his unequalled cultic power and privilege. His bathing reiterates his

---

3. For a critique of this method of interpretation, see Gilders's (2004) study of the meaning of blood rites in biblical ritual, especially pp. 2-8. Gilders's work has greatly affected both the methodology and intent of this paper.

4. See the list of scholars in Gane (2005: 186 n. 81; 188 n. 94) who hold this view. Gane's discussion of the issue illustrates many of the difficulties in trying to ascertain the meaning of the rite (Gane 2005: 186-91).

5. E.g. Bell (1992).

cultic involvement and emphasizes his access to the sacred. This meaning may be even more clear in the mishnaic interpretation of the high priest's bathing: according to m. *Yom*. 3.3, he must bathe five times and wash his hands and feet fifteen times. This extreme amount of bathing correlates with the most prestigious religious activity and helps to point up its importance. The repeated acts of bathing by the high priest thus aver again and again his cultic acceptability and prominence.

Bathing rites also contribute to social constructs in other ways. In Exod. 19.10-11, where the Israelites must wash their clothes before the theophany at Sinai, they are not told do so because their clothes are dirty, or because the people are impure, but in order to 'be ready' (ויהיו נכנים) for the event. It is unclear exactly what 'being ready' means. In this instance it is related to consecration, investiture and purification, but those states are also effected by other actions, such as abstaining from sex. Again, instead of looking for a stable meaning for the washing (i.e. trying to figure out what they have washed off), it is more useful to see that the laundering defines the cultically privileged group (i.e. those who will encounter God and make a covenant with the divine) and changes the status of those who have gone from common people to chosen people, thereby differentiating the Israelites from others. In the context of Exodus 19, the bathing and laundering rites that help to forge the ritual community of Israelites also create a distinction between men and women. In 19.15, after the 'Israelites' have washed, Moses tells them, 'Be ready for the third day; do not go near a woman', thus indicating that those who have just washed are not women, are different from women, and that their washing is related to separation from women.[6] Bathing helps to define the practising community, which in this situation also correlates to gender and its relative cultic status.

Any attempt to interpret the power dynamics inherent in biblical ritual is limited by the fact that these ritual actions cannot be directly observed and are mediated and narrated by the author of the text in question. The literary presentation of ritual not only changes its very nature but can make opaque many aspects of ritual that readers would like to know, such as how it is related to specific people that the text does not discuss. For those of us wanting to know more about the roles of women in biblical and Israelite religion, this textual presentation forces some methodological questions, such as whether we can assume that laws which do not specifically mention women in the text implicitly include them in practice. For example, in Leviticus 15 it is unclear whether the laws of purification for those who contact the impurity of a זב

---

6. The exclusion of women from Sinai that seems inherent in this passage has been problematic for Judaism in general and for Jewish women's theology in particular. The rabbis were uncomfortable with the textual implication that women were not there. For an introductory discussion, see Plaskow (1990: 25-28).

(a man with an impure genital discharge) by touching him and his bedding apply only to men. Verse 5, which is the first set of these instructions, uses the specific term איש (man) to describe the person who must undergo such a purification. The impurity of a woman who may come into contact with the זב is not specified and the laws do not describe the ritual consequences of having intercourse with a זב, which would be a concern for women (Wegner 1998: 86; Wright 1987: 195). Thus the contamination of men is the author's primary concern. We do not know if the laws apply evenly to women, or if they do not, how they vary for women.

A common means of interpreting such gaps in ritual instruction is to assume that the same prescriptions apply to women when not expressly stated. However, acknowledging the gap and exploring it leads to better articulation of what is unclear and to interpretative possibilities for the omission and its effects. In the case of Leviticus 15, for example, one can then question whether women were thought somehow to have a different relationship to impurity from the one that men do. They may have been expected to defile themselves by touching ill men in a way that men might not have been expected to touch women or other men. A focus on what the text articulates and what it does not opens up opportunities for analysis and forces more scrutiny of the interests of its author. The example of Exodus 19 makes clear that female participation in cultic activity cannot necessarily be assumed.

Men and Bathing

In priestly texts, the rites of bathing and laundering are most commonly done by men. Men are required to bathe during rites of consecration or ordination, when participating in unusual cultic events or in the rites of sacrifice, or when approaching the altar. Those who wash in these contexts become raised in status over other members of the community. For example, when the Levites are consecrated in Numbers 8, they are told to launder their garments, purify themselves with ritual water, and shave their entire bodies (8.6-7). They then are presented as a wave offering and they offer their own sacrifices (8.8-13). In this way, God tells the Israelites, 'you shall set the Levites apart from the other Israelites and the Levites shall be mine' (Num. 8.14). Although the consecration of the Levities is a complicated ritual, one primary aspect of their consecration and setting apart is laundering and bathing.

Similarly, at the consecration of Aaron and his sons for the priesthood in Exodus 29, the priests wash in water at the door to the tent of meeting (29.4). They then change their clothes, are anointed with oil, and perform sacrifices. As the first ritual act, it is the bathing that begins their change to an elevated status; without it the other rites would seem not to be efficacious. Aaron and his sons also bathe at the consecration of the tabernacle, and thus at the institution of their vocation there (Exod. 40.12), as well as in their ordination in Leviticus

8 (v. 6). Indeed, every time the priests do their work or enter the tent of meeting they bathe their hands and feet from the lavers (Exod. 40.30-32). The bathing is the first step in the ritual process of their being distinguished from other men and thus in the creation of their higher cultic status.

As mentioned above, bathing rites also mark off the activity of the high priest from the other priests on Yom Kippur, where the high priest bathes twice (Lev. 16.4, 24) when he alone conducts unusual rites in the holy of holies. The first time is at the very beginning of the procedure, when he puts on his special linen clothes; he does it again after he leaves the adytum and takes off the linen. These actions contribute to his distinctiveness from the other priests, who never perform this duty, and emphasize the unique and important nature of his ritual practice.

The act of ritual bathing can also set apart a non-priestly man from other men from the laity. The man who leads away the goat for Azazel on Yom Kippur, for example, must bathe himself and his clothes upon returning (Lev. 16.26), as must the man who burns the remains of the communal חטאת outside the camp on that day (16.28). Likewise, the ordinary men involved in the creation of the ashes of the red cow in Numbers 19 bathe or launder after their work (19.8, 10, 21). Those who participate in the red cow rite are specifically called impure (19.8, 10, 21), but the text is unclear as to whether the men involved in the Yom Kippur rites, like the high priest, bathe because they are impure, or because they have contacted holiness from touching sancta, or for some other reason. But one effect of bathing for all these men is that it sets them apart from other people as involved in special cultic activity so that they become like priests but unlike other men. In all of these instances bathing is thus coordinated with elevated cultic participation and status.

By contrast, women are never said to bathe or launder their clothes as a part of any rite of consecration or ordination, nor are they required to bathe as a result of some ritual activity, such as creating the ashes of the red heifer. Women are not required to bathe even if they become Nazirites: the elaborate rites described in Numbers 6 do not require bathing at all. So men who bathe in the course of ritual action assert status over other men who do not have their same cultic prerogatives as well as over all women, who would not have the opportunity to carry out any of these cultic tasks.

Bathing, Gender and Impurity

While bathing for men is important to these more positive and exceptional ritual activities, the most common reason for bathing in ritual law is as an antidote for coming into contact with impurity. Impurity can be contracted from unclean animal carcasses, skin disease, some forms of genital discharge and corpses, or people or things that are carriers of such impurities (Leviticus 11–15, 17; Numbers 19). Men are specifically said to bathe or launder as antidotes to all of them.⁷ However, it is unclear how these laws apply to women; many seem to be gender neutral, but then show surprising disparities.⁸ In Numbers 19, for example, the language of the text seems to imply that the prescriptions for death impurity, including bathing, would apply evenly to men and women, but at the end of the passage we are told, 'Any man (איש) who becomes unclean and does not cleanse himself will be cut off from the congregation, for he has defiled the LORD's sanctuary' (v. 20). Does this use of איש here mean that all along this law only applied to men? Or does it mean that women are implicitly subsumed under the category of 'man'? Or does it mean that the law applied to all people but not following it results in the כרת of only men? If so, does the author of this text understand the punishment of being cut off from the congregation to be one that is only really applicable to men?

The only specific instance of women washing in the laws of death impurity or skin disease is in one subsection of the 'leprosy' laws where men and women are declared clean and must launder their clothes if a scall on their head or cheek does not spread after fourteen days (Lev. 13.28-37).⁹ The inclusion of women here, coupled with the use of the term אדם throughout chapters 13–14 to describe the afflicted person, most likely implies that all of the laws of skin disease pertain to women and that the extensive restorative rituals in Leviticus 14 consistently apply to them as well. However, Lev. 13.40-44, which addresses the purity of baldness for men alone, leaves open the possibility that baldness in women is an impurity. Moreover, the fact that a person recovering from skin disease must shave the beard (Lev. 14.9) indicates that these laws must vary to some degree for women. Such gaps accent the ambiguity of women's ritual status even in this relatively straightforward set of laws.

---

7. Lev. 11.25, 28, 40; 13.6, 34; 14.8, 9; 15.5, 6, 7, 8, 10, 11, 13, 16, 18, 21, 22, 27; 17.15-16; Num. 19.19.

8. Num. 5.1-4 describes a different treatment from that in Leviticus for those suffering from genital and death impurities, so that they must all reside outside the camp along with the skin-diseased person. Unlike Leviticus, this passage emphasizes that these purity laws apply to females as well as males: verse 3 states, 'Remove male and female alike; put them outside the camp so that they do not defile the camp of those in whose midst I dwell' (NJPS). The following section in Numbers 5, which concerns the confession and restitution for those who commit a wrong, also emphasizes that the law pertains to females as well (v. 6). One wonders whether the emphasis is due to the lack of clarity about the extent of legal application to women generally and in the parallel Leviticus texts in particular.

9. Women are also explicitly mentioned in the following subsection in vv. 38-39, which discusses a similar minor instance of skin disease. Milgrom (1991) posits that the reason for differentiating men and women in v. 29 is because only a man would have a beard and yet the law on disease in hair follicles would apply also to women's head hair (794). He argues that the gender specifications in v. 38 are affected by the form of the previous pericope (798), and that men alone are discussed in the following section on baldness (vv. 40-44) because usually only men become bald (800).

Specific purity rituals for women are mostly of concern in Leviticus 12 and 15 which address the genital impurities of childbirth, menstruation, semen, and abnormal discharge. Though genitalia are the source of life, and possibly for that reason cause impurity, they are also the site of sex differentiation, which may be a more fundamental basis for their ability to defile and the need to regulate them through ritual action. Gender definition, as part of social status, is also intrinsic to ritual status. The laws for the parturient in Leviticus 12 are highly gendered: there are no comparable rites for a new father. A new father is not required to make any sacrifices or wait for a period of time before rejoining the worshipping community. Moreover, the mother's status is determined in part by the gender of what she bears: if she has a son she is impure for 40 days, if a daughter, she is impure for 80 days (12.2, 4-5). But unlike people who become unclean through death impurity or skin disease, the text never requires a new mother to bathe or launder her clothes. She is obligated to bring sacrifices at the end of her impurity (12.6-8), but the only purificatory act she must undertake before bringing these is to wait for the passage of time. The waiting period seems to make her sufficiently ritually clean to bring her offering. Therefore, in this passage, bathing is not part of the ritual remedy for the specifically female impurity of childbirth. Even if the ritual system behind these laws assumes that she must bathe, the text takes no concern to emphasize bathing as part of female ritual procedure in the same way that it stresses the rite of bathing for other cultic situations and characters. This omission of bathing for other female impurities occurs also in Leviticus 15, where neither a menstruant nor a woman with an abnormal genital condition is said to bathe.

Leviticus 15

In contrast to Leviticus 12, Leviticus 15 contains extended discussion of the genital impurity of both men and women. The passage is often understood to be an instance of gender unity and equality since it has a chiastic and seemingly symmetrical form of male and female impurities (Wenham 1979: 217; Ellens 2000: 124, 130; 2003: 35). The chapter is sometimes divided into six sections: an introduction in vv. 1-2a and a conclusion in vv. 31-33; two sections on male discharges, the first containing the laws of the זב (vv. 2b-15) and the second concerning the impurity of ejaculation (vv. 16-18); and two sections on female discharges, addressing the menstruant (vv. 19-24) and the זבה, or woman with an irregular or extended flow of uterine blood (vv. 25-30). This gives the following chiastic structure:

1-2a Introduction
    A 2b-15 Laws of the זב
        B 16-18 Laws of ejaculation
        B' 19-24 Laws of the menstruant
    A' 25-30 Laws of the זבה
31-33 Conclusion

Gordon Wenham was the first to discuss the chiastic form of the passage. He showed that the sections I have here called A and A' discuss the abnormal and long-term genital impurities of both males and females while sections B and B' legislate for the normal and transient impurities of both sexes. The structure of the passage, he said, shows the unity and interdependence of the sexes by treating them similarly (Wenham 1979: 217). Deborah Ellens offers a more detailed structural analysis based on the fact that v. 18 is matched by v. 24, both of which discuss intercourse and its effects on purity. She too understands the structure of the chapter to indicate likeness; she says, 'Structural symmetry constitutes gender symmetry' (Ellens 2000: 130; 2003: 35). However one describes the passage, its structure does seem to show a parity between men and women in that they are both sources of genital impurity, they each have normal and pathological impurities, and that genitalia themselves, whether male or female, are problematic for the author. Nevertheless, the structure of the law also encourages a close comparison between male and female impurities and their cultic treatments, since each category of genital impurity has its unique stipulations. There are many differences among them.

For the purposes of this paper, there are two most pressing ways in which the laws are different for men and women. The first is that the stipulations on the communicability of the impurity of a זב, which are found in vv. 7-12, are far more extensive than those for a זבה. The זב is portrayed as spitting on people, riding on a saddle, touching people and contaminating a cooking vessel. Since these stipulations are unmatched for the זבה, it is unclear whether they would apply to her as well, or even whether a woman would be understood to engage in these activities. The second difference regards purificatory rites. When men are the source of impurity, as with the זב and the man with an emission of semen, they are required to bathe (vv. 13, 16, 18). The זב must bathe after counting off seven days following the end of his impurity and before offering sacrifices. The man who emits semen, whether in intercourse or otherwise, must bathe and wash it off any cloth or hide on which it lands, and then be unclean until sundown. But, like the parturient, women are never required to bathe when they are the source of genital impurity. Neither the menstruant nor the זבה has to bathe or launder her clothes. The menstruant must only wait the allotted seven days and then she resumes her normal status (v. 19). The ritual treatment for the זבה, when she is cleansed from her impurity, is exactly the same as for a זב, except that she does not bathe. She brings the same sacrifices as the זב to the sanctuary at the end of her impurity, and she counts off seven days between the end of her flowing and the offering of those sacrifices, just as the זב does, but nowhere does the text require that she bathe. Comparison of the two sets of ritual instructions makes this clear; the purificatory rites for the זב and זבה are shown below, with the elements unique to the זב highlighted:[10]

---

10. See also Wegner (1998: 83).

> Leviticus 15.13 When one with a discharge becomes clean of his discharge, he shall count off seven days *for his cleansing, wash his clothes, and bathe his body in fresh water;* then he shall be clean. 14 On the eighth day he shall take two turtledoves or two pigeons *and come before the* LORD at the entrance of the Tent of Meeting and *give them to the priest.* 15 The priest shall offer them, the one as a sin offering and the other as a burnt offering. Thus the priest shall make expiation on his behalf, for his discharge, before the LORD.
>
> 15.28 When she becomes clean of her discharge, she shall count off seven days, and after that she shall be clean. 29 On the eighth day she shall take two turtledoves or two pigeons, and bring them to the priest at the entrance of the Tent of Meeting. 30 The priest shall offer the one as a sin offering and the other as a burnt offering; and the priest shall make expiation on her behalf, for her unclean discharge, before the LORD (NJPS).

In addition to this omission, the rules for the זב in vv. 7-12 that are unmatched for the זבה show that the impurity of the זב can be mitigated by water in other ways: he can be prevented from contaminating others by touch as long as he first rinses his hands, and a wood vessel he touches is cleaned with water (15.11, 12). In contrast, the contagion of the זבה is not said to ease if she washes her hands, nor is it said that a vessel she touches must either be burnt or washed in water. These differences raise questions about how the writer understood a זבה to act in the world in general, as well as in the world of ritual. The author may not have imagined her to touch other people as commonly or publicly as a man might. Or perhaps some responsibility for preparing food would have affected the author's understanding of the woman's relationship to wooden vessels. In any event, these stipulations for the זב concerning water do reinforce the pattern of ritual washing as male activity.

Many interpreters have assumed that menstruants, parturients and women with irregular flows of blood are in fact required to bathe at the end of their impurity.[11] Deborah Ellens and others argue that the laws of the זב extend to the זבה by analogy or by what Ellens calls a 'shorthand technique' of assuming that all the stipulations of a longer law are implied in similar shorter laws, and that the text therefore implies that women should bathe (Ellens 2000: 141). Milgrom states that the laws for women in Leviticus 15 are completely dependent upon the laws for men and thus the order and structure of Leviticus 15 is of great importance: the main law of genital impurity is laid out first in the law of the זב, and the subsequent laws of the זבה and the menstruant follow its details (Milgrom 1991: 905, 925). But if that is the case it is unclear why only these certain parts of the law of the זב would be repeated in the rules for the menstruant and זבה, and what criteria the author employed for repetition. Moreover, Milgrom assumes that the parturient would also need to bathe because the law of the parturient in Leviticus 12 refers to menstrual impurity (v. 2) (Milgrom

---

11. E.g. Milgrom 1991: 746, 756, 924, 934-35, 944; Wright 1987: 191.

1991: 745), but that chapter is clearly not structurally dependent upon the first section of Leviticus 15.

Other scholars, such as Cohen, Frymer-Kensky and Meacham,[12] do take the text at face value and see that the menstruant, the זבה, and the parturient are not required to bathe, but they offer little interpretation of the omission. The most systematic explanation of the difference between men's and women's bathing rituals is offered by Judith Romney Wegner, who argues that the reason the זב and the ejaculator are required to bathe but the menstruant, parturient and זבה are not, is because men give (נתן) their sacrifices to the priest 'before the LORD' (לפני יהוה) at the entrance to the tent of meeting, but the unclean woman only *brings* (הביאה) her sacrifices to the priest at the entrance to the tent of meeting without handing them directly to the priest and without coming 'before the LORD' (Wegner 1988: 147; 1992: 42-43; 1998: 83-86). This discrepancy can be seen in the difference between vv. 14 and 30. Though they offer the same sacrifices, the זב and זבה have different relationships to the divine presence, with that of the זב being before God. Wegner interprets the disparity in cultic practice to be the reason for the disparity in bathing rituals: because women do not actually encounter the presence of the LORD, their cultic cleanness is not required. As she says, 'The priestly system mandates ritual purity only for the performance of cultic acts. Ritual purity is required of one who will be either literally or figuratively *entering the presence of Yhwh*. But, unlike the זב, the זבה does *not* come symbolically לפני יהוה, because as a woman she is ineligible to do so; consequently, *in this context*, her state of cultic purity is irrelevant' (Wegner 1998: 85). For Wegner, the discrepancy in relation to the divine presence also 'undoubtedly reflects the priestly view of women's ineligibility to enter, still more participate in, the public domain of the cult' and shows that the woman's act of sacrifice is not 'of the same cultic quality' as the man's (Wegner 1998: 84).

Wegner's interpretation is important: it adheres to the literal wording of the text, it puts forth a systematic reason for the omission of women's bathing rituals, and it considers women's cultic actions with integrity. It also shows that ritual actions express power relations and create hierarchy in status. However, it is not the case that the זבה or other women who do not wash have an irrelevant cultic status. The parturient, menstruant and זבה must all become pure. Even though they do not bathe, they are specifically said to become clean (טהרה), either through acts of sacrifice, as in Lev. 12.8, or a waiting time, as the זבה does in 15.28. Lev. 12.4 also implies that clean women touch at least some holy things and enter the sanctuary, and thus perform cultic acts. The bringing of a sacrifice itself, whether 'before the LORD' or not, is still a cultic act, but it is one that exhibits a lesser status than that of a man.

12. Cohen 1991: 275; 1999: 83; Frymer-Kensky 1983: 402, 413 n. 9; Meacham 1999: 24, 26-28.

Even within the laws of impurity, then, it is still difficult to find a stable meaning for bathing rites. Wegner seems to imply that bathing functions as a precursor to coming 'before the LORD', but this meaning cannot always hold, since there are men who bathe but are not said to come into the divine presence (e.g. Lev. 17.15-16; Num. 19.8, 10) and since women are said to bathe in some ritual circumstances (see below and in Lev. 13.34) even though Wegner implies that they would never come into the divine presence.[13] Moreover, as Wegner herself points out, it is uncertain precisely what 'coming before the LORD' describes. Both the זב and the זבה take their sacrifices to the same place in the tabernacle area, to the priest at the door of the tent of meeting, so that spatially it is unclear just how that differs for the man and for the woman. It may be, as Wegner suggests, that the idea of being 'before the LORD' is more of a metaphorical location and that coming before the LORD is not a particular action, but a way of being, an indication of status that emphasizes connection with the divine (Wegner 1998: 82; 1992: 42-43). Thus the omission of a statement on the woman's presence 'before the LORD', even if it does not indicate a different cultic act or location, de-emphasizes her relationship with the divine. The lack of a female bathing ritual, or at least the lack of a textual statement on it, may work in the same way: it may not affect the woman's ability to perform a cultic action, such as bringing a sacrifice, but it does emphasize distance from the divine, and thus cultic inferiority, simply because the omission fails to affirm a certain status. The bathing is an additional cultic action that marks the זב off from the זבה as more cultically complex and consequently reveals his higher status. He more resembles the priests and other functionaries who bathe. The lack of a bathing rite for a woman, in this case, is not an indication of an irrelevant cultic status but of a lesser cultic status. I disagree with Wegner that (lack of) bathing in this case affects the ability to take certain cultic actions, but I think she has amply highlighted that both bathing and being 'before the LORD' are indications of ritual hierarchy and of differentiation between the genders in a cultic setting.

The omission of bathing rituals for women in Leviticus 12 and 15 is not a mere editorial technique to eliminate repetition, but evidence of a deeper structure. The omission is far too systematic to be some sort of coincidence: the only people in priestly law who are not said to bathe or launder their clothes after a major impurity are women who undergo the specifically female impurities of

---

13. Wegner (1998) states that only the suspected adulteress of Num. 5.11-31 would come before the deity, but then as a passive object instead of ritual actor (86-87). However, if the laws of skin disease and its purification do apply equally to women, then a woman recovering from that impurity would come into the divine presence (Lev. 14.11). This exception highlights the uncertainty around the application of the laws of skin disease to women, as does the fact that the female 'leper' would be the only woman to come into direct contact with sacrificial and other purificatory animal blood when the blood of the אשם offering is daubed on her body and she is sprinkled with the bird's blood mixture (Lev. 14. 7, 14).

menstruation, childbirth and excessive uterine bleeding. It is difficult to know the exact meaning of the underlying deeper structure, however. The omission of the bathing rite may only be literary, and it may have been implicitly understood by the author that the women should bathe. But even if the rite is assumed by the authors, the fact that it is not mentioned or stressed in these laws contributes to a literary characterization of these women as less cultically involved and less directly related to the presence of the divine. However, it also seems quite likely that the priestly writer omitted the rite of bathing for these women because of a belief that women undergoing the particular impurities brought about by female genital blood relate differently to the cultic system than those with other types of impurities, and this belief is represented in the ritual itself. In either case, whether the discrepancy is on the literary level or the ritual level, the effect is a characterization of women as having inferior cultic status and as being more closely related to the low status of impurity. Without a bathing rite to demarcate the shift from impure to pure, the זבה, menstruant and parturient have a less clear distinction as to when their bodies are in each of these two states. The line between the clean and unclean female is less dramatic and more ambiguous when only the passage of time marks the difference. Similarly, if a man must wash after touching an impure woman or her bedding, but the woman need not wash herself after her own impurity, he is more separated from that impurity than she is. She also appears to be more of an object that defiles and less like an autonomous subject who must be removed from defilement. In these ways, the act of ritual bathing enacts the relative status of men and women.

Two Exceptions

Although there are no stipulations requiring women to bathe after their own genital fluxes, one law in Leviticus 15 requires a woman to bathe: v. 18 states that she must wash after having ejaculatory sexual intercourse with a man. This law parallels another example of gender-irregular cultic behaviour in chapter 15, namely, that of the man who has sex with a menstruant (v. 24). He is the only man who does *not* bathe after contacting a genital impurity, and indeed he is the only man in all of priestly law who does not bathe or launder after contacting a severe impurity of any type.

Both of these examples come at the end of sections on normal discharges: the woman who bathes appears at the end of the section on the impurity of semen (v. 18), and the man who does not bathe comes at the end of the section on the menstruating woman (v. 24). Both cases show that intercourse affects the cultic status of one's partner. In each case, the partner acquires an impurity identical to its source and requires the same cultic remedy for it as the person whose body initially contains the impurity, regardless of sex. When a woman has ejaculatory intercourse with a man, she becomes impure in the same way as he does. Like the man she must bathe and she remains unclean for only one day. A man who has sex with a menstruant becomes impure like a menstruant. Although he does not actually shed blood, he is unclean for seven days and contaminates his bedding in the same ways as a menstruant. Like her, he is not said to bathe at the end of the seven-day period (v. 24). In this way he becomes, cultically speaking, like a woman. He also becomes different from a normal man, who bathes when coming in contact with a female impurity (vv. 19-23, 26-27). In inverse fashion, a woman who has intercourse with a man that results in ejaculation is ritually and textually treated like a man in terms of her short period of impurity and the requirement to bathe.[14]

These two cases raise interesting questions about how intercourse influences the nature of gender itself. The sources of genital impurity are highly gender-specific, that is, only a woman who has a flow of blood for seven days or less is actually a menstruant; a man who bleeds genitally is not in נדה, and is not even impure. Similarly, only a man who emits semen (not blood or some other substance) causes the impurity of ejaculation. But the act of intercourse can make these sex-specific impurities contagious in the unique way of making the contactor like the source itself. The sexual partner contacts the same impurity as the source and has the same ritual treatment. Thus, ritually speaking, intercourse has the power to change a sexual partner into a person of the opposite gender. This hierarchical gender status is enacted in the ritual remedies for its impurity. The woman who has sex can attain a higher cultic status: she is now treated like a man who bathes. It might be argued that to some extent a woman is cultically rewarded by engaging in normal sex. Conversely, a man who engages in intercourse with a menstruant is cultically degraded by being treated like a woman. The remedy for his resumption of purity does not include bathing. In sex, a man has the ability to raise a woman's status but she only has the ability to undo his. It is this ability to make gender flexible and contagious, I believe, that makes sexuality and its impurities most frightening.

Conclusion

In this paper I have shown that bathing rites, like all rituals, enact and create status and power. The ritual production of status also contributes to the creation and support of gender ideologies. In priestly law men bathe as a regular part of their ritual action, but the priestly texts do not describe bathing as a purity rite for women when they are unclean in the particularly feminine ways of menstruation, childbirth and special forms of genital illness. These omissions

---

14. One could argue that, like the cloths and skins in the preceding verse, the woman is merely a repository for semen that needs to be washed, but the form of the verbs would contradict such a reading. In v. 18b the man and woman are treated together as active subjects in the plural verbal forms for bathing 'they bathe (ורחצו) and they are unclean (וטמאו)'. In intercourse both the man and the woman are active and momentarily treated equally. If the woman were thought of as merely a place that semen lands, it is unlikely that she would be spoken of in this way.

add to hierarchal ideas about the relative ritual practices of men and women. The laws of gender-neutral impurities are at times vague in their application to women, thus creating ambiguity and uncertainty over the existence of women's bathing rites and hence over women's cultic practice and status.

It should be mentioned that my conclusions on bathing and gender for the biblical laws may be contradictory to those of the Jewish laws of *miqveh*. Though that ritual bathing is done for various reasons by both men and women, the most wide-spread use of the *miqveh* is by married women after menstruation and childbirth.[15] Bathing marks the beginning of sexual availability to one's husband. Among women who participate in the rites of the *miqveh*, it is thus often perceived as a marker or even validator of female sexuality and female sexual practice. In contrast, the biblical laws of ritual bathing often act not as an expression of femaleness or female sexuality, but of male sexuality, and male privilege.

BIBLIOGRAPHY

Bell, Catherine
    1992   *Ritual Theory, Ritual Practice* (New York: Oxford University Press).

Cohen, Shaye J.D.
    1991   'Menstruants and the Sacred in Judaism and Christianity', in Sarah B. Pomeroy (ed.), *Women's History and Ancient History* (Chapel Hill: University of North Carolina Press): 273-99.
    1999   'Purity, Piety, and Polemic: Medieval Rabbinic Denunciations of "Incorrect" Purification Practices', in Wasserfall 1999: 82-100.

Ellens, Deborah L.
    2000   'Leviticus 15: Contrasting Conceptual Associations regarding Women', in Wonil Kim, Deborah Ellens, Michael Floyd and Marvin A. Sweeney (eds.), *Reading the Hebrew Bible for a New Millennium: Form, Concept and Theological Perspective. Volume 2: Exegetical and Theological Studies* (Studies in Antiquity and Christianity; Harrison, PA: Trinity Press International): 124-51.
    2003   'Menstrual Impurity and Innovation in Leviticus 15', in Kristin De Troyer, Judith A. Herbert, Judith Ann Johnson and Anne-Marie Korte (eds.), *Wholly Woman, Holy Blood: A Feminist Critique of Purity and Impurity* (Studies in Antiquity and Christianity; Harrisburg, PA: Trinity Press International): 29-43.

Frymer-Kensky, Tikva
    1983   'Pollution, Purification, and Purgation in Biblical Israel', in Carol L. Meyers and M. O'Connor (eds.), *The Word of the Lord Shall Go Forth: Essays in Honor of David Noel Freedman* (Winona Lake, IN: Eisenbrauns): 399-414.

Gane, Roy
    2005   *Cult and Character: Purification Offerings, Day of Atonement, and Theodicy* (Winona Lake, IN: Eisenbrauns).

---

15. For a helpful discussion of the uses and interpretations of *miqveh* and menstruation, see the essays in Wasserfall (1999).

Gilders, William K.
> 2005 *Blood Ritual in the Hebrew Bible: Meaning and Power* (Baltimore: The Johns Hopkins University Press).

Maccoby, Hyam
> 1999 *Ritual and Morality: The Ritual Purity System and its Place in Judaism* (Cambridge: Cambridge University Press).

Meacham, Tirzah
> 1999 'An Abbreviated History of the Development of the Jewish Menstrual Laws', in Wasserfall 1999: 23-29.

Milgrom, Jacob
> 1991 *Leviticus 1–16* (AB, 3; New York: Doubleday).

Plaskow, Judith
> 1990 *Standing Again at Sinai: Judaism from a Feminist Perspective* (San Francisco: HarperSanFrancisco).

Wasserfall, Rahel R. (ed.)
> 1999 *Women and Water: Menstruation in Jewish Life and Law* (Brandeis Series on Jewish Women; Hanover, NH: Brandeis University Press).

Wegner, Judith Romney
> 1988 *Chattel or Person?: The Status of Women in the Mishnah* (New York: Oxford University Press).
> 1992 'Leviticus', in Carol A. Newsom and Sharon H. Ringe (eds.), *The Women's Bible Commentary* (Louisville, KY: Westminster/John Knox Press): 36-44.
> 1998 'Coming before the LORD: לפני יהוה and the Exclusion of Women from the Divine Presence', in Jodi Magness and Seymour Gitin (eds.), *Hesed ve-Emet: Studies in Honor of Ernest S. Frerichs* (BJS, 320; Atlanta: Scholars Press): 81-91.

Wenham, Gordon J.
> 1979 *The Book of Leviticus* (NICOT, 3; Grand Rapids, MI: Eerdmans).

Wright, David P.
> 1987 *The Disposal of Impurity: Elimination Rites in the Bible and in Hittite and Mesopotamian Literature* (SBLDS, 101; Atlanta: Scholars Press).
> 1992 'Unclean and Clean (OT)', *ABD* VI: 729-41.

Part III
Ethnological and Anthropological Approaches to Gender

CONTESTING THE NOTION OF PATRIARCHY: ANTHROPOLOGY
AND THE THEORIZING OF GENDER IN ANCIENT ISRAEL*

Carol Meyers

Introduction

Social science methods and models, including social anthropology, have long been a part of biblical studies.[1] Among the well-known pioneers in this enterprise are William Robertson Smith, Max Weber, Herbert Spencer, Julius Wellhausen and Johannes Pedersen. In addition, many scholars who do not explicitly apply social-science methods nevertheless indirectly or unconsciously engage them.[2] Albrecht Alt, for example, used many of Weber's major formulations in his analysis of charismatic biblical figures, as did Martin Noth in portraying Israel as an oath-bound covenant community.[3] This interdisciplinarity has become increasingly prominent in the decades since Mendenhall and Gottwald used social science paradigms to offer new perspective on Israelite beginnings (Mendenhall 1962; Gottwald 1979).

The study of gender in the Bible and the biblical world has likewise engaged the social sciences since the emergence of feminist biblical study in the late 1970s, although relatively few scholars have followed this path. Among them is Naomi Steinberg, whose study of family structure in Genesis is informed by anthropological kinship theory (Steinberg 1993). Phyllis Bird draws on cross-cultural studies for her work on women and the Israelite cultus (Bird 1987). My own work, beginning with *Discovering Eve*,[4] invokes the findings of social anthropology as a way to understand the social reality of women's lives in ancient Israel.

My premise was, and is, that using the Bible alone to study Israelite women provides a distorted if not erroneous view of social reality because of (1) the

---

* This essay is adapted from a study (Meyers 2006) published in a Festschrift for William G. Dever and appears here with the kind permission of the editors (S. Gitin, J.E. Wright, and J.P. Dessel) of that volume.

1. For a brief summary of social-science criticism in biblical studies see Steinberg (2004); for an extensive review see McNutt (1999); and for an anthology of examples, see Carter and Meyers (1996).

2. So Esler (2006: 21).

3. See Mayes (1989: 49-54).

4. Meyers 1988; and see most recently Meyers (2005).

inherently androcentric perspective of the texts, (2) the national (rather than family) focus of the texts, and (3) the urban context of many of its authors—priests, prophets, and courtiers—as opposed to the agrarian setting in which as much as 90% of the population lived throughout the biblical period. Therefore, using a multi-disciplinary approach, perhaps best represented by the term 'ethnohistory', allows the researcher to reconstruct various aspects of women's lives, especially their economic contributions to family life, their social networking possibilities, their professional roles in the larger community, and their household religious activities.[5] An anthropological—or more specifically an ethnohistorical—approach to the study of Israelite women eschews the notion that the use of anthropology in biblical studies is simply a matter of interpreting anthropologically biblical texts mentioning women. Instead of being determined by the agendas of the biblical text, anthropological research agendas are independent efforts to reconstruct and also to evaluate women's lives.

Perhaps one of the thorniest issues in the consideration of gender in biblical Israel is the habitual characterization of Israelite society as *patriarchal*. Feminist biblical scholarship has tended to appropriate western interpretative traditions that explicitly or implicitly assume that the Bible reflects an Israelite society characterized by female inferiority or submissiveness and male domination. Those traditions—shaped by two millennia of post-biblical Judaism and Christianity, during which social realities were very different from those of the agrarian, Iron Age communities of the Israelites—have inevitably influenced views of gender roles in the biblical period. But applying the term 'patriarchy' to ancient Israel is problematic.[6] Examining and challenging assumptions about universals, dualistic modelling of gender differentiation, and valuations of gendered roles and status means arguing against a facile application of 'patriarchy' to ancient Israel, or to any traditional society for that matter. The term is tainted by nineteenth-century Marxist critiques of industrialized European society; it is thus arguably inaccurate as a descriptor of premodern agrarian societies and too often misrepresents the dynamics of their daily life. Moreover, as a term denoting generalized male dominance, *patriarchy* is inappropriate because it masks or otherwise fails to take into account the complexity of social structures in Iron Age Israel, as in other traditional societies. Ancient Israelite society may seem simpler to us than our own, as we view it from the twenty-first century. But nonetheless it *was* complex.

The notion of patriarchy, embedded as it is in hierarchical models, must now be contested in an even more fundamental way. By drawing upon the results of the last few decades of feminist biblical scholarship and scholarship on ancient Israel, as they are both informed by social science research, the very notion of ancient Israel as hierarchical can be problematized. Furthermore,

---

5. Ethnohistory is embedded in the discipline of anthropology; see Meyers (forthcoming).
6. See Meyers (1988: 24-46) (ch. 2: 'The Problem of Patriarchy').

informed by models drawn from anthropology, another conceptualization—which acknowledges women's roles and attendant power and better accommodates the knowledge we now have about the various functions of women in Israelite society—can be proposed.

Current Models: Looking at Patriarchy and Hierarchy

The analysis of ancient societies by social scientists typically involves the use of models drawn from more recent periods. These models are heuristically invaluable, but they are nonetheless problematic because they may distort our perceptions of ancient cultures by introducing social and political arrangements that are much less analogous to the societies of antiquity than we would like to believe. A case in point—and an example outside the question of gender relations—is the use of the term *monarchy* for the Judaean and Israelite kingdoms. This word connotes structures as well as economic arrangements and political dynamics that are based on what we know from European history since the medieval period. Consequently, using *monarchy* and concomitantly the terms *monarchic state* and *state formation* is problematic; for these terms—and what they mean in relation to documented medieval-to-modern history—vary in their direct applicability to ancient Israelite or Judaean polities or to any other archaic states.[7] Although some aspects of our conception of monarchic states may be relevant to ancient Levantine polities, other features may be quite different from what these terms signify to us. Nonetheless, these terms continue to appear in the discourse about Israelite forms of governance, albeit more guardedly in recent years. Indeed, it has recently been suggested that 'Near Eastern patrimonialism', which excludes European feudal models, is a more suitable designation for the polities featured in the Hebrew Bible.[8]

Similarly, the literature on family structures in ancient Israel assumes that the term *patriarchy* is applicable to the Israelites of the biblical period. Yet this term is derived from the analysis of social structures of relatively recent times and may be just as problematic as is the term *monarchy* for describing Israelite society. Moreover, it is not always clear what biblical scholars mean when they use *patriarchy*. Defining it is difficult, for its meaning varies considerably, depending upon the discipline in which it is being used.

To some, the idea of patriarchy is related to its literal meaning, 'rule of the father' as head of the family (*paterfamilias*), and to the institutionalized male power concomitant with the notion of *patria potestas* as the embodiment of patriarchal authority. This understanding is drawn from studies of ancient Roman society, where elite males apparently had absolute and even tyrannical legal and economic power in the family. However, not all societies are

---

7. Pointed out by Schäfer-Lichtenberger (1996: 83).
8. Schloen (2001), drawing on Weber; cf. Schäfer-Lichtenberger (1996: 85-87).

organized as Roman society was understood to have been, and the paradigm of patriarchal authority is not holding up well even for the study of ancient Rome.[9] To others, patriarchy more broadly represents an ideology of male dominance, thought by some to have originated in male control of female sexuality and fertility, and manifest in systems of ranking male leadership.[10] In point of fact, these two perspectives often converge and evince other emphases. Gerda Lerner, for example, relates patriarchy to the emerging Near Eastern states of the third millennium BCE, and insists that patriarchy means that men control all the important institutions of a society and that women are denied access to such power.[11]

In any case, the term 'patriarchy' clearly invokes overlapping structural and ideological values that are rarely elucidated in discussions of gender in ancient Israel and its literature. For the most part, it seems that both aspects of patriarchy are implied in reconstructions of ancient Israel. The literal meaning, 'rule by fathers,' is understood to imply a system in which male rulership, or 'power over', is central and in which men have absolute control and women are subordinated. It is thus assumed that patriarchy signifies 'power relations that systematically oppress women through structural mechanisms of male authority over social, political, and economic institutions'.[12]

The terms 'patriarchy' and 'patriarchal society' are so entrenched and taken for granted in discussions of ancient Israel and its texts, especially in feminist discourse, that it is important to look at how they entered biblical scholarship. Their use can be traced back at least to the 1880s, when the German scholar Bernhard Stade published a large-scale and influential social and political history of ancient Israel, *Geschichte des Volkes Israel* (1887–88). Stade drew on the work of the early French theorist Numa Fustel de Coulanges, who had published a book in 1864, *La cité antique,* claiming that the patriarchal family was the fundamental form of social life. The subtitle of that book (*Etude sur le culte, le droit, les institutions de la Grèce et de Rome*, 'study on the religion, laws, and institutions of Greece and Rome') makes it explicit that his notion of ancient society is based on the literature of the classical world. Influenced by *La cité antique*, Stade posited the intrinsic role of religion in the Israelite family, which was dominated by the father's power. Moreover, despite the occasional appearance of the idea—classically stated in J.J. Bachofen's *Das Mutterrecht* in 1861—that the family was originally matriarchal, most other important theorists were proponents of the concept of patriarchy. William Robertson Smith, for

---

9. So Saller (1994: 74-132) (ch. 5: '*Pietas* and *Patria Potestas*: Obligation and Power in the Roman Household').
10. E.g. Rowbotham 1979; cf. Lerner (1986: 238-42) and Gross (1996: 23).
11. But see Kray's (2002) cogent critique of Lerner's methodology.
12. So Gilchrist (1999: xvi), who is a powerful voice in discussions of gender in premodern societies. Gilchrist's list should also include religious institutions.

example, asserted that Hebrew society was dominated by the universal form of the patriarchal family (Smith 1885). His portrayal of Semitic patriarchy, based on Western male observations of nineteenth-century Arab tribal life as well as on classical models, was adopted by Julius Wellhausen, his contemporaries, and his followers, in their reconstructions of Israelite society.[13]

As already noted, contemporary biblical scholarship continues to characterize ancient Israel as 'patriarchal'. Stager and King's recent book on *Life in Biblical Israel*, although outstanding in many aspects of its reconstruction of daily life in the biblical period, unproblematically refers to Israelite society as patriarchal, with the father as the *paterfamilias*.[14] This follows in the tradition of such classics as de Vaux's *Ancient Israel*, which is emphatic in calling Israelite society patriarchal, with absolute authority resting in the male head of the family (de Vaux 1961: 20). In his cogent arguments for the patrimonial household as the most suitable paradigm for ancient Near Eastern sociopolitical systems, including those of ancient Israel and Canaan, even Schloen adopts the Weberian notion that patrimonialism originates in the 'patriarchal household government'; yet he never examines the appropriateness of the word 'patriarchal' (Schloen 2001: 52).

Feminist biblical scholarship likewise tends to assume the existence of biblical and/or Israelite patriarchal forms without considering the pitfalls of using a term originating in the analysis of classical society with an overlay of Bedouin life. Frymer-Kensky, for example, insists that feminism's contribution to biblical studies has been the recognition that 'the Bible is a patriarchal document from a patriarchal society' (Frymer-Kensky 1994: 17). Ringe refers to the 'patriarchal values embedded in all of the biblical writings' and to the patriarchal nature of the society surrounding scripture in her discussion of feminist interpretative strategies (Ringe1998: 4-5). Fuchs stridently asserts that the Bible is a political document that justifies the subordination of women and thereby promotes a patriarchal ideology of male supremacy (Fuchs 2000: 11-16). Although Bird similarly looks at biblical women against the backdrop of the 'patriarchal character of the society', her juxtaposition of 'patrilineal' with 'patriarchal' signifies her sense that descent and kinship may be more salient in considering models for social organization (Bird 1992: 949). But 'patriarchy' as a descriptor of ancient Israel is flawed, not only for the reasons adduced in *Discovering Eve*, but also because it is part of a hierarchical model of social structure.

'Hierarchy'—as anthropologists define it—is a term designating an organizational structure in which, on the basis of certain factors, some elements are subordinate to others and are typically ranked (Crumley 1979: 144). Hierarchies are often represented spatially as being nested or conical vertical structures, giving rise to such phrases as 'filtering down the hierarchy', 'moving up in

---

13. So Rogerson (1978: 15, 27).
14. King and Stager (2001: 38) actually use the Latin term.

the hierarchy', or 'climbing the social [hierarchical] ladder' (Crumley 1995: 3). Most anthropologists, and also historians whose work draws upon their analyses, uncritically invoke the hierarchical model in conceptualizing state societies, chiefdoms and even tribal societies, all apparently male-controlled. Socio-political hierarchies are thus considered pervasive structural systems, even representing order itself; and the opposite of order, namely chaos, is presumed to exist in the absence of an organizing hierarchical structure (Crumley 1995: 2). The hierarchical model was appropriated by a number of prominent mid-twentieth century evolutionary theorists of sociopolitical development, who in turn influenced biblical scholars such as Mendenhall and Gottwald.[15]

But is the hierarchical model valid? Does it help or hinder our understanding of premodern societies, especially with respect to gender and its assumptions of male control of all levels in the hierarchy? Recent developments in anthropological theory can help answer those questions.

In the past few decades some anthropologists, drawing upon archaeological materials, have challenged both evolutionary theories and the related hierarchical model.[16] Especially relevant is their observation that not all structures—biological or social—are organized hierarchically (Stein 1998: 5-8). Moreover, many of the assumptions associated with the hierarchy model—such as that ranking is permanent and always present, and that the ranking of elements according to various criteria will always coincide—can legitimately be challenged (Brumfiel 1995: 125-26). It has become clear that, as a reductionist metaphor for order, the concept of hierarchy has distorted and misrepresented the social reality of complex premodern societies. Yet the almost unconscious assumption of hierarchy still often remains unexamined among many social scientists studying complex societies. And it is especially common in biblical studies for scholars to assume unproblematically a pervasive hierarchical structure linking the various levels of Israelite society.

Of particular concern, with respect to gender, about the validity of hierarchy as a metaphor for Israelite society lies in the way in which it absorbs the 'patriarchy' concept and assumes that gender-based hierarchy is at the heart of patriarchy.[17] If the patrimonial monarchy or, for the premonarchic period, a tribal federation, is at the top of a hierarchical structure, with tribes (שׁבטים) at the next level down, followed by clans or lineages (groups of extended families [מׁשׁפחות]), then family households (בית אב) are de facto at the bottom. The Bible itself seems to portray this hierarchy in its segmented genealogies (McNutt 1999: 77-78), which represent ancient Israel in terms of an overarching kinship structure in which women rarely appear. Moreover, discussions of

15. Those theorists include Elman Service (Service 1962), Morton Fried (Fried 1967), and Allen W. Johnson and Timothy Earle (Johnson and Earle 1987).
16. See the summary of these critiques in Stein (1998).
17. So Fuchs (2000: 13).

family structure in the social science appraisals of ancient Israel assume that the hierarchy extends into the family household (בית אב), with the dominance of men over women. For example, in looking at Pentateuchal legislation, McNutt mentions the ascription of powerlessness to women in various studies; and her summary of research on the family stories in Genesis with respect to gender suggests a 'clearly patriarchal society' (McNutt 1999: 94). King and Stager likewise claim, as already noted, that the *paterfamilias* exercised control over *all* women of their household (King and Stager 2001: 36-38).

The long and pervasive tradition of calling Israelite society patriarchal is based on biblical texts (both legal passages and narratives) interpreted in light of older anthropological theories about premodern societies. But it lags behind advances in anthropology in two ways. First, it does not take into account the reconstruction of family dynamics that is now possible by utilizing the burgeoning engendered research in anthropological archaeology and ethnography,[18] research that time and again contests existing notions of hierarchies involving patriarchal dominance. Second, it does not engage a newer heuristic model that can replace the flawed hierarchical one in attempts to reconstruct Israelite society. I will propose remedies for each of these deficiencies in turn.

Re-assessing Patriarchy with Respect to Women's Roles and Power Dynamics

An examination of the social, economic, and religious roles of Israelite women—and the attendant power dynamics—draws upon ethnographic data and models provided by feminist anthropologists, whose work has revolutionized their discipline over the last forty or so years.[19] Using information from the Bible, archaeology, and ethnography, women's organizational structures—which operated on both formal and informal levels and would have crosscut household (בית אב) and clan (משפחה) structures—can be identified (Meyers 1999). Yet women's organizational structures are virtually unrecognized in analyses of Israelite sociopolitical arrangements, which virtually always examine associations formed by men for military, economic, political, or religious purposes. Perhaps because men's formal organizations are the ones directly mentioned in the ancient texts, and also because patriarchal models are dominant, male organizational structures are the only ones afforded legitimacy in the eyes of observers and scholars. Consequently, women's structures, with their own hierarchies, have gone largely unnoticed. But 'unnoticed' does not mean 'nonexistent'. Indeed, the existence of both formal and informal women's

---

18. See Meyers (2003b) for a summary of the engendered nature of contemporary anthropology and anthropological archaeology.

19. For summaries of the early years of this transformation, see Lamphere (1977) and Quinn (1977); for a review of more recent developments, see di Leonardo (1991).

groups calls into question the validity of overarching hierarchical models and of patriarchal control.

To consider, first, women's formal supra-family groups, it is useful to characterize them as guilds whose members provided essential services to the Israelite populace. To be sure, 'guild' is often used narrowly as a designation for a union of people involved in the same trade or craft; but it can also be used more broadly to denote any association of people for the promotion of common interests.[20] In the latter sense it is an appropriate term for groups of female professionals—those who have expertise gained through study, training, and experience and who transmit their expertise to newer members or apprentices. The existence of guilds of professional women can be posited in relation to at least five different skills—all mentioned in biblical texts:

(a) musical traditions (singers and various instrumentalists);[21]

(b) prophetic roles, including soothsaying and necromancy (and sorcery?), some of which may have been linked to health-care or fertility concerns, others to legal matters;[22]

(c) funerary services (i.e. professional keeners or reciters of dirges);[23]

(d) psychological care, counselling, and conflict resolution as provided by wise women;[24]

(e) midwifery and other forms of health care; cf. (b).[25]

Women who were experts in these professions may not have been occupied full-time with them—more likely they practised them sporadically, as the need arose, while otherwise carrying out household tasks. Age was no doubt a factor in how much of a woman's time was allotted to specialized activities; midwives, for example, would probably have been past childbearing years. What is important about these professional women, as is apparent when considering ethnographic correlates, is that, in offering needed services to their local, regional, and even national communities, they would have been part of loose organizational structures that had their own internal hierarchies operating apart from other institutions in Israelite society.

20. So Mendelsohn (1940).
21. Goitein 1988; Meyers 1993.
22. Avalos 1995: 295-97; Brenner 1997: 84-86; Carter 1997; Bowen 1999; Meyers 2000a.
23. Meyers 2000c. The call in Jer. 9.19 for female keeners to 'teach your daughters wailing' probably uses 'daughters' to designate young, or apprentice, members of the 'guild' of female mourners rather than their biological daughters, although it is of course possible that this profession was transmitted in families; cf. the use of the phrase 'son of prophets' (e.g. 1 Kgs 20.35, translated by NJPS as 'disciple of prophets') in reference to prophetic groups.
24. Camp 2000a, 2000b; Fontaine 1995, 2002.
25. Meyers 2000b; Fontaine 2002: 71-80. Herbalists, who are usually female because of women's role in horticulture, would also have been health care providers.

Such organizational structures are typically present in traditional societies in professions, such as the ones enumerated, that involve specialized knowledge—knowledge of techniques, substances, rituals, equipment, and in some cases vocal utterances such as prayers, incantations, chants, dirges, or songs. That is, 'professional' women depend on a corpus of information that had to be conveyed to new members of the guild as older ones became inactive or died; thus younger women learned the techniques of their profession by working with older experts. Also, some of these professions involved group activity (performance), which involved joint preparation (rehearsal), presumably led by those with greatest expertise. Expertise and skill, loosely correlated with age, create hierarchies in these loosely organized guilds.

Just as important as women's professional groups but virtually invisible in the Hebrew Bible were the *informal networks* of Israelite women that are typical of women's relationships in peasant societies such as ancient Israel. These networks can be posited on the basis of archaeological evidence. Most Israelite women lived in agricultural settlements, and their daily tasks differed from those of men. The social corollary of that labour differential can be ascertained by examining Iron Age dwellings. For example, the positioning of the implements and the installations used in bread production, a female task, shows that women from several households would have worked together in the tedious series of processes required to change grain into bread (Meyers 2002a). The same is probably true for some components of domestic textile production (Meyers 2003a: 432-34) and perhaps for other aspects of the household economy. Ethnographic analogues allow us to understand that the cooperation and companionship experienced by women in carrying out their routine daily and seasonal tasks typically fosters female solidarity and the concomitant formation of informal networks.

The significance of these networks can also be ascertained from ethnographic correlates. Women's informal networks provide vital functions for community and even intercommunity life—functions rarely visible to outside observers. For example, women in neighbouring households who work together on a daily basis are well aware when a woman or man in any of their households, or even households somewhat farther away, becomes ill or injured and is unable to carry out essential child-care or subsistence tasks. They can then deploy labour to compensate for the inability of individuals to do their work (March and Taqqu 1986: 54-59). Informal networks of this sort constitute infrastructures that help maintain family and community life. They are vital modes of communication in a world without e-mail and telephones. Moreover, they exhibit certain organizational properties whereby some women, usually on the basis of age and experience (as with formal associations), characteristically exert leadership in organizing the various services that women provide across households. In short, in traditional societies informal women's networks are not simply a trivial web of acquaintances or friendships but rather are alliances that provide critical social linkages and thus carry considerable weight (Maher 1976: 52-53; March and Taqqu 1986: 16).

Studies of Israelite society have indeed noted that cooperation, reciprocity, and mutual assistance across families and even communities were essential for maintaining stability and for providing aid in time of personal, political, or economic travail.[26] But what has not been recognized is that at least some of the groundwork for such interfamily and intercommunity cooperation would have been provided by the connections forged by women.[27] Moreover, women in ancient Israel were better positioned than men to establish and maintain such connections, not only because of their labour patterns but also because ancient Israel was a patrilocal society. That is, when a woman married into a family, she thereby had linkages with two descent groups: the *natal* family of her parents and the *residential* family of her husband, who usually remained with his natal family and consequently had only one set of connections.

Israelite women, with two sets of family ties as well as with sociable work patterns, were thus uniquely positioned to facilitate inter-group relationships. Informal networks of this sort are found in Ruth 4.17, which refers to שׁכנות—a group of connected women gathered for socio-medical purposes, namely, facilitating childbirth and the naming of the newborn—and thus reflects the community female solidarity of traditional societies (Meyers 2000d). This solidarity was especially important in communities, such as the agrarian highland communities of ancient Israel, that exist at the subsistence level.

The fact that women's informal networks in ancient Israel would have performed essential social functions has implications for the assessment of gender-linked power. Gender-sensitive ethnographic information, even from societies otherwise considered strongly male dominant, suggests that the contributions of Israelite women to the larger welfare of the community would have afforded them considerable power.[28] Also, female responsibility for critical subsistence technologies, such as bread and textile production, signifies the presence of gender-linked power, as does female control of important aspects of household religious culture—aspects deemed critical for family survival.[29] Such female power, albeit less formal and visible than that of men, has usually been ignored or marginalized in Western scholarship with its traditional focus on formal and visible institutions. Yet, in terms of the dynamics of daily life, these informal power relations are just as important as, and perhaps even more important than, formal relations of power (Sweely 1999). All told, formal professional women's

---

26. See Gottwald (1979: 267, 316).
27. See Zonabend (1996: 25-39).
28. See the examples in Rogers 1975 and Maher 1976.
29. Power linked to women's subsistence tasks is discussed in Meyers (2002a: 30-32), and power resulting from women's household religious activities is discussed in Meyers (2005: 68-69).

guilds and informal women's networks originating in household activities were significant organizational structures, not only because of the services they provided to their families and communities but also because of the power that accrued to the women involved.

But women's organizational structures are especially significant for this consideration of patriarchy as part of a hierarchical model because, as noted, they have their own hierarchies that crosscut other sociopolitical structures. In this regard, the existence of other female Israelite hierarchies, based on sociopolitical class rather on than professional skills or neighbourhood leadership, is also relevant. Such women likely exercised political or religious control over underlings. In the royal household, at least, women probably held a variety of religious, managerial, and political roles and as such can be understood as 'hierarchically organized female functionaries'.[30]

All told, the presence in Israelite society of all these hierarchies of women challenges the appropriateness of the model of all-pervasive male hierarchies—or patriarchy—as adequate or accurate for representing Israelite and probably any other complex traditional society. Just as status cannot be generalized for all systems across a culture—for example, in preindustrial societies, the low status of women in one area of economic, social, sexual, or religious life correlates negatively with status in other social domains (Whyte 1978)—so too authority and control in one domain do not entail authority and control in all domains. That is, the hierarchical model is deficient by not acknowledging the function of structures that do not fit into its nested or conical vertical contours. But there are other heuristic models that can better represent diverse structures.

Heterarchy: Another Heuristic Model

One possible alternative to hierarchy offered by anthropological assessments of traditional cultures, at least with respect to gender, is *complementarity*, which recognizes the interdependence and/or equality of women and men for certain economic and social functions.[31] But viewing social systems in this binary fashion is itself problematic because it does not take into account women's roles beyond the ones in which complementarity can be demonstrated. Like hierarchy, complementarity is an inadequate model in that it characterizes social

---

30. Solvang 2003: 65; see also Ackerman (1993) and Cushman (2006). Examples of female functionaries would be royal women in general, the 'queen-mother' (גבירה) in particular; and the spouses of highly ranked priests or other officers.

31. E.g. Bodenhorn 1990 and Joyce 1996. Complementarity, or gender interdependence (and also intergenerational interdependence) can be posited for the household level with respect to certain economic or social functions. For this possibility in Israelite households, see Meyers (1988: 168-73; 1997: 32-35); my comments in these studies concern early Israel but most likely apply to agrarian households throughout the biblical period.

systems in grossly generalized ways that do not accommodate the complexities of gendered social reality in complex societies.

More nuanced or flexible models, which take into account the fact that behavioural patterns—such as control and knowledge, authority and autonomy—are not static but are found in highly variable ways among members of any social group, must be considered. An appropriate model must recognize that ideologies of prestige, status, and power associated with a supposedly dominant (male) group are often contradicted by practical structures that crosscut formal arrangements and afford the supposedly subordinate group (women) the ability to have a modicum of autonomous activity and to control certain resources (Gero and Scattolin 2002). Another heuristic model, namely *heterarchy*, does just that. It is a model that includes the recognition of hierarchies but is more flexible than hierarchy alone for acknowledging the variability, context, and fluctuation of power structures in premodern societies.

The term 'heterarchy' was first applied in a modern context in the 1940s by a biophysicist studying multiple human neural structures that are not organized hierarchically; 'heterarchy' was used to represent their collective interactions (McCulloch 1945). This model revolutionized the neural study of the brain and ultimately led to the solution of major problems in the fields of artificial intelligence and computers.[32] But it was not used for the study of human society until 1979, when it was introduced by the anthropologist Carole Crumley as an alternative to central place theory or other locational models in analyzing settlement patterns (Crumley 1979). Following her lead, many anthropological archaeologists have realized the power of the heterarchy model for representing complex social structures for which the hierarchical model is inadequate. Indeed, the annual meeting of the American Anthropological Association held a symposium devoted entirely to the concept of heterarchy in 1993.[33]

What exactly is meant by 'heterarchy' as introduced by Crumley in relation to human organizational structures? She defines heterarchy as an 'organizational structure ... in which each element possesses the potential of being unranked (relative to other elements) or ranked in a number of different ways, depending on systemic requirements'. Instead of the system consisting of an overall nested or conical set of ranked structures, as in a hierarchy, it is seen as consisting of many structures that are most simply envisioned as laterally connected and not vertically connected, as in the case of hierarchy. Moreover, a 'horizontally' connected set of systems precludes the notion of ranking that is implicit in the notion of hierarchy—all systems in a heterarchy are understood to have a unique good and are thus equally important all together for the functioning of the society.[34]

---

32. So Minsky and Papert (1972).
33. For the proceedings, see Ehrenreich, Crumley and Levy (1995).
34. Crumley 1979: 144-45; cf. Crumley (1995).

Crumley first invoked heterarchy in her study of the locational arrangements of Iron Age settlements in Europe. Subsequently, as the result of increased epistemological attention to models of sociocultural complexity, heterarchy has been interpreted and employed in many different ways. It is a model that takes into account the flaws, already noted, in assuming that ranking is permanent or that the ranking of elements according to different criteria will coincide; and it provides a way to accommodate the variety of patterns found across cultures in organizational structures and the ranking of structures vis-à-vis each other (Brumfiel 1995: 125). Examples of four different structural forms that the concept of heterarchy can represent are instructive:

(a) Heterarchy can represent the membership of elements in many different unranked interaction systems, with participation in each system determined by the needs of each element. It has been used in this way in a study of tribal interactions in the prehistoric Yadkin Valley in the American southeast and in an analysis of iconographic motifs and gender relations in Bronze Age Denmark.[35]

(b) Heterarchy can represent membership in many different systems of ranking in which the same element occupies a different rank in the different systems. Three studies—one examining individual status in southeast Asia, another looking at production sites and settlement functions among the Classic Maya, and a third analysing economic and political hierarchies in ancient Greece—use heterarchy in this way.[36]

(c) The heterarchy model can represent the existence of two or more discrete hierarchies that interact as equals. It has been used in this way in a study of iconographic motifs and gender relations in Bronze Age Denmark and in one on church–state relationships in Mediaeval Ireland.[37]

(d) Heterarchy can represent the existence of two or more functionally discrete but unranked systems that interact as equals. It is used in this way in a study of production sites and settlement functions among the Classic Maya and in a study of tribal relations in south India.[38]

---

35. For the Yadkin Valley, see Rogers (1995); for Bronze Age Denmark, see Levy (1995).

36. The southeast Asia example appears in White (1995); the Mayan one is in Potter and King (1995); and Small (1995) presents the case from ancient Greece.

37. Levy (1995) examines Bronze Age Denmark, and Wailes (1995) presents mediaeval Ireland.

38. For the Classic Maya, see Potter and King (1995); and for south India, see Zagarell (1995).

These four different ways of invoking the concept of heterarchy are not mutually exclusive—note that the Denmark and Maya studies each appear in two different examples. A thorough analysis of the various ranked and crosscutting systems of ancient Israel would likely produce similar results, and the second example is perhaps the one that would be most congenial to theorizing Israelite society.

Discussion

The heterarchy model is compelling in considering ancient Israelite society, for many reasons. One is that it avoids the binary problem implicit in the idea of hierarchies alone. That is, because hierarchical is understood to be the opposite of egalitarian, labelling a society hierarchical means that it is not egalitarian and thus is automatically oppressive. When *Tribes of Yahweh* first appeared in 1979, Gottwald was criticized for using the term 'egalitarian,' by which he meant 'lack of ranking stratification' (not the modern concept of the legally established rights of individuals).[39] His idealistic ascription of social equality to the premonarchic period and perhaps as an ideal in prophetic literature was rightly challenged.[40] But the discussions of his work would have looked very different if they had not assumed that if early Israel was not truly egalitarian—which it almost certainly was not, as recent studies of Iron I settlement patterns and related deposits of luxury goods have demonstrated (Miller 2005)—then it was hierarchically stratified and thus oppressive.[41]

Perhaps the most attractive feature of the heterarchy model is that it recognizes a variety of hierarchies, such as those of the formal and informal associations of women, that would otherwise go unnoticed; and it admits the possible existence of multiple hierarchies in discrete but overlapping systems. It allows for each of these hierarchies to manifest rankings that are different from and even antithetical to those of other systems in the society and that may operate as equals in some instances or in various unequal relationships for other functions. In other words, invoking the heterarchy concept does not entail eliminating the hierarchy model. Heterarchies and hierarchies are not necessarily independent or mutually exclusive concepts but rather stand in dialectical relationship to each other.[42] Heterarchy sees various social units—including individuals, households, guilds of professionals, kinship-groups, and village communities—as involved in multiple vertical and lateral relationships.

---

39. Gottwald (1979: 798 n. 634) is drawing upon the discussion of egalitarian social structures in Fried (1967: 52, 61).

40. Already by Buss (1979).

41. For further discussion of the *Tribes of Yahweh* issue, see Meyers (2002b).

42. Crumley 2005: 40. Crumley also calls heterarchy a condition as well as a structure (Crumley 2005: 39).

In this way, the heterarchy model obviates the tendency to privilege stratification as the hallmark of a complex society. Archaeological or textual evidence of one kind of domination, the kind of evidence usually marshalled in claiming biblical or Israelite patriarchy, does not entail generalized rankings or absolute patterns of subordination. Rather, a multiplicity of interwoven systems means that a social unit, even an individual, can rank simultaneously high in one modality and low in another. Furthermore, some rankings, such as those that are age-related, are fluid and would vary over time.

With respect to gender, the heterarchy model challenges the notion of patriarchy by recognizing that certain systems associated with women, each with its own set of rankings, privileges, and statuses, would hold authoritative roles vis-à-vis other systems. The awareness that many systems could coexist would contest the interpretative tradition in biblical studies that tends to privilege male roles and assume anachronistically that the gender hierarchies present in biblically based Judaism and Christianity were already in place during the Iron Age. In other words, the conventional wisdom about male dominance in pervasive hierarchical structures affecting all domains of human interaction would be subverted and give way to the recognition that there were multiple systems and multiple loci of power, with women as well as men shaping society.[43]

In short, the heterarchy model is a more plastic concept than hierarchy alone and thus offers great potential as a heuristic model for understanding the diversity and complexity of Israelite society. It can bring a fresh perspective and provide a corrective to the hierarchy models, with their embedded assumptions of patriarchy, that dominate studies of ancient Israel.[44] It would allow us to attain a more nuanced and probably more accurate view of ancient Israel for any period in its history—a view that would preclude the claim that any one group completely dominated another, and a view that would recognize domains of female agency. More specifically, an integrated hierarchy and heterarchy model would represent the multiplicity of organizational structures in Israelite society and allow for the differential effects that varied organizational structures inevitably have on one another.[45] Acknowledging the interplay of such structures over time, in the relationships of individuals and groups organized in overlapping and interlocking spheres of activities and exchanges, means that we can avoid the limiting and problematic implications of the patriarchy label.[46]

---

43. Cf. Nelson (1997).

44. The applicability of the heterarchy model for ancient Israel is suggested by Zevit (2001: 648), who finds features—including 'different heterarchical authorities'—of the tribal kingdoms of Transjordan (as reported in LaBianca [1998]) congruent with his own findings.

45. Cf. Zagarell (1995).

46. Labelling the Hebrew Bible or ancient Israel 'patriarchal' involves a tendency to 'blame' Jews, or their biblical ancestors, for 'inventing patriarchy'; see the classic statement on this problem in Plaskow (1980), which is focused on the rabbinic period but begins with a statement about the 'myth' that the ancient Hebrews invented patriarchy. This claim is typically related,

It is important to keep in mind that like any model, the heterarchic one is a heuristic tool for facilitating comparisons and asking new questions of existing data. In and of itself, it cannot be deemed either true or false.[47] Rather, its value lies in how helpful it is for viewing a society for which direct observation is not possible. Models must be modified or replaced if they cease to be helpful or if another model becomes more relevant. The hierarchic model has outlived its usefulness, especially in the way it sustains the notion of patriarchy. Perhaps the heterarchic one will endure—for invoking 'heterarchy' in our reconstructions of ancient Israel allows us to recognize that the lives of women, and men, were more interesting and complex than could otherwise have been imagined.

Bibliography

Ackerman, Susan
    2003   'The Queen Mother and the Cult in Ancient Israel', *JBL* 112: 385-401.

Avalos, Hector
    1995   *Illness and Health Care in the Ancient Near East: The Role of the Temple in Greece, Mesopotamia, and Israel* (HSM, 54; Atlanta: Scholars Press).

Bachofen, J.J.
    1861   *Das Mutterrecht: Eine Untersuchung über die Gynaikokratie der alten Welt nach ihrer religiösen und rectlichen Natur* (Stuttgart: Hoffmann).

Binford, Lewis R. (ed.)
    1977   *For Theory Building in Archaeology: Essays on Faunal Remains, Aquatic Resources, Spatial Analysis, and Systemic Modeling* (New York: Academic Press).

Bird, Phyllis A.
    1987   'The Place of Women in the Israelite Cultus', in Patrick D. Miller, Jr, Paul D. Hanson and S. Dean McBride (eds.), *Ancient Israelite Religion: Essays in Honor of Frank Moore Cross* (Philadelphia: Fortress Press): 397-419.
    1992   'Women, Old Testament', *ABD* VI: 951-57.

Bodenhorn, Barbara
    1990   'I'm not the Great Hunter, my Wife Is', *Etudes/Inuit/Studies* 14: 55-74.

Bowen, Nancy R.
    1999   'The Daughters of your People: Female Prophets in Ezekiel 13: 17-23', *JBL* 118: 417-33.

Brenner, Athalya
    1997   *The Intercourse of Knowledge: On Gendering Desire and 'Sexuality' in the Hebrew Bible* (Biblical Interpretation Series, 26; Leiden: E.J. Brill).

Brumfiel, Elizabeth M.
    1995   'Heterarchy and the Analysis of Complex Societies: Comments', in Ehrenreich, Crumley and Levy (1995): 125-31.

---

especially in pop anthropology and among goddess-religion proponents, to the notion of a male deity as model for social male dominance (cf. the critique of the idea of a harmonious, prehistoric mother-goddess society in Ruether [2005]).

    47. Cf. Esler (2005: 4).

Buss, M.
   1979   'Literary-critical Critique', paper presented at a symposium on Norman Gottwald's *Tribes of Yahweh,* Society of Biblical Literature Annual Meeting (New York).
Camp, Claudia
   2000a   'Wise Woman of Tekoa (2 Sam 14:1-20)', in Meyers, Craven and Kraemer (2000): 263.
   2000b   'Wise Woman of Abel Beth-maacah (2 Sam 20:14-22)', in Meyers, Craven and Kraemer (2000): 266-67.
Carter, Charles E.
   1997   'Huldah as Prophet and Legal Authority: A Linguistic and Social Science Approach,' paper presented at the American Academy of Religion/Society of Biblical Literature/American Schools of Oriental Research Annual Meeting (San Francisco).
Carter, Charles E., and Carol L. Meyers (eds.)
   1996   *Community, Identity, and Ideology: Social-Scientific Approaches to the Hebrew Bible* (Sources for Biblical and Theological Study, 6; Winona Lake, IN: Eisenbrauns).
Crumley, Carole L.
   1979   'Three Locational Models: An Epistemological Assessment of Anthropology and Archaeology', in Michael B. Schiffer (ed.), *Advances in Archaeological Method and Theory Volume 2* (New York: Academic Press): 141-73.
   1987   'A Dialectical Critique of Hierarchy', in Thomas C. Patterson and Christine W. Gailey (eds.), *Power Relations and State Formation* (Washington, DC: American Anthropological Association): 155-69.
   1995   'Heterarchy and the Analysis of Complex Societies', in Ehrenreich, Crumley and Levy (1995): 1-5.
   2005   'Remember How to Organize: Heterarchy across Disciplines', in Christopher S. Beekman and William W. Baden (eds.), *Nonlinear Models for Archaeology and Anthropology: Continuing the Revolution* (Aldershot: Ashgate Publishing): 35-50.
Cushman, Beverly W.
   2006   'The Politics of the Royal Harem and the Case of Bat-Sheba', *JSOT* 30: 327-43.
Dever, William G.
   1993   'Biblical Archaeology: Death and Rebirth', in Avraham Biran and Joseph Aviram (eds.), *Biblical Archaeology Today, 1990: Proceedings of the Second International Congress on Biblical Archaeology* (Jerusalem: Israel Exploration Society): 706-22.
   1997   'Biblical Archaeology', in Eric M. Meyers (ed.), *Oxford Encyclopedia of Archaeology in the Near East* (5 vols.; New York: Oxford University Press): I, 315-19.
di Leonardo, Micaela (ed.)
   1991   *Gender at the Crossroads of Knowledge: Feminist Anthropology in the Postmodern Era* (Berkeley: University of California Press).
Ehrenreich, Robert M., Carole L. Crumley and Janet E. Levy (eds.)
   1995   *Heterarchy and the Analysis of Complex Societies* (Archeological Papers of the American Anthropological Association, 6; Arlington, VA: American Anthropological Association).

Esler, Philip F.
 2006 'Social-Scientific Models in Biblical Interpretation', in Philip F. Esler (ed.), *Ancient Israel: The Old Testament in its Social Context* (Minneapolis: Fortress Press): 3-32.

Fontaine, Carole R.
 1995 'The Social Roles of Women in the World of Wisdom', in Athalya Brenner (ed.), *A Feminist Companion to Wisdom Literature* (FCB, 9: Sheffield: Sheffield Academic Press): 24-49.
 2002 *Smooth Words: Women, Proverbs and Performance in Biblical Wisdom* (JSOTSup, 356; Sheffield: Sheffield Academic Press).

Fried, Morton
 1967 *The Evolution of Political Society: An Essay in Political Anthropology* II (New York: Random House).

Frymer-Kensky, Tikva
 1994 'The Bible and Women's Studies', in Lynn Davidman and Shelly Tenenbaum (eds.), *Feminist Perspectives on Jewish Studies* (New Haven: Yale University Press): 16-39.

Fuchs, Esther
 2000 *Sexual Politics in the Hebrew Bible: Reading the Hebrew Bible as a Woman* (JSOTSup, 310; Sheffield: Sheffield Academic Press).

Fustel de Coulanges, N.D.
 1864 *La cité antique: étude sur le culte, le droit, les institutions de la Grèce et de Rome* (Paris: Hachette).

Gero, Joan M., and Cristina M. Scatollin
 2002 'Beyond Complementarity and Hierarchy: New Definitions for Archaeological Gender Relations', in Sarah Milledge Nelson and Myriam Rosen-Ayalon (eds.), *In Pursuit of Gender: Worldwide Archaeological Approaches* (Gender and Archaeology Series, 1; Walnut Creek, CA: AltaMira Press): 155-71.

Gilchrist, Roberta
 1999 *Gender and Archaeology: Contesting the Past* (London: Routledge).

Goitein, S.D.
 1988 'Women as Creators of Biblical Genres', *Prooftexts* 8: 1-33.

Gottwald, Norman K.
 1979 *The Tribes of Yahweh: A Sociology of the Religion of Liberated Israel, 1250–1050 B.C.* (Maryknoll, NY: Orbis Books).

Gross, Rita M.
 1996 *Feminism and Religion: An Introduction* (Boston: Beacon Press, 2nd edn).

Hodder, Ian
 1986 *Reading the Past: Current Approaches to Interpretation in Archaeology* (Cambridge: Cambridge University Press).

Johnson, Allen W., and Timothy Earle
 1987 *The Evolution of Human Societies: From Foraging Groups to Agrarian State* (Stanford: Stanford University Press).

Joyce, Rosemary A.
 1996 'The Construction of Gender in Classic Maya Monuments', in Rita P. Wright (ed.), *Gender and Archaeology* (Philadelphia: University of Pennsylvania Press): 167-95.

King, Philip J., and Lawrence E. Stager
 2001 *Life in Biblical Israel* (Library of Ancient Israel; Louisville, KY: Westminster/John Knox Press).

Kray, Susan
    2002   ' "New Mode of Feminist Historical Analysis"—Or Just Another Collusion with "Patriarchal" Bias?', *Shofar* 20: 66-90.

LaBianca, Øystein S.
    1998   'Iron Age Tribal Kingdoms in the Southern Levant: Ten Hypotheses', paper presented at the Annual Meeting of the American Schools of Oriental Research (Orlando, FL).

Lamphere, Louise
    1977   'Review Essay: Anthropology', *Signs* 2: 612-27.

Lerner, Gerda
    1986   *The Creation of Patriarchy* (New York: Oxford University Press).

Levy, Janet E.
    1995   'Heterarchy in Bronze Age Denmark: Settlement Pattern, Gender, and Ritual', in Ehrenreich, Crumley and Levy (1995): 41-54.

Maher, Vanessa
    1976   'Kin, Clients and Accomplices: Relationships among Women in Morocco', in Diana Leonard Barker and Sheila Allen (eds.), *Sexual Divisions and Society: Process and Change* (Explorations in Sociology, 6; London: Tavistock): 52-75.

March, Kathryn S., and Rachelle L. Taqqu
    1986   *Women's Informal Associations in Developing Countries: Catalysts for Change?* (Women in Cross-Cultural Perspective; Boulder, CO: Westview Press).

Mayes, A.D.H.
    1989   *The Old Testament in Sociological Perspective* (London: Marshall Pickering).

McCulloch, Warren S.
    1945   'A Heterarchy of Values Determined by the Topology of Neural Nets', *Bulletin of Mathematical Biophysics* 4: 88-93.

McNutt, Paula M.
    1999   *Reconstructing the Society of Ancient Israel* (Louisville, KY: Westminster/John Knox Press).

Mendelsohn, I.
    1940   'Guilds in Ancient Palestine', *BASOR* 80: 17-21.

Mendenhall, George E.
    1962   'The Hebrew Conquest of Palestine', *BA* 25: 66-87.

Meyers, Carol
    1988   *Discovering Eve: Ancient Israelite Women in Context* (New York: Oxford University Press).
    1993   'The Drum-Dance-Song Ensemble: Women's Performance in Biblical Israel', in Kimberly Marshall (ed.), *Rediscovering the Muses: Women's Musical Traditions* (Boston: Northeastern University Press): 49-67, 234-38.
    1997   'The Family in Early Israel', in Leo G. Perdue, Joseph Blenkinsopp, John J. Collins and Carol Meyers, *Families in Ancient Israel* (Family, Religion and Culture; Louisville, KY: Westminster/John Knox Press): 1-47.
    1999   'Guilds and Gatherings: Women's Groups in Ancient Israel', in Prescott H. Williams and Theodore Hiebert (eds.), *Realia Dei: Essays in Archaeology and Biblical Interpretation in Honor of Edward F. Campbell, Jr. at His Retirement* (Atlanta: Scholars Press): 154-84.
    2000a   'Female Sorcerer (Exod 22:18; Isa 57:3)', in Meyers, Craven and Kraemer (2000): 197.

2000b	'Midwife (Gen 35:17; 38:28)', in Meyers, Craven and Kraemer (2000): 182-83.
2000c	'Mourning Women (Jer 9:17-20; Ezek 32:16)', in Meyers, Craven and Kraemer (2000): 327-28.
2000d	'"Women of the Neighborhood (Ruth 4.17)": Informal Female Networks in Ancient Israel', in Athalya Brenner (ed.), *Ruth and Esther* (FCB 2, 3; Sheffield: Sheffield Academic Press): 110-27.
2002a	'Having their Space and Eating There Too: Bread Production and Female Power in Ancient Israelite Households', *Nashim* 5: 14-44.
2002b	'Tribes and Tribulations: Retheorizing Earliest Israel', in Roland Boer (ed.), *Tracking 'The Tribes of Yahweh': On the Trail of a Classic* (JSOTSup, 351; London: Sheffield Academic Press): 34-45.
2003a	'Material Remains and Social Relations: Women's Culture in Agrarian Households of the Iron Age', in William G. Dever and Seymour Gitin (eds.), *Symbiosis, Symbolism, and the Power of the Past: Canaan, Ancient Israel, and Their Neighbors from the Late Bronze Age through Roman Palaestina* (Winona Lake, IN: Eisenbrauns): 425-44.
2003b	'Engendering Syro-Palestinian Archaeology', *Near Eastern Archaeology* 66: 185-97.
2005	*Households and Holiness: The Religious Culture of Israelite Women* (Facets; Minneapolis: Fortress Press).
2006	'Hierarchy or Heterarchy? Archaeology and the Theorizing of Israelite Society', in Seymour Gitin, J. Edward Wright and J.P. Dessel (eds.), *Confronting the Past: Archaeological and Historical Essays in Honor of William G. Dever* (Winona Lake, IN: Eisenbrauns): 245-54.
Forthcoming	'Beyond the Bible: Feminist Ethnohistory and the Recovery of Israelite Women', in Esther Fuchs (ed.), *Biblical Feminisms* (New Brunswick, NJ: Rutgers University Press).

Meyers, Carol, Toni Craven and Ross S. Kraemer (eds.)
    2000   *Women in Scripture: A Dictionary of Named and Unnamed Women in the Hebrew Bible, the Apocryphal/Deuterocanonical Books, and the New Testament* (Boston: Houghton Mifflin).

Miller, Robert D., II
    2005   *Chieftains of the Highland Clans: A History of Israel in the Twelfth and Eleventh Centuries B.C.* (The Bible in its World; Grand Rapids, MI: Eerdmans).

Minsky, Marvin, and Seymour Papert
    1972   *Artificial Intelligence Progress Report* (Artificial Intelligence Memo, 252; Cambridge, MA: Massachusetts Institute of Technology).

Nelson, Sarah Milledge
    2000   *Gender in Archaeology: Analyzing Power and Prestige* (Walnut Creek, CA: AltaMira Press).

Plaskow, Judith
    1980   'Blaming Jews…for the Birth of Patriarchy', *Lilith* 7: 11-13.

Potter, Daniel R., and Eleanor M. King
    1995   'Heterarchical Approach to Lowland Maya Socioeconomics', in Ehrenreich, Crumley and Levy (1995): 17-32.

Quinn, Naomi
    1997   'Anthropological Studies of Women's Status', *Annual Review of Anthropology* 6: 181-225.

Ringe, Sharon H.
    1998   'When Women Interpret the Bible', in Carol A. Newsom and Sharon H. Ringe (eds.), *Women's Bible Commentary* (Louisville, KY: Westminster/John Knox Press, expanded edn): 1-9.

Rogers, Rhea J.
    1995   'Tribes as Heterarchy: A Case Study from the Prehistoric Southeastern United States', in Ehrenreich, Crumley and Levy (1995): 7-16.

Rogers, Susan Carol
    1975   'Female Forms of Power and the Myth of Male Dominance: A Model of Female/Male Interactions in a Peasant Society', *American Ethnologist* 2: 741-54.

Rogerson, J.W.
    1978   *Anthropology and the Old Testament* (Growing Points in Theology; Oxford: Blackwell).

Rowbotham, Sheila
    1979   'The Trouble with Patriarchy', *New Statesman,* December 21/28, 970-71.

Ruether, Rosemary Radford
    2005   *Goddesses and the Divine Feminine: A Western Religious History* (Berkeley: University of California Press).

Saller, Richard P.
    1994   *Patriarchy, Property, and Death in the Roman Family* (Cambridge Studies in Population, Economy, and Society in Past Time, 25; Cambridge: Cambridge University Press).

Schäfer-Lichtenberger, Christa
    1996   'Sociological and Biblical Views of the Early State', in Volkmar Fritz and Philip R. Davies (eds.), *The Origins of the Ancient Israelite States* (JSOTSup, 228, Sheffield: Sheffield Academic Press): 78-105.

Schloen, J. David
    2001   *The House of the Father as Fact and Symbol: Patrimonialism in Ugarit and the Ancient Near East* (Studies in the Archaeology and History of the Levant, 2; Winona Lake, IN: Eisenbrauns).

Service, Elman
    1962   *Primitive Social Organization: An Evolutionary Perspective* (New York: Random House).

Small, David B.
    1995   'Heterarchical Paths to Evolution: The Role of External Economies', in Ehrenreich, Crumley and Levy (1995): 71-86.

Smith, W. Robertson
    1885   *Kinship and Marriage in Early Arabia* (Cambridge: Cambridge University Press).

Solvang, Elna K.
    2003   *A Woman's Place is in the House: Royal Women of Judah and their Involvement in the House of David* (JSOTSup, 348; London: Sheffield Academic Press).

Stade, Bernhard
    1887–88   *Geschichte des Volkes Israel* (Berlin: Groote).

Stein, Gil J.
    1998   'Heterogeneity, Power, and Political Economy: Some Current Research Issues in the Archaeology of Old World Complex Societies', *Journal of Archaeological Research* 6: 1-44.

Steinberg, Naomi
    1993   *Kinship and Marriage in Genesis: A Household Economics Perspective* (Minneapolis: Fortress Press).
    2004   'Social-Scientific Criticism', in *Methods of Biblical Interpretation* (excerpted from John H. Hayes [ed.], *Dictionary of Biblical Interpretation*; Nashville, TN: Abingdon Press): 275-79.

Strathern, Marilyn
    1972   *Women in Between: Female Roles in a Male World* (Seminar Studies in Anthropology, 2; London: Seminar Press).

Sweely, Tracy L.
    1999   'Gender, Space, People, and Power at Cerèn, El Salvador', in Tracy L. Sweely (ed.), *Manifesting Power: Gender and the Interpretation of Power in Archaeology* (London: Routledge): 155-71.

Vaux, Roland de
    1961   *Ancient Israel: Its Life and Institutions* (trans. John McHugh; New York: McGraw Hill).

Wailes, Bernard
    1995   'A Case of Heterarchy in Complex Societies: Early Medieval Ireland and its Archaeological Implications', in Ehrenreich, Crumley, and Levy (1995): 55-70.

White, Joyce C.
    1995   'Incorporating Heterarchy into Theory on Socio-Political Development: The Case for Southeast Asia', in Ehrenreich, Crumley and Levy (1995): 101-24.

Whyte, Martin King
    1978   *The Status of Women in Pre-industrial Societies* (Princeton, NJ: Princeton University Press).

Zagarell, Allen
    1995   'Hierarchy and Heterarchy: The Unity of Opposites', in Ehrenreich, Crumley and Levy (1995): 87-100.

Zevit, Ziony
    2001   *The Religions of Ancient Israel: A Synthesis of Parallactic Approaches* (London: Continuum).

Zonabend, François
    1996   'An Anthropological Perspective on Kinship and the Family', in André Burghière, Christiane Klapisch-Zuber, Martine Segalen and François Zonabend (eds.), *A History of the Family*. I. *Distant Worlds, Ancient World* (trans. Sarah Hanbury Tenison, Rosemary Morris and Andrew Wilson; Cambridge: Belknap Press of Harvard University Press): 8-68.

THE SILENCED SONGS OF VICTORY: POWER, GENDER AND MEMORY
IN THE CONQUEST NARRATIVE OF JOSHUA (JOSHUA 1–12)*

Ovidiu Creangă

This essay addresses the absence of women's singing to commemorate Joshua's victories in the conquest of the land, as narrated in Joshua 1–12. The type of musical performance under discussion has been associated usually with women who welcome the returning troops with songs of praise and dancing. This phenomenon is well documented throughout the ancient Near East, as well as in the Hebrew Bible where it concludes some of Israel's famous wars.[1] Well-known biblical examples include Jephthah's daughter who, upon the return of her victorious father from battle, comes out to meet him 'dancing to the sound of tambourines' (Judg. 11.34). Similarly, women in Jerusalem welcome King Saul and David with song, dance and shouts of joy accompanied by musical instruments as the two return from defeating the Philistine army (1 Sam. 18.6). More elaborate descriptions of female musical performance in connection with military victory are Miriam's Song of the Sea (Exod. 15.1-21)[2] and Deborah's victory song (Judg. 5.1-31). The Song of the Sea celebrates the crossing of the Israelites through the Red Sea and depicts Miriam leading a female crowd in jubilant dancing that involved playing the tambourines and singing praises to the Lord 'who has thrown horse and rider into the sea' (Exod. 15.1, 21). However, the joyful songs of women who have gathered to celebrate Israel's taking of the land never occur in the conquest narrative (or in the book of Joshua) as one might expect given the magnitude of Joshua's military success.[3]

---

*   This paper has benefited from feedback received from Dr Deborah Rooke, my doctoral supervisor. During the conference 'A Question of Sex? Gender and Difference in the Hebrew Bible', where this paper was first read, Professor Carol Meyers, Professor Tal Ilan and Dr Diana Lipton provided valuable encouragement and further guidance, for which I am thankful. Any shortcomings that remain are solely my own.

1. Some relevant studies are Seibert (1974), Poethig (1985) and Braun (2002).

2. In defence of attributing the whole song (Exod. 15.1-21) to Miriam, see Meyers (2005b: 116) and Brenner (1985: 52-56).

3. Mixed gender gatherings after victorious military campaigns occur near Mt Gerizim and Mt Ebal (Josh. 8.30-35) and at Shechem (Josh. 24.1-26). In the first passage the presence of women is clearly stated (8.35), but in the second it is uncertain. כל־שבטי ישראל (24.1a) could be a gender-inclusive designation similar to כל־העם in 23.2 denoting the whole com-

This glaring absence becomes even more intriguing in light of the fact that men's musical and poetic performances *are* recorded. War-related shouting (תרועה) occurs repeatedly before the battle of Jericho (6.5) and, on a different occasion, Joshua utters words of poetry as he asks Yhwh to stop the time to allow him to fully defeat the Amorite coalition (10.12-13). Strange, too, is the fact that the fabulous nature of some of the events occurring in Joshua's battles does not provoke women to sing, as similar miracles in other narratives of war do, for example, the parting of the River Jordan (Josh. 3.13) and the parting of the Sea (Exod. 14.16-17; 15.8-9) or the defeat of Goliath (1 Sam. 17.48-54 in conjunction with 18.7) and the fall of Jericho's walls (Josh. 6.20). Likewise, the idea that Yhwh grants victory 'through the hand of a woman' shapes the defeat both of the Canaanites led by Sisera (Judg. 4) and of those led by the king of Jericho (Josh. 2), but only in one instance does this belief move people to sing about it (Judg. 5). Women are conspicuously silent in the conquest narrative, even if Yhwh is repeatedly said to fight for Israel.[4] Why this silence on the part of women regarding Joshua's victories?

Context and Method

One could suggest, with some degree of speculation, that records of female victory songs of the conquest may have been part of the poems contained in the now lost 'book of Jashar' (ספר הישר) mentioned in Josh. 10.14 (and also in 2 Sam. 1.19). Scholars believe this 'book of the upright' to have been a collection of poems and national songs celebrating 'righteous' individuals, like Joshua, or their great deeds (e.g. the stopping of time in Josh. 10.12-14).[5] Another, perhaps less speculative, hypothesis is to assert that at some point under the monarchy or later, earlier conquest hymns composed or sung by women to welcome troops back home were collected, reworked and eventually attributed to male musicians (David, Asaph) without women receiving

---

munity that gathered 'before God' (24.1). The mention in 24.1b of 'elders', 'heads', 'judges', and 'officers' following the mention of 'all the tribes of Israel' seems to suggest the opposite, but this may not necessarily be the case. However, there is no mention of joyous singing at either of these gatherings. This is curious because even if the Shechem ברית is a covenant of recommitment following military confrontations, as Jackson suggests (2000: 235), it still lacks the joyful celebration expected at a gathering of this kind (cf. 2 Chron. 15.12-15). On the other hand, according to the Qumranic reading of the book of Joshua, the end of the conquest is celebrated in 8.30-35 following circumcision (5.2-10) to resemble the pattern laid down in Genesis 15–17 where the promise of the land is sealed through a covenant (Genesis 15) and then celebrated in ritual circumcision (Genesis 17). See Kempinski (1993). Yet no matter which interpretative tradition is followed, there is no explicit indication of female joyous singing following or concluding the conquest.

4. Josh. 5.13-14; 10.14, 42; 11.20.
5. Cf. Harris, Brown and Moore (2000: 66). See also Freedman (1970: 56).

credit for it. In the Psalter they function as songs of praise in honour of Yhwh for giving Canaan and/or the Canaanites over to Israel.[6] The failure of these views to address the possibility of a motivated silence of women's voices is noteworthy. This latter shift in perspective reflects an awareness that public musical performances are bound up with relations of power between the members of the community. Even if female victory-hymn singing ultimately advances certain inequalities in society (in the sense that women celebrate *men*'s victories), public musical performances create alternative centres of leadership in the persona of leading female singers. It is no coincidence that the presence of strong female leading singers in the narrative of Exodus and Judges (Miriam and Deborah who are also among the leaders of the community) next to male leaders (Moses and Barak) has made many interpreters point to the anxiety of men over their prerogatives to power.[7] And, of course, the easiest way to remove the threat of female musicians is to credit men with composing and singing their songs of victory, as is attempted in Exod. 15.1 ('Moses and the children of Israel sang') and Judg. 5.1 ('Deborah and Barak sang that day').[8] It may well be, then, that the writers of the conquest narrative follow a somewhat similar tactic through recording only men's poetic expressions. Moreover, embedded in the idealism and androcentrism surrounding the person of Joshua is the desire of the writers to put men (Joshua) at the centre of the transmission of the group's heroic or authoritative (legislative) past, as clearly seen in Joshua 23 and 24. However, recall of the past is at the heart of victory hymn singing as well (see below), and thus in order to eliminate the genealogy of female power that derives from transmitting the group's past, women's acts of recall are suppressed, or utilized confessionally to stress the submission of foreigners to Yhwh, as in the case of Rahab (Josh. 2.9-11).[9] My aim in the following sections of this work is twofold. First, I want to demonstrate that the 'power' of female singers is a product of both their social networking, and of becoming recognized cultural performers of memory through singing the group's heroic past. This form of 'power' is limited but real nevertheless. Secondly, I argue that the suppression of women's singing has to do partly with the desire to idealize Joshua's undisputed leadership over 'all Israel' and partly with the construction of his masculinity in remembering the past.[10] Four short observations on the gendered language of memory are offered in defence of this claim.

    6. See, for instance, Pss. 78.54-55; 80.8-11; 105.44-45; 135.10-12.
    7. See Exum (2003).
    8. Especially Trible (1994).
    9. For more on Joshua's power and the submission of the 'foreigner', see Rowlett (1996).
    10. These observations represent my initial findings into the relationship between gender and memory in the conquest narrative that will be further developed in my PhD thesis, 'The Conquest of Memory: Israel's Identity and the Commemoration of the Past in the Conquest Narrative of Joshua (chaps. 1–12)'.

Song, Gender and Memory

The central idea of studying gender and memory together owes its origin to the fact that 'memory is influenced by the particular social, cultural, and historical conditions in which individuals find themselves' (Neubauer and Geyer-Ryan 2000: 6). These conditions are very much the product of society (i.e. they are socially constructed) and vary between men and women. This explains why men's memories are often different from women's. Studies on oral history and autobiography make this point very clear.[11] However, memory is not only an activity shaped by the social, cultural and sexual 'location' of the rememberer,[12] but also something people use to define their gender. Because gender, as West and Zimmerman indicate, is 'not simply an aspect of what one is, but, more fundamentally, it is something that one *does*, and does recurrently in interaction with others' (West and Zimmerman 1991: 27), remembering can be a way in which gender is constructed. So, for instance, in places where public commemoration of the past is primarily understood as a male function, for women to recall the past in public, or for men to fail to do so when needed, is to negotiate between genders. The 'remembering behaviours' characteristic of each gender, i.e. who remembers what and in what context, can be—and indeed are—continuously enforced or negotiated when men and women sustain, reproduce or change their gender. The scholarly field of gendered memory, therefore, studies both the location from which individuals or collectives remember, and the impact of remembering on the gender of the rememberer.

These theoretical observations can be brought to bear on the central idea of Meyers's still-influential study *Discovering Eve* (Meyers 1988). At its heart, this book suggests that the androcentric, male-elitist bias of the editors/writers is to be blamed for the scant attention given to the life of women in the biblical text. The Hebrew Bible, in other words, is the product of androcentric memory. This type of memory levels over local memories and histories of women (*and* men) in pursuing the (male) public figures of history and of the organizations and institutions that support male hegemony in the public world (which is the only world that is made to matter). Meyers, however, uses archaeology in an attempt to unearth dormant memories of forgotten women and their local, domestic social and cultural life from ancient Israel. In so doing, her study provides 'counter-memories' to the official, textual memory of public historiography.[13]

---

11. See Hirsch and Smith (2002), and Leydesdorff, Passerini and Thompson (2005) and the bibliography therein.

12. 'Locating' in relation to remembering means asking 'by whom, where, in which context and against what?'. See Davis and Starn (1989: 2).

13. A recent survey on the politics of counter-remembering is Kirk (2005: 11-13). Also suggestive is Hendel's discussion of 'counter-memory' in relation to the various portrayals of Abraham in the Hebrew Bible (Hendel 2005: 41-43).

Relating this to the issue at hand, the account of the conquest is far from 'historical'; rather, it is better seen as 'mnemohistory', which according to Jan Assmann 'is concerned not with the past as such, but only with the past as it is remembered' (Assmann 1997: 9). Reading the conquest narrative as mnemohistory does not mean that the tradition, or the traditions that coalesce into this narrative, are true, but rather that they are a phenomenon of collective memory that reconstructs the past selectively. A strand in the tradition of Israel's emergence in the land, and the product of a group of scholars who constructed Israel's past as 'conquest of the land', the whole book of Joshua and not just the conquest narrative is an androcentric text that renders women's cultural habits and products invisible and inaudible as men's words and deeds—that is, men's memory—is preserved. With the exception of the foreign prostitute Rahab (Joshua 2), all women in the conquest narrative are unnamed individuals whose identity derives from being related to a man (father, husband, brother).[14] These women are subsumed under large monolithic tropes such as כל קהל ישראל, כל ישראל, כל העם or בני ישראל that hide more than they reveal about how Israelite women lived.[15] Simply put, their history is levelled over and left unrecorded, as if nothing of worth could come from those who belong with the children and herds (cf. Josh. 1.14).[16] This representation of gender—nurturing women and warrior/cultural men—is considered 'natural' in the conquest narrative, a reflection of 'enduring dispositions' (West and Zimmerman 1991: 32-33). As a construct, however, patriarchy is constantly under the threat of being undermined by the very structure that sustains it, as Eilberg-Schwartz and Cheryl Exum show in their respective studies. According to these scholars, patriarchy resorts to various techniques—from visible and aggressive (force and threat) to subtle and hidden (sexualization, motherhood)—in order to secure women's cooperation.[17] Vocal and courageous, the foreign female prostitute Rahab is an example of the women who challenge the association between masculinity and memory, as she recalls Israel's past 'like a man' (Josh. 2.9-11). She does not escape the control of patriarchy, first in the sexualization of her body (זונה, Josh. 2.1), then

---

14. See the entries under 'unnamed women' in the book of Joshua, in Meyers, Craven and Kraemer (2000: 236-38).

15. The referents implied by these tropes are often male. 'Women' are only explicitly mentioned once in Josh. 8.35. See also n. 3 above.

16. Until recently, private life was not considered part of the collective memory of the community and so people and activities associated with it become almost invisible. The advantage of linking gender and memory is that it allows for consideration of the specific context in which remembering occurs, and so private life can be rediscovered. For further details, see Hirsch and Smith (2002: 6, 11-13). This point is taken up by Meyers in relation to ancient Israelite women's religious culture (Meyers 2005a). Similarly, Larranaga (2005) documents the unrecorded history of female singers in the Basque singing tradition that has traditionally been associated with men but in which the author discovers that many women (actual singers or the mothers/singers of male singers) have been a part.

17. See Exum (2003: 133-34); Eilberg-Schwartz (1995a: 2, 9; 1995b: 166).

in the controlling of her speech (vv. 14, 17-21) before she is allocated a place in the patriarchal order symbolized by the camp (Josh. 6.25); but she nevertheless embodies a threat that needs to be 'tamed'.

As Meyers corroborates through archaeological evidence, descriptions of women in ancient Israel are often at odds with the representation of women in the Hebrew Bible. Ancient Israelite women appear to have performed a wide range of cultural and intellectual activities, some public, some in the privacy of their household, with which biblical women are only rarely associated, and even then, it is done pejoratively.[18] The example of victory hymn singing is a good case study. To unmask the ideological and hegemonic interests that may be inherent in the omission of female singing from the conquest narrative it is important to understand the nature of the power of female musicians and the way this power is achieved.

Power and Public Singing

In her study entitled 'Miriam the Musician' (Meyers 1994), Meyers reflects on the social and political ramifications of musical performance. She maps out two salient features implicit in the texts dealing with women's victory-hymn performance, namely (a) the expectation that following a military victory the returning forces would be met by women who had the musical skills to regale them in a particular way, and (b) the public context of the ensuing performance, which would take place before the leaders of Israel—Moses, Jephthah, Saul, and so on (Meyers 1994: 225). The performance, therefore, is an artistic event (comprising performers, setting and audience) centred on an artistic action (the creation or performing of an artistic production). The social power of female singers results from the intersection of the artistic event with the artistic action. This combination allowed women (singers) to 'exercise control of themselves and their worlds and thus enjoy a sense of power rather than powerlessness'

---

18. Meyers presents the emancipation of women in agrarian societies of premonarchic Israel as deriving from women's equal participation in the demanding economies of production, procreation and protection—a theoretical thread which she develops in an earlier study (1983). This position has gathered many adherents, but there is, of course, still disagreement among scholars about the extent to which women were really equal to men in many areas of influence despite their equal contribution to the life of the community. Still, by rooting her analysis in women's social life (e.g. female guilds) Meyers has established a good basis from which to reconstruct the complex relations of inter-dependence and support that are assumed to have existed among the members of premonarchic Israelite communities. See, for instance, Meyers (1999a, 1999b). Furthermore, reconstructing women's religious culture allows Meyers to dispute the assumption of superiority of male religious duties and practices (cf. Bird 1999). She shows that household religious practices performed by women were central to the wellbeing of their households, especially as regards the performance of rituals surrounding fertility, pregnancy, labour, birth, postpartum lactation, infant care and circumcision, and so on. For further details, see Meyers (2005a).

(Meyers 1994: 227-28). This was true because production (artistic action) required competence, training, rehearsals, and regular contact with other female peers that allowed women to incur 'social capital' (Meyers 1994: 227). Moreover, drawing from feminist ethnomusicology (the study of the relationship between music behaviour and gender behaviour), Meyers points out that '(t)he nature of a society's gender structure impacts upon women's expressive forms, and those forms in turn reflect and symbolize gender structures'.[19]

Given that it is a common feature of ideal men to deliver public orations and poems (Jacob, Moses, Joshua and David all do so), for women to do so means to aspire to a position of power similar to that of men. That is why female public singing is a place of negotiating power and asserting control in the public sphere. Of course, the power of victory hymn singers is an acceptable form of empowerment that relates to public performance. In other words, it is power confined to the occasion, but this is not to say that it is not real. During the period of performing, power is divided and shared between male leaders and female leading musicians who mobilize for singing probably a good part of the place's female population ('all the women followed Miriam', Exod. 15.20), and perhaps even those men who have not been able to join the army (the young and the old). As Meyers clearly explains, 'the performance has the capacity, at least for the moment of the communicative and professional activity ... to transform social structure' (Meyers 1994: 228). While this transformative power may be limited in time and space, the memory of leading singers who have mobilized large masses of people is likely to be remembered by the community as well as by its leaders beyond the event itself. It is therefore reasonable to expect musicians of this kind to receive further recognition and respect, thus allowing them more bargaining power in other matters of the society.

Another issue related to female public singing concerns the question of who retells publicly the nation's heroic past (which is, of course, a religious past as well). In whose 'gender trajectory' does the 'remembering behaviour' of public retelling fall? Generally, men are depicted as recollectors of Israel's memory. The Song of the Sea and Deborah's victory ode, however, depict women retelling in a poetic language the victory that was achieved on the battlefield. This position of women as retellers of the past seems everywhere in conflict with the gender hierarchy dominant in the narratives where female singing occurs (Exodus, Judges, 1 Samuel). It is also in conflict with the gender structure dominant in the conquest narrative. There, Joshua figures as the only authorized disseminator

---

19. Meyers 1994: 226. Meyers links the organization of women in ancient Israel in guilds with the transmission of practical knowledge and skills, including societal beliefs and ideas that go hand in hand with skill learning. See Meyers (1999a). This connection between female guilds and the transmission of societal cultural traditions is worth more investigation, as it is a fertile point of intersection between women as cultural actors and the transmission of cultural memory. On habits and the transmission of cultural memory, see Bourdieu (1977) and Connerton (1989). For a critical analysis of their theoretical models, see Strathern (1996: 26-32).

of the Law (Josh. 1.8), the person through whom Yhwh communicates more directly with his people (Josh. 3.8, 9-13; 4.2-7; 5.2, 3; 6.2-5, 6-11, etc.) and the leader who revisits Israel's past (cf. Josh. 22.13-20; 24.2-15). When Rahab returns to Israel's past in Josh. 2.9-11, she certainly undermines many of the narrative's assumptions about the privileged position of Israel's male leaders to recall their past. In fact, by doing so, Rahab undermines the very construction of male gender that is based on the link between memory and masculinity[20]—as do victory hymn singers who are, after all, singers of Israel's past.

Because Rahab links Israel's past to her present, she—just like Miriam and Deborah—is a cultural actor, and much more than that. Indeed, Rahab becomes a performer of Israel's cultural memory, in regard both to the past she evokes (exodus from Egypt and subsequent victories in Transjordania) and to the fact that *she*, an epitomic 'other', does it. Robert Polzin explains the change in perspective that occurs in Rahab's performance of Israel's memory as she adopts the point of view of the invaders in this way: 'the story of Rahab is really the story of Israel told from the point of view of a non-Israelite'.[21] Therefore, Bal appears to be right in linking recollection of memory with performing it, for, as she puts it, 'cultural recall is not merely something of which you happen to be a bearer, but something that you actually perform, even if, in many instances, such acts are not consciously and wilfully contrived' (Bal 1999: vii). The struggle of biblical (and later rabbinical) authors and contemporary biblical scholars to acknowledge that women, too, narrate (and even embody) the identity and history of their people is a sub-theme of Alice Bach's article 'With a Song in her Heart: Listening to Scholars Listening for Miriam'.[22]

Having thus identified the root of women musicians' power in the artistic performance of the group's cultural memory, it now appears more clearly why the writer(s) of this narrative preferred to tell the story of the conquest under Joshua in the way they did: to secure Joshua's (and their) hegemony. As will be seen in the following section, at the heart of male hegemony lies an androcentric memory that results from various linkages between masculinity and remembering. To this I now turn.

Masculinity and Memory

1. *The Gender of Memory*. As well as being a 'warrior' (גבור) and a 'man of war' (איש מלחמה),[23] a second important feature defining masculinity in this narrative is to commemorate the past. The first set of public commemorations

---

20. Another example of a woman 'unmanning' men by performing what is usually seen as belonging to men, is Yael in Judg. 4. 17-21. See Yee (1993).
21. Polzin 1980: 88. Polzin interprets the whole episode of the encounter with Rahab in light of his 'shift in perspective', and as a plea against an authoritarian dogmatism represented by Deuteronomy's law of חרם (Deut. 7. 1-5; 20. 16-18). See Polzin 1980: 84-91.
22. See Bach (1999b: 420).
23. Josh. 4.13; 5.4, 6; 6.3, 7, 9, 13; 8.3, 11; 10.7.

of the past takes place at Gilgal, the place chosen for the establishment of the camp and the place from which, and to which, most military expeditions set out and return. It is here that Joshua has the twelve large stones that were picked up from the Jordan assembled as a 'memorial for ever' (זכרון עד־עולם) in order to commemorate the fact that 'Israel crossed the Jordan on dry ground' (Josh. 4.7, 20-22). Then the episode of circumcision of adult males (זכרים) appears, in connection with 'rolling away the reproach of Egypt' (5.9). Circumcision, as scholars have noted, is a sign of belonging to God's people, a symbol of masculinity and, not least, a physical reminder of the patriarchal covenant.[24] Even though the precise nature of this 'reproach' is unclear (some kind of shame or disgrace caused by Egypt is implied[25]), the removal of it conveys a desire to suppress it. Finally, there is the remembering of the exodus from Egypt in the Passover celebration (5.10-12). These commemorations of the past prior to the start of the Cisjordanian conquest are paralleled by others during the conquest. These latter are usually associated with the marking of sites of victory or destruction, as well as burial places that mark the event for the future. They appear in this order: the ruins of Jericho (6.26), the burial site of Achan and his family (7.25-26), the ruins of Ai and the burial site of its king (8.26), and the place where the five Amorite kings where captured and killed by Joshua near the cave of Makkedah (10.22-27). One has to include here the oral reading of the Law and its inscription on a stone altar near Mount Ebal (8.32-35). Commemoration, in all of these instances, serves various purposes in the narrative, both to legitimize a collective identity (Israel) or an individual role (Joshua as the leader), and also to motivate action (the conquest). It is important to note the recollection of violence—divine and human—that many of the above 'sites of memory' evoke or even mark for future recall.

The recent work of scholars like Washington and Clines on violence and masculinity in the Hebrew Bible[26] underline the fact that physical violence is gendered in so far as it is indexed as a feature of one, or both, sexes (but one usually associated with men), and engendering in so far as it affirms the associated sex (usually manhood). These studies reinforce the point that physical violence is constitutive of masculinity. But so is the commemoration of violence by men. Men commemorate violence in order to legitimize their identity as איש גבור, 'strong, mighty man', as well as to maintain their social prerogatives that are linked with knowledge of the past (e.g. membership in the community). For these reasons, if for no others, men remember their heroic past.

---

24. See Eilberg-Schwartz (1990: 141-77) and Hendel (2005: 20-33). This is not without its problems, particularly as regards women's sense of belonging to the covenant community. For a feminist critique of circumcision as a (male) sign of the covenant, see Plaskow (1991: 82-84; 1999). Two other studies that offer an explanation of this tension are Goldingay (2000) and Cohen (1997).

25. Various explanations have been offered: slavery, uncircumcision, disobedience, landlessness. See Nelson (1997: 76); Hawk (2000: 81); Mitchell (1993: 46).

26. Washington (1998) (which develops from Washington [1997]) and Clines (1995).

2. *Mnemonic Violence.* It is important to highlight further the fact that the conquest of Canaan is framed as an event recalling divine promises made in the past. Because of this understanding of the conquest, Israel's violence is 'mnemonic', i.e. it relates back to, and brings forward, the promise to the fathers with which it is directly linked in Josh. 1.6: 'Be strong (חזק) and courageous (אמץ) because you will lead this people to inherit the land which I swore (שבע) to their fathers to give them'. Similarly, a few verses later, Joshua calls the armed men of the two and a half tribes who reside in Transjordania to 'remember (זכור) what Moses commanded (צוה) you' and help the rest of the people in the conquest of Cisjordania (1.13-15). My interest here is not to restate what is known all too well, namely that various theological threads running through the Pentateuch (e.g. the 'pledge to the fathers' mentioned above) are picked up in the conquest narrative. Rather, I want to stress the mnemonic relationship that exists between the conquest and the divine promise to the patriarchs. Just as in the ceremony of circumcision the Israelites are reminded of the patriarchal promise (Josh. 5.2-9), so then the conquest of the land recalls earlier promises as it fulfils them. This idea transpires more clearly in Joshua's final valedictory addresses where he clearly indicates that הדברים הטובים אשר דבר יהוה אלהיכם עליכם הכל באו לכם לא־נפל ממנו דבר אחד ('not one promise failed from all the good promises that Yhwh your God spoke, but all have been fulfilled, not a single one has failed') (23.14). In the same chapter 23, speaking in retrospect, Joshua explains that Yhwh has fought for Israel in accordance with what Yhwh had said earlier (לכם כאשר דבר, 23.10). Joshua himself, too, has conquered the nations of the land in order to keep all that is written in the ספר תורת משה (23.4, 6; also 11.15, 23). Similarly, a chapter later, Joshua recapitulates Israel's past history, stating that Yhwh 'took Abraham from beyond the River, multiplied his seed, gave him Isaac ... (and) Jacob ... and Jacob and his children went down into Egypt' (24.3, 4). The following verses enumerate a series of acts of deliverance—from Egypt (24.6, 7), the Amorites (24.8), Moabites (Balak and Balaam, 24.9), and seven nations living in the land, including the Jerichonites (24.11)—that can reasonably be assumed to have derived from Yhwh's commitment to the 'the fathers' even if this is not explicitly stated. This rhetoric of explaining the present in light of the past links men's fighting with bringing to completion past promises or causing them to happen, and so fulfilment of the past becomes embedded in the type of masculinity Joshua and his troops embody.

3. *Masculinization of Memory and the Feminization of Oblivion.* A number of important studies on warfare in the ancient world have focused on the sexualized language of war and its relationship to gender construction.[27] This has been

---

27. For the gendered language of warfare relating to the Israelite-Assyrian encounter, see the important work of Chapman (2004). See also Washington (1997, 1998) for gendered language in the biblical law of war (Deuteronomy 20-21). For later accounts of conquest, see Goldstein (2001: 333-62); Cohn (1993); Trexler (1995: 12-37).

an important move in showing the extent to which, in the words of Harold Washington, 'violence and domination are central to the discursive production of the gendered subject' (Washington 1998: 193). Again, there are ramifications of how violence participates in the construction of the gendered subject, and my aim in this subsection is to explore how the gendered language of warfare links up with remembering and forgetting as it constructs gender. The language in the Deuteronomic law of warfare (Deuteronomy 20–21) in its imagery and grammar pictures the territories to be conquered as feminine. Military invasions are imagined as rape and cities under siege as women undergoing sexual assault (Washington 1998: 200). As in other narratives of war, the conquest narrative of Joshua, too, renders the defeated as feminine and victors as masculine.[28] The description of Jericho prior to its conquest is likened to that of a virgin whose entry point (vagina) is tightly shut up (סגרת ומסגרת, Josh. 6.1) before being penetrated. The city of Ai falls into Joshua's hands when the men in the ambush manage to 'enter' (בוא, Josh 8.19) it.[29] This use of the feminine in the Deuteronomic language of warfare, as Washington points out, relegates 'woman' to a secondary status (penetrated) in relation to 'man' (penetrator).[30]

But there is more that can be said about the connotations of feminine language in the Deuteronomic law of warfare. What is the connotation of 'woman' in light of the total destruction required by the law of חרם (Deut. 20.16-18)? Is anything added to the concept of 'woman' by the fact that the she-city is not only penetrated and humiliated, but finally utterly destroyed? I think it is, and I do not think Washington goes far enough to make this connection. Yet it seems logical to push the imagery to the limits allowed by Deuteronomy 20. Deut. 20.16-18 adds to the concept of 'woman' an extreme form of defeat, i.e. the erasure of the enemy's human and material traces (see also Deut. 7.2-5). In light of this addition, the image of 'woman' denotes a sequence of siege-penetration-defeat-erasure (or forgetfulness). There are three clearly indicated cities that Joshua puts to the חרם: Jericho (Josh. 6.17, 21), Ai (Josh. 8.26), Makkedah (Josh. 10.28) and Hazor (Josh. 11.11). Common to all these instances of חרם are the decimation of their citizens, slaughter of their king (and his army) and total ruination of the city (the extent of destruction in the case of Makkedah is not stated).[31] Even in the case of cities that are not put under the ban of חרם, the attempt to rename them is an

---

28. As Goldstein (2001) puts it, 'war borrows gender as a code for domination-submission relationships... Enemies and subordinates are gendered feminine' (333).

29. See also the story of the prostitute Rahab (Josh. 2.1) where the narrator plays on בוא to entertain the possibility that Joshua's spies may have entered not only the house of the harlot but also 'into' her (that is, had sex with her).

30. Washington 1997: 345. See also Washington (1998: 193-94).

31. This is, of course, also true for Achan who perishes together with all his belongings, including his family, in what appears to be a proper application of the law of חרם as a result of violating it (Josh. 7.1, 11-13, 25-27).

act of erasure of cultural traces of their former inhabitants (e.g. Kiriath-sepher changed to Debir or Luz changed to Bethel).³²

If, then, 'woman' stands for that which is obliterated by חרם, does 'man' indicate that which resists physical erasure? Clearly, the conquest narrative links masculinity with physical monuments that recall Joshua's victims as well as his victories. Examples of this are the large stone heaps (גל־אבנים גדול) raised over the dead bodies of Achan (Josh. 7.26) and the king of Ai (8.29), the stones at the mouth of the cave containing the bodies of the five Amorite kings (10.27), and the monument marking the victory of the male god, Yhwh, over the waters of the Jordan (4.7, 23-24). These stone structures bear witness 'to this day' (עד היום הזה, Josh. 7.26; 8.28; 10.27) and 'for ever' (עד עולם, Josh. 4.7) to the memory of what they came to mark, but also of Joshua's achievements (cf. Josh. 4.14; 6.27). The choice of the material and architecture to mark his success indicates the desire for lasting memory. Perhaps even more can be suggested, namely, that the verticality of these commemorative monuments constructs a phallic symbol representing Joshua's masculinity. The idea that masculinity and public commemoration are linked is reinforced by physical monuments. Conversely, physical erasure of memory as a result of complete destruction enters the domain of the 'feminine'.

4. *Public vs. Private.* In a study on the cultural poetics of gender and nationhood, Don Seeman employs the notion of 'space' as a category for analysing how masculinity and femininity are constructed in the patriarchal narratives (Seeman 1998). Looking at the narrative of heir announcement in Genesis 18, Seeman finds that 'closure in tent' is indicative of the failure on the part of Abraham and Sarah to achieve their masculinity and femininity, respectively. When the three unexpected guests approach the couple, Sarah is inside the tent while Abraham sits by the entrance of the tent (Gen. 18.1, 6). According to Seeman, their position inside the tent (Sarah) and near the door (Abraham) mirrors the 'closure' of their bodies to fertility (Seeman 1998: 8-9). The announcement of progeny comes only after Abraham changes locations, moving away from the door of the tent into the field where he welcomes the messengers (Gen. 18.2, 7-8). Sarah, too, progressively moves from inside the tent to the tent's door (Gen. 18.9-10)—that place fraught with both danger and blessings. In his analysis, Seeman identifies two symbolic vectors in relation to 'tent': on the one hand, a male centrifugal vector characterized by a movement towards 'outside', the field, a space of vitality, and on the other hand, a centripetal vector, a movement towards 'inside', interiority, and lack of vitality. While successful masculinity (fatherhood in this case) is represented by the centrifugal vector, moving away from the domestic habitat into the 'field' where men achieve true masculinity, the example of Sarah indicates that women, too, will achieve their femininity

---

32. For more on this topic, see Fewell and Gunn (1995).

(motherhood in this case) by moving outwardly, towards the door of the tent, even if maintaining a degree of 'interiority'. Women become valuable social actors when their interiority is relative and not absolute.[33]

For the most part, the conquest narrative portrays Israelite women in a state of near 'absolute interiority'. Despite this fact, a small degree of 'relative interiority' can be inferred from the two instances in which women are mentioned in connection with domestic responsibility (Josh. 1.14) and participation in the cult (Josh. 8.35). Like Sarah in the Genesis narrative, women in the book of Joshua struggle to achieve 'cultural' fertility. Patriarchy would want women to stay away from the public world (and care for children, Josh. 1.14) and, at the most, be called to hear the recitation of the Law (8.35). This describes cultural infertility.[34]

The conquest narrative deploys space and movements across space to construct masculinity (in opposition to femininity). For instance, Joshua and his army are consistently depicted as moving away from the camp of residence to the battlefield and returning there victorious.[35] This movement reaffirms their masculinity. To flee from before the enemy, i.e. to turn one's back and move inward, 'discredits' in masculine contests of war, as the first set-back at Ai shows. In the first instance, the men of Ai put Joshua's troops on the run. The following characterization describes well the use of spatial movements to construct gender: 'and they fled (נוס) before the men of Ai... and the hearts of the people melted (מסס) and became like water' (Josh. 7.5). Real men do not run away in the face of the enemy and their courage does not dissipate, unless one has become a 'woman'.[36] Similarly, for men to be 'sitting down in the camp', וישבו תחתם במחנה (presumably in tents), symbolizes physical weakness (after circumcision) and vulnerability to deceit (the Gibeonites' trick).[37] These examples suggest that interiority and restricted mobility 'unmans' men

33. Seeman 1998: 14-15. As Seeman puts it '...if centrifugal motion is the sign of male vitality in the Hebrew Bible, centripetal motion and relative interiority are the setting for successful motherhood' (115). Returning to Joshua's conquest narrative, Rahab fits the description of a successful woman because she moves in and out of her house: from the roof to the door of her house to hide Joshua's men and deal with the king's messengers (Josh. 2.3-6). Another example of 'relative interiority' is Jael who is a tent dweller ('the tent of Jael', אהל יעל) but she 'goes out' (יצא) to meet her visitors Sisera and Barak (Judg. 4.18, 22). For the latter example, see Bal 1988a:169-96.

34. It is worth noting the similar description of the women of the land who, with the exception of Rahab, are equally absent and voiceless. They appear secluded behind city walls before becoming victims of war, חרם (Josh. 6.21; 8.25-26).

35. Gilgal is the starting and finishing point of all the three expeditions, in the central (Josh. 5.10; 9.6), southern (Josh. 10.6, 15; 10.43) and northern parts of the land (Josh. 11.4).

36. Here 'manhood' represents the opposite of 'melting', 'flowing' and 'water'. This illustrates the earlier point that durable, immutable monuments of stone symbolize masculinity.

37. Josh. 5.8; 9.6-27. Bal (1988b) traces the 'unmanning' of Sisera to entering the 'tent of Jael' (121-23).

and womanizes them. This is certainly true for the five Amorite kings who hide from Joshua in a cave before being captured by Joshua's men and imprisoned in it. Their gesture transforms them into 'women' failing to confront Joshua on the battlefield. They end up being humiliated even more (10.16, 22-26).[38] Hence, as Seeman observes above, moving outward, away from one's immediate residence, into the 'field', symbolizes masculinity; moving centripetally signifies femininity.

These observations are important when read alongside the fact that most commemorations and 'sites' of memory are located outside of the camp or tent and on the battlefield. The fact that women are not on the battlefield where victories are won and where monuments are erected to commemorate men's victories does not fully explain why, upon their return, Joshua's troops were not welcomed with joyful singing (the women in Jerusalem gathered after the battle to acclaim Saul and David, 1 Sam. 18. 6). But this fact raises the question, which will have to await a further study, whether monumental war commemoration competes with, if not replaces, women's commemorative singing in this narrative of the conquest.

Conclusion

Seeing the lack of female jubilant singing in the conquest narrative of Joshua as motivated rather than accidental, this essay has argued that the desire to idealize Joshua by presenting him as the only legitimate leader of 'all Israel' has led the writer(s) of this narrative to marginalize a female musical tradition of victory hymn singing because of its emphasis on female power. Instead, the writers made commemoration of violence an activity of men and an attribute of their masculinity. However, this vast marginalization of women and of their cultural products reveals anxiety over male leadership and especially its vulnerability in the face of women like Rahab, who, even if a product of patriarchy, can act and think 'like a man'. This study has also shown the preference of patriarchy conveniently to remember only what suits its structures ('mnemohistory') in order to create an 'androcentric' memory that fosters male hegemony. This project, too, can be turned upside-down by female performers of memory who exhibit knowledge of the past comparable to that of men.

---

38. Other examples of masculine tasks and attributes could be found in Joshua's portrayal in the book of Joshua, which seems to have been influenced by notions of masculinity prevalent in Assyrian royal texts. See, for instance, Chapman (2004: 28-37). For a more general and less gender-informed comparison between the account of Joshua's conquests (especially Joshua 9-12) and related texts from ancient Near Eastern literature of war, see Younger (1990: 197-266).

BIBLIOGRAPHY

Assmann, Jan
    1997   *Moses the Egyptian: The Memory of Egypt in Western Monotheism* (Cambridge, MA: Harvard University Press).

Bach, Alice (ed.)
    1999a   *Women in the Hebrew Bible: A Reader* (London: Routledge).
    1999b   'With a Song in her Heart: Listening to Scholars Listening for Miriam', in Bach 1999a: 419-27.

Bal, Mieke
    1988a   *Death and Dissymmetry: The Politics of Coherence in the Book of Judges* (Chicago Studies in the History of Judaism; Chicago: Chicago University Press).
    1988b   *Murder and Difference: Gender, Genre and Scholarship on Sisera's Death* (trans. Matthew Gumpert; Bloomington and Indianapolis: Indiana University Press).
    1999   'Introduction', in Mieke Bal, Jonathan. Crewe and Leo Spitzer (eds.), *Acts of Memory: Cultural Recall in the Present* (Hanover, NH: University Press of New England): vii-xvii.

Bird, Phyllis
    1999   'The Place of Women in the Israelite Cultus', in Bach 1999a: 3-20.

Bourdieu, Pierre
    1977   *Outline of a Theory of Practice* (trans. Richard Nice; Cambridge Studies in Social and Cultural Anthropology, 16; Cambridge: Cambridge University Press).

Braun, Joachim
    2002   *Music in Ancient Israel/Palestine: Archaeological, Written, and Comparative Sources* (trans. Douglas W. Scott; Grand Rapids, MI: Eerdmans).

Brenner, Athalya
    1985   *Israelite Woman: Social Role and Literary Type in Biblical Narrative* (Biblical Seminar; Sheffield: JSOT Press).

Brenner, Athalya (ed.)
    1994   *A Feminist Companion to Exodus to Deuteronomy* (FCB, 6; Sheffield: Sheffield Academic Press).

Chapman, Cynthia R.
    2004   *The Gendered Language of Warfare in the Israelite-Assyrian Encounter* (HSM, 62; Winona Lake: Eisenbrauns).

Clines, David J.A.
    1995   'David the Man: The Construction of Masculinity in the Hebrew Bible', in David J.A. Clines (ed.), *Interested Parties: The Ideology of Writers and Readers of the Hebrew Bible* (JSOTSup, 205/GCT, 1; Sheffield: Sheffield Academic Press): 212-43.

Cohen, Shaye J.D.
    1997   'Why Aren't Jewish Women Circumcised?', *Gender and History* 9: 560-78.

Cohn, Carol
    1993   'War, Wimps, and Women: Talking Gender and Thinking War', in Miriam Cooke and Angela Woollacott (eds.), *Gendering War Talk* (Princeton, NJ: Princeton University Press): 227-46.

Connerton, Paul
    1989   *How Societies Remember* (Cambridge: Cambridge University Press).
Davis, Natalie Z., and Randolph Starn
    1989   'Introduction: Memory and Counter-Memory', *Representations* 26: 1-6.
Eilberg-Schwartz, Howard
    1990   *The Savage in Judaism: An Anthropology of Israelite Religion and Ancient Judaism* (Bloomington, IN: Indiana University Press).
    1995a   'Introduction: The Spectacle of the Female Head', in Eilberg-Schwartz and Doniger 1995: 1-13.
    1995b   'The Nakedness of a Woman's Voice, The Pleasure in a Man's Mouth: An Oral History of Ancient Judaism', in Eilberg Schwarz and Doniger 1995: 165-84.
Eilberg-Schwartz, Howard, and Wendy Doniger (eds.)
    1995   *Off With her Head: The Denial of Women's Identity in Myth, Religion, and Culture* (Berkeley: University of California Press).
Exum, J. Cheryl
    2003   'The Hand That Rocks the Cradle', in Janet Martin Soskice and Diana Lipton (eds.), *Feminism and Theology* (Oxford Readings in Feminism; Oxford University Press): 123-43.
Fewell, Danna Nolan, and David M. Gunn
    1995   'Achsah and the (E)razed City of Writing', in Gale A. Yee (ed.), *Judges and Method: New Approaches in Biblical Studies* (Minneapolis: Fortress Press): 119-45.
Freedman, Harry
    1970   'Joshua: Introduction and Commentary', in Abraham Cohen (ed.), *Joshua and Judges: Hebrew Text and English Translation with Introduction and Commentary* (Soncino Books of the Bible; London: The Soncino Press) 1-151.
Goldingay, John
    2000   'The Significance of Circumcision', *JSOT* 88: 3-18.
Goldstein, Joshua S.
    2001   *War and Gender: How Gender Shapes the War System and vice versa* (Cambridge: Cambridge University Press).
Harris, J. Gordon, Cheryl A. Brown and Michael S. Moore
    2000   *Joshua, Judges, Ruth* (NIBCOT, 5; Peabody, MA: Hendrickson).
Hawk, L. Daniel
    2000   *Joshua* (Berit Olam; Collegeville, MN: Liturgical Press).
Hendel, Ronald
    2005   *Remembering Abraham: Culture, Memory, and History in the Hebrew Bible* (Oxford: Oxford University Press).
Hirsch, Marianne, and Valerie Smith
    2002   'Feminism and Cultural Memory: An Introduction', *Signs* 28: 1-20.
Jackson, Bernard S.
    2000   *Studies in the Semiotics of Biblical Law* (JSOTSup, 314; Sheffield: Sheffield Academic Press).
Kempinski, Aharon
    1993   'When History Sleeps, Theology Arises: A Note on Joshua 8:30-35 and the Archaeology of the Settlement Period', *Eretz Israel* 24: 175-83 (Hebrew).

Kirk, Alan
    2005   'Social and Cultural Memory', in Alan Kirk and Tom Thatcher (eds.), *Memory, Tradition, and Text: Uses of the Past in Early Christianity* (Leiden: E.J. Brill): 1-24.

Larranaga, Carmen
    2005   'Ubiquitous but Invisible: The Presence of Women Singers within a Basque Male Tradition', in Leydesdorff, Passerini and Thompson 2005: 59-70.

Leydesdorff, Selma, Luisa Passerini and Paul Thompson
    2005   'Introduction', in Selma Leydesdorff, Luisa Passerini and Paul Thompson (eds.), *Gender and Memory* (Memory and Narrative Series; New Brunswick and London: Transaction Publishers): 1-16.

Meyers, Carol
    1983   'Procreation, Production and Protection: Male-Female Balance in Early Israel', *Journal of the American Academy of Religion* 51: 569-93.
    1988   *Discovering Eve: Ancient Israelite Women in Context* (New York/Oxford: Oxford University Press).
    1994   'Miriam the Musician', in Brenner 1994: 207-30.
    1999a   'Guilds and Gatherings: Women's Groups in Ancient Israel', in Prescott H. Williams and Theodore Hiebert (eds.), *Realia Dei: Essays in Archaeology and Biblical Interpretation in Honor of Edward F. Campbell, Jr. at his Retirement* (Atlanta: Scholars Press): 161-70.
    1999b   'Women and the Domestic Economy of Early Israel', in Bach 1999a: 33-43.
    2005a   *Households and Holiness: The Religious Culture of Israelite Women* (Facets Series; Minneapolis: Fortress Press).
    2005b   *Exodus* (NCBC; Cambridge: Cambridge University Press).

Meyers, Carol, Toni Craven and Ross S. Kraemer (eds.)
    2001   *Women in Scripture: A Dictionary of Named and Unnamed Women in the Hebrew Bible, the Apocryphal/Deuterocanonical Books and the New Testament* (Grand Rapids, MI: Eerdmans).

Mitchell, Gordon
    1993   *Together in the Land: A Reading of the Book of Joshua* (JSOTS, 134; Sheffield: Sheffield Academic Press).

Nelson, Richard D.
    1997   *Joshua: A Commentary* (OTL; Louisville, KY: Westminster/John Knox Press).

Neubauer, John, and Helga Geyer-Ryan
    2000   'Introduction—Gender, Memory, Literature', in John Neubauer and Helga Geyer-Ryan (eds.), *Gendered Memories* (Proceedings of the xvth Congress of the International Comparative Literature Association 'Literature as Cultural Memory', Leiden 16-22 August 1997; Amsterdam-Atlanta, GA: Radopi): 5-8.

Plaskow, Judith
    1991   *Standing Again at Sinai: Judaism from a Feminist Perspective* (New York: HarperCollins).
    1999   'Transforming the Nature of Community: Toward a Feminist People of Israel', in Bach 1999b: 403-18.

Poethig, Eunice B.
    1985   *The Victory Song Tradition of the Women of Israel* (PhD dissertation, Union Theological Seminary, New York).

Polzin, Robert
    1980   *Moses and the Deuteronomist: A Literary Study of the Deuteronomistic History. Part One: Deuteronomy, Joshua, Judges* (New York: The Seabury Press).

Rowlett, Lori L.
    1996   *Joshua and the Rhetoric of Violence: A New Historicist Analysis* (JSOTSup, 226; Sheffield: Sheffield Academic Press).

Seeman, Don
    1998   ' "Where is Sarah Your Wife?" Cultural Poetics of Gender and Nationhood in the Hebrew Bible', *HTR* 91/2: 103-25.

Seibert, Ilse
    1974   *Woman in Ancient Near East* (trans. Marianne Herzfeld; Leipzig: Fortschritt Erfuhrt).

Strathern, Andrew J.
    1996   *Body Thoughts* (Ann Arbor: University of Michigan Press).

Trexler, Richard C.
    1995   *Sex and Conquest: Gendered Violence, Political Order, and the European Conquest of the Americas* (Cambridge: Polity Press).

Trible, Phyllis
    1994   'Bringing Miriam Out of the Shadows', in Brenner 1994: 166-86.

Washington, Harold C.
    1997   'Violence and the Construction of Gender in the Hebrew Bible', *Biblical Interpretation* 5: 324-63.
    1998   ' "Lest He Die in the Battle and Another Man Take Her": Violence and the Construction of Gender in the Laws of Deuteronomy 20–22', in Victor H. Matthews, Bernard M. Levinson and Tikva Frymer-Kensky (eds.), *Gender and Law in the Hebrew Bible and the Ancient Near East* (JSOTSup, 262; Sheffield: Sheffield Academic Press): 185-213.

West, Candice, and Don H. Zimmerman
    1991   'Doing Gender', in Judith Lorber and Susan A. Farrell (eds.), *The Social Construction of Gender* (Newbury Park: Sage): 13-37.

Yee, Gale A.
    1993   'By the Hand of a Woman: The Metaphor of the Woman Warrior in Judges 4', *Semeia* 61: 99-132.

Younger, K. Lawson, Jr.
    1990   *Ancient Conquest Accounts: A Study in Ancient Near Eastern and Biblical History Writing* (JSOTSup, 98; Sheffield: JSOT Press).

PART IV
GENDER IN POST-BIBLICAL LITERATURE

WOMEN IN THE APOCRYPHA AND THE PSEUDEPIGRAPHA

Tal Ilan

It is nothing new to say that the Apocrypha and Pseudepigrapha cannot easily be defined. Consider first the definition of them as Second Temple Jewish literature, which is a standard Jewish definition. Jewish tradition defines this literature as books that were written by Jews after the return from the Babylonian exile, and before the foundation of the rabbinic movement and formation of rabbinic literature. The latter superseded and ultimately suppressed the former. Second Temple literature was considered by the rabbis too late to be canonized, and too theologically incompatible with rabbinic ideology to be studied and preserved. Thus these books are termed 'external books', ספרים חיצוניים (Kahana 1937: vi-xvii; Hartum 1958: 6-7). However, this definition runs into problems on both sides of the chronological divide. If Cyrus' declaration and the return from the Babylonian exile is taken as a starting point, a fair number of biblical books too will have to be considered as Second Temple literature. This means not just the book of Daniel, which is Hellenistic by all accounts (Hartman and Di Lella 1978: 9-18), but probably most of the Ketuvim and, according to some European scholars, a great deal more than those as well (Lemche 1993; Grabbe 1997). If the destruction of the Second Temple is taken as the end point for defining Second Temple literature, a large number of books which are of the same cloth from a literary-genre perspective, and clearly Jewish, will have to be excluded, such as the apocalypses of Baruch and Ezra, which are both to be seen as reactions to the destruction of the Second Temple (Myers 1974: 129-31; Klijn 1976: 107). This definition would also require including in the count the writings of the historian Josephus and of the philosopher Philo, who were both Jews, both wrote during the Second Temple period (in Greek) and were both rejected by their Jewish audience, only to be cherished and preserved by the Christian church.

If this literature is considered as chronologically intertestamental, according to a Christian theological outlook, another set of problems emerges, namely which of the books in this category are really Jewish? It is usually agreed that the books known as the 'Apocrypha', which are canonized by the Catholic Church, are indeed Jewish and date to the Second Temple period (Charles 1913: vii-x), but aside from them, other Christian churches have canonized or preserved a large number of other intertestamental documents, some of them Jewish and dating to the Second Temple period, but certainly not all. Thus, the Ethiopian church has preserved and canonized the book of *Jubilees* (VanderKam 1989: II, xviii-xix). This sectarian document is Jewish and dates to the Second Temple period, as can now be proven by its discovery in Hebrew in the Qumran library (VanderKam and Milik 1994). However, a kindred composition bearing a similar message, namely, the *Testaments of the Twelve Patriarchs*, is a Christian reworking of a Jewish document, in which the borders between Jewish and Christian are blurred to such an extent that the Jewish document is not quite recognizable any more (Hollander and de Jonge 1985: 82-85). Jewishness is also not clearly defined. Thus, while some scholars consider the Syriac *Apocalypse of Baruch* Jewish and almost contemporary with the destruction of the Second Temple (Klijn 1976: 107), a minority opinion considers it Christian and late (Nir 2003). While most scholars think *Joseph and Aseneth* Jewish and Hellenistic-Alexandrian (Chesnutt 1995: 80-85), Ross Kraemer suggested reading it as Syriac-Christian, dating to the sixth century (Kraemer 1998).

For the subject of this essay, this last example is particularly relevant. Several scholars have noted in the past that, unlike in First Temple literature, in Second Temple times women became the subject of a number of compositions. Two biblical books are named after women—Ruth and Esther. One of these (Esther) dates itself to Second Temple times and the other is dated by most scholars to the same period. Similarly, two apocryphal compositions—Judith and Susannah—cast women as their heroines. Several scholars have devoted studies to Second Temple women based on a combination of some or all of these books (LaCocque 1990; Brenner 1995). Larry Wills, in his 1995 study, discussed Esther, Judith and Susanna, together with the book *Joseph and Aseneth* as belonging to the same genre (Wills 1995). Unlike Ross Kraemer, he obviously did not consider the book Christian, or late.

When speaking about Jewish women in the Second Temple period, one would constantly be inquiring, what evidence may be used in order to create a picture, make an argument, put forward a theory? Let me demonstrate this methodological quandary with reference to the last book I mentioned, namely *Joseph and Aseneth*. If we wish to speak about an important issue that is very relevant to Second Temple Judaism, namely, conversion, and if we wish to say something meaningful about women's conversion to Judaism, it would serve as a useful document. Using the biblical figure of Joseph, it tells of his marriage to the daughter of an Egyptian priest (a detail mentioned in a single verse in the Bible) and of her conversion to Judaism in order to meet his standards (an issue that was of no interest to, and therefore completely ignored by, the Bible). If, together with Larry Wills, we consider this document as Jewish and early we could deduce from it quite a number of things about women and Judaism in Second Temple times. We could infer, first, that intermarriage was a burning issue for Jews in the Hellenistic Diaspora, especially in Alexandria (Zlotnick 2002: 92-102); second, that in the Second Temple period women as well as men were required to convert (Chesnutt 1995: 153-84); and third, that this conversion entailed a process and ritual later completely rejected by rabbinic Judaism in favour of other measures (Kee 1983). If, on the other hand, together with Ross Kraemer we consider this document as Christian and late, we may perhaps be able to deduce from it that Christianity required the conversion of women, which would be unsurprising and no novelty.

I have presented this example so as to demonstrate some of the methodological problems confronted by scholars of Second Temple literature in general and of Jewish women in the Second Temple in particular. I will now briefly define the corpus of texts I have chosen to use, and defend my approach as concisely as possible, after which I will move on to discuss in some detail a number of chosen themes, which will both demonstrate the issue at hand and give a very general idea about how the lot of Jewish women as it appears in this literature differed, on the one hand from that of their biblical foremothers, and on the other from that of their rabbinic descendants.

For my purpose, Second Temple Jewish literature is defined as follows. The chief, undeniably Jewish texts are those of Josephus and Philo. Both were apologists for Judaism, and both strove to present it to their non-Jewish audience as a complete, ideal system. As such, their treatment of Jewish women is more direct and less incidental than that of other compositions. Next, I consider the writings of the Qumran library as Jewish. While the Qumranites were, in my opinion, clearly a well defined and unique Jewish sect, with unconventional and marginal approaches to Judaism and its various components (including women), they also preserved a large non-sectarian library, which included many texts that are relevant to the issue at hand. Both groups of documents are important in this context—the sectarian documents as an example of an alternative branch of Judaism that died out (and thus 'the way not taken' in the approach to women), and the other documents so as to help define the Jewish corpus of the Apocrypha and Pseudepigrapha. The well-defined corpus of the Catholic Apocrypha comes next. This collection of books was singled out early by the Christian church as the missing link between biblical Judaism and the New Testament, because they are already part of the Septuagint, the earliest translation of the Hebrew Bible into Greek. It includes 1 and 2 Maccabees, clearly historical compositions devoted to Second Temple times. 1 Maccabees is also cited by Josephus, as is 3 Ezra, another book contained in the Apocrypha. Other fictional books from this collection can also be dated to the same period, such as Ben Sira, copies of which have been found in Hebrew both in Masada and in the Cairo Genizah, and fragments of which have been found in Qumran,[1] and Tobit, the Aramaic vorlage of which was also discovered in Qumran (Fitzmyer 1995). I take it on trust that the other compositions in this collection are also of the same cloth,

---

1. Historical Dictionary of the Hebrew Language 1973.

particularly since they do not display any Christian theological proclivities. Thus, we gain as Jewish compositions the two books whose heroines are women, Judith and Susanna. Apocryphal compositions not directly associated with the Catholic Apocrypha I treat with more caution. *Jubilees* and *1 Enoch* have a Hebrew and Aramaic *Vorlage* in Qumran (VanderKam 1989; Milik 1976). They are certainly Jewish and Second Temple. *3 Maccabees* and the *Letter of Aristeas* are quoted by Josephus (*Ant.* 12.11-118; *Apion* 2.52-54), proving their antiquity. All other texts (including *Joseph and Aseneth*) require further proof before they can be considered relevant for my corpus. I also generally speaking take as Second Temple Jewish literature the fragments of Hellenistic Jewish writers preserved by Alexander Polyhistor via the Church father Eusebius,[2] but these are not very relevant for gender issues.

It has been noted by Neusner that the Hebrew Bible has no system of women, but that rabbinic literature does (Neusner 1980). This means that in the Hebrew Bible women are mentioned randomly, without a theoretical framework to explain and define their unique position vis-à-vis men. Rabbinic literature, on the other hand, beginning with the Mishnah, devoted a sixth of its corpus (*Seder Nashim*) to women. The rabbis created a system in which women, as a complex issue, were theoretically and then practically defined. I take it as a given that this system is not a *creatio ex nihilo*, and I consider Second Temple literature the experimental ground on which various theories about women were tested and then discarded or adopted on the way to becoming the formative Judaism of the Mishnah. Some of these theories I will demonstrate here.

Let me start with women's creation. The second creation story of Genesis (Genesis 2), together with the story of the sin in Eden and the fall (Genesis 3), are the closest the Hebrew Bible comes to forming some philosophical existential explanation for the differences between men and women. However, as noted by many (Meyers 1988: 72-78), this story was for a long time of marginal existence in Jewish consciousness. Thus, it is nowhere quoted in the Hebrew Bible itself as a justification for the position of women. Even in post-biblical literature, as demonstrated by scholars, Jews preferred the story of Genesis 6 about the copulation of the sons of God with the daughters of man as a way of explaining sin and suffering in this world (Schwartz 2001: 74-87). Ben Sira, who can be dated by his own admission to the first half of the second century BCE, is probably the first author to mention the idea that humankind's fall was brought about by a woman. He says, 'From woman does sin emerge, and because of her we will all die' (25.24). This verse has usually been interpreted as referring to the temptation of Eve by the serpent, and to the punishment humankind has suffered as a result. However, the reference is not explicit. No names are mentioned, neither are the Garden of Eden, nor the Tree of Knowledge nor the serpent. One scholar, John Levison, actually made so bold as to suggest that

---

2. See in particular Holladay (1983–96).

this reference is not to the creation story at all; rather, he argued that since it is embedded in the discussion of a bad wife, it refers to the harmful actions of a wife, which bring death to her husband (Levison 1985). In any case, as shown by Trenchard (Trenchard 1983), Ben Sira has a very low opinion of women, and this text can be seen as no more than another one of his own virulent misogynistic observations, based on no precedent at all.

The story of woman's creation and the fall is, however, retold by three Second Temple compositions, the earliest being the book of *Jubilees*, followed by Philo and Josephus. In all three, the biblical story is not much expanded. In *Jubilees* 3 the story of the temptation and fall agrees almost word for word with Genesis 3. However, an interesting variant is displayed in the formulation of the punishment meted out to the woman (cf. Gen. 3.16). She is informed that her 'return' rather than her 'desire' will be to her man, and thus he will rule over her (*Jub.* 3.24). This alternative reading is obviously based on an alternative Hebrew *Vorlage* that had the word תשובתך instead of תשוקתך in it, and this manuscript variant is also evident in other early biblical witnesses such as the Septuagint (καὶ πρὸς τὸν ἄνδρα σου ἡ ἀποστροφή σου) and Onkelos translations (ולות בעליך תיובתיך). It may be interpreted as having minor theological repercussions. 'Return', תשובה, can be interpreted as repentance. If the woman is to repent to her man, rather than to God, this may suggest that God is placing the man in an intermediary position between himself and the woman, creating a sharper hierarchy than the one described in the Masoretic Bible. However, even if this is a correct reading of the *Jubilees* text, it should be remembered that this variant is not unique to *Jubilees*, is very old, and may preserve the original intention of the biblical author.

Instead, what *Jubilees* is clearly interested in is using the creation story to explain the differences in women's impurity resulting from the birth or a son or a daughter. For a son she is unclean for one week, and for a daughter, two (*Jub.* 3.8-14). Yet these differences are already spelt out in the Bible itself (Lev. 12.1-5), so that *Jubilees* neither adds to nor detracts from the biblical picture of women's role in the suffering of mankind. The novelty here is in the use of the creation story to justify gender inequality described elsewhere in the Bible. As we shall see, this 'midrashic' tendency becomes full-blown in rabbinic literature.

Josephus is even less innovative than *Jubilees* in his reworking of the Adam and Eve story. It is an exact paraphrase of the biblical story, told with less grace. If anything, the role of the woman is diminished rather than enhanced. She is punished with birth-pangs, but her subordination to her husband is downplayed (*Ant.* 1.49).

Philo introduces some interesting and meaningful philosophical innovations in his use of this story to conceptualize the existential position of women. In accordance with Aristotelian philosophy, Philo held the opinion that women were essentially inferior to men. Thus, he writes with regard to the special Jewish laws:

> ... the male is more complete, more dominant than the female, closer akin to causal activity, for the female is incomplete and in subjugation and belongs to the category of passive rather than active. So too with the two ingredients which constitute our life principle, the rational and the irrational; the rational which belongs to mind and reason is of the masculine gender, the irrational, the province of the sense, is of the feminine. Mind belongs to a genus as wholly superior to sense as man is to woman (*Spec. leg.* 1.37 [201]).[3]

Due to this conception, and to his allegorical understanding of the biblical narrative, he writes of the creation of woman:

> And woman becomes for (Adam) the beginning of blameworthy life. For as long as he was by himself, as accorded with such solitude, he went on growing like to the world and like God, and receiving in his soul the impressions made by the nature of each ... (*Op. mund.* 53 [151]).

This statement seems to contradict God's biblical observation that 'It is not good for Adam to be alone (לא טוב היות האדם לבדו)' (Gen. 2.18). It continues, however, with the words,

> But when woman too had been made, beholding a figure like his own and a kindred form, he was gladdened by the sight, and approached and greeted her... Love supervenes, brings together and fits into one the divided halves, as it were, of a single living creature, and sets up in each of them a desire for fellowship... (*Op. mund.* 53 [151-2]).

One might well wonder what could be so bad about that. Philo proceeds to explain: 'And this desire begat likewise bodily pleasure, that pleasure which is the beginning of wrongs and violation of the law' (*Op. mund.* 53 [152]). According to Philo the very creation of woman upsets the neat order of a male world. This construction does not complement but actually contradicts the ethos of the creation story in Genesis. Thus, when the woman yields to the serpent's temptations, Philo explains this as follows:

> It is said that she, without looking into the suggestion, prompted by a mind devoid of steadfastness and firm foundation, gave her consent and ate of the fruit and gave some of it to her husband (*Op. mund.* 55 [156]).

Yet Philo's understanding of this story is overtly allegorical. He continues:

> Pleasure does not venture to bring her wiles and deceptions to bear on the man, but on the woman, and by her means on him ... for in us mind corresponds to man, the senses to woman; and pleasure encounters and holds parley with the senses first and through them cheats ... the sovereign mind itself (*Op. mund.* 59 [165]).

Thus, Adam is not really Adam and Eve is not really Eve, and the purpose of this biblical account is not to account for the subordinate position of women

---

3. Interestingly, Philo resorts to this gender division in his analysis of male and female sacrificial animals. On Philo and gender in general see Wegner (1991); Sly (1990); Mattila (1996); Baynes (2002).

in the world. This position is, according to Philo, self-evident. The biblical account is an allegory for the human psyche, and how the senses work on the mind and corrupt it. It uses the well-known subordination of women in order to explain more complex psychological theories. I would conclude that Philo's contribution to the conceptualization of the creation narrative as formative for the position of women in Judaism is his use of women's self-evident inferiority allegorically. Such thinking was obviously pervasive in his days. It was taken over from the Greek Aristotelian philosophical discourse and endorsed by Jewish Hellenistic thinkers.

Thus, for example, in the *Letter of Aristeas*, when the Jewish sages who will eventually translate the Bible into Greek meet with the Ptolemaic King in a symposium, one of them remarks, '[R]ealizing that the female sex are rash and energetic in pursuing their desire, and fickle through fallacious reasoning and of naturally weak constitution, [o]ne must deal with them sanely...' (*Aristeas* 250).

At this point it is worth noting that although a full blown Adam-and-Eve literature did develop in post-biblical times, and has been extensively researched and discussed within the context of apocryphal literature, none of it can be definitively dated to the intertestamental, or Second Temple, period, or definitively proven to be Jewish rather than Christian.[4] Christian fascination with Eve and the fall is notorious. These texts will, therefore, not be further discussed in this context.

In rabbinic literature, Eve's role as seductress and the source of all evil in the world is fully developed. In Genesis Rabbah we read,

> They asked Rabbi Joshua: Why does a man have sex with his face downward, and the woman with her face upward? He said to them: The man looks at the place of his creation and the woman to the place of her creation. Why does a woman need perfume while the man does not? He said to them: Adam was created from earth, and earth does not stink, but Eve was created from a bone, and if you leave meat standing for three days without salt it begins to stink. Why is a woman's voice high, and a man's is not? He said to them this is like a bowl filled with meat. If you shake it, it makes no noise, once you place a bone in it, immediately it makes a noise. Why is the man easily tempted, but the woman is not? He said: Adam was created from earth. If you spill even a drop of water on it, immediately it absorbs it, but Eve was created from a bone and even if you submerge it in water several days, it does not absorb the water. Why does a man approach a woman sexually but not vice versa? He said to them: To what may this be likened? To someone who has lost something. He searches for his loss, but it does not search for him ... Why does a man go out with his head uncovered but a woman does not? He said to them: This is like one who sinned and is ashamed, therefore she goes out with her head covered. Why do they go first in a funeral? He said to them: Since they brought death to the world, therefore they go first in a funeral ... Why were they given the commandment of menstruation? Because she spilled the blood of Adam, therefore the commandment

---

4. See the careful analysis of the issue in Stone (1992: 42-74).

of menstruation was given to her. And why was the commandment of Hallah-dough given to her? He said to them: Because she spoiled Adam, who was the Hallah-dough of the world, therefore was the Hallah-dough commandment given to her. And why was the commandment of the Sabbath candle given to her? He said to them, because she extinguished the soul of Adam, who was the world's candle (*Gen. R.* 17.8).

This text systematically reworks the Genesis narrative so as to indict woman for bringing death into the world, and to explain her resultant subordinate and lowly position. Even the three commandments which the rabbis identified as unique to women—menstruation, Hallah-dough and lighting the Sabbath candle—are seen here as punishments for her sin (*m. Šab.* 2.6). The late midrash of Abot de Rabbi Nathan adds to this catalogue of punishments:

> With ten curses was Eve cursed at that time: 'I shall multiply your pains' (Genesis 3.16) these are two bloods: Pains of the blood of menstruation and pains of the blood of virginity. 'Your pregnancies' (*ibid.*) this is the pain of pregnancy. 'In pain you shall bear sons' (*ibid.*) as is plainly stated. 'To your husband is your desire' indicates that a woman longs for her husband when he is away. 'And he shall rule over you'—the man demands the woman verbally, but she can only demand him in her heart. She is wrapped up like a mourner and locked in prison, and is banned from all people (*ARN* 1.1).

One could argue that the rabbis' fascination with the fall story is influenced by their Christian neighbours, but this does not detract from the systematic approach to this story that can be observed in their writings.

As noted, the book of *Jubilees* downplays the role of Eve in the bringing of evil into the world. Instead it blames the fall of humankind on the actions of the sons of God mentioned in Genesis 6, who in *Jubilees* are identified with fallen angels (4.15, 22; 5.1-2, 6-11). These, we are told in the Bible, observed the daughters of man from above, became enamoured of them and seduced them, begetting giant offspring (Gen. 6.1-4). This alternative fall story was particularly popular in certain circles in Second Temple times. This is indicated not just by the book of *Jubilees*, but also by the story's presence in the Book of the Watchers, the earliest part of *1 Enoch*, which is generally dated to the third century BCE and is the earliest recognizable Jewish apocalypse (VanderKam 1984: 111-14). This book initiated a millennium-long period of speculation about the enigmatic figure of the biblical Enoch. That it was adopted as authoritative by the Qumran sectarians demonstrates its radical, anti-establishment nature. It has a fuller and more instructive discussion of the second fall account than *Jubilees*, particularly in relation to the role of women. In the biblical account women are also involved in the second fall story, but they could be construed as the victims of rape at the hands of the sons of God. In Enoch's version they play a more active role, and are also allotted a more central position in the cosmic order. We are told that the fallen angels taught the daughters of man a number of useful skills: the wearing of jewellery and make-up (*1 Enoch* 8.1), obviously in order to allure men; the properties of roots and plants, for medicinal purposes, but obviously also for poisoning; and witchcraft (7.1).

Enoch's accusation against women that they are the initiators and originators of magic in this world is not the oldest such claim. Already in the Book of the Covenant in Exodus we read, 'You shall not suffer a witch (מכשפה) to live' (Exod. 22.17). The form מכשפה is feminine. Thus, this legal injunction may be understood as singling out women as engaging in witchcraft. However, this may not be the only possible interpretation of this text. The word מכשפה can be understood as an abstract noun, in the same way as a Hebrew word like מגפה, 'disease', in which case it would refer to witchcraft in general, and the phrase could be translated as 'you shall not tolerate witchcraft'. When King Saul initiates the earliest witch-hunt in history we are told that he removed the sorcerers and necromancers (האובות והידעונים) (1 Sam. 28.3), who are designated using masculine nouns. Thus, the description in *1 Enoch* is probably the earliest wholesale association of magic with women in Jewish literature. In rabbinic literature this association is endorsed and justified. In answer to the question of why the biblical text particularly singles out witches and not wizards, the rabbis answer with resounding clarity that the law refers to both males and females, but 'witchcraft was named after women … because most women engage in witchcraft' (*y. San.* 7.19, 25d; *b. San.* 67b), or, in an alternative version, 'most witchcraft is found among women' (*Mek. SbY.* 22.17).[5] The development from the Bible to rabbinic literature, and the middle position evident in post-biblical *1 Enoch* is, in this case, clear.

Judith Plaskow's book on feminist Jewish theology bears the title *Standing again at Sinai*. She chose this title because she observed the interesting phenomenon that the biblical text of מתן תורה—the giving of the Torah at Mt Sinai—implies that only men were its recipients. She deduces this from the verse in Exodus which describes Moses' injunction to the Israelites: 'Be ready in three days, do not go near a woman' (Exod. 19.15), that those who should be ready for the revelation are also those who should not go near a woman, namely men. The question of Jewish women's full participation in the covenant, and through it in Judaism itself, is open. The Jewish covenant consists first of all of circumcision, in which women have no part, and secondly in the fulfilment of the Torah. If women were not among the recipients of the Torah, they certainly are not required to fulfil it to the same degree as do men. This issue is systematically conceptualized by the rabbis, whose awareness of this conundrum is great. It is of some interest to see how Second Temple literature tackled this problem. Thus, both Josephus and Philo assume the presence of women at the convocation in Sinai. Josephus writes, 'Withal they partook of more sumptuous fare and arrayed themselves, along with their *wives* and children, in splendid attire' (*Ant.* 3.78). Philo's words are as follows: 'The ten words or oracles, in reality laws or statutes, were delivered by the Father of All when the nation, men and women alike, were assembled together' (*Dec.* 9 [32]).

---

5. For more on this see Ilan (2006: 214-58).

It is not difficult to show that, for the rabbis too, the question of women's participation in the Sinai event was of vital importance. Thus, the *Mekilta de Rabbi Ishmael* observed that, based on the verse 'Do not go near a woman' (Exod. 19.15), 'a woman who emits semen on the third day (after intercourse) is pure. This is proven from Sinai' (*Mek.,* Yitro, Bahodesh 3). This text implies that the men did not go near women for three days, so that women as well as men would be pure at the moment of the Torah revelation. Thus, the assumptions of both Josephus and Philo are mirrored in the writings of the rabbinic school of Rabbi Ishmael, indicating a continuum of concerns regarding gender and the covenant. However, this midrash is only found in the *Mekilta de Rabbi Ishmael* and may be a minority opinion. The Mishnah and the Babylonian Talmud do not emphasize women's presence at Sinai. On the contrary, one can infer from their interpretation of the seventh-year gathering devoted to Torah study that is described in Deuteronomy something of their attitude to women in the Sinai revelation as well. On the verse 'Gather the people, men, women and children' (Deut. 31.12), the rabbis ask, 'If the men come to learn and the women to listen, why do children come?' (*b. Hag.* 3a). This question is first and foremost intended to indicate a hierarchical participation in the gathering event, where women's presence, according to the rabbis (but not according to the Bible), is of an inferior value to men's.

The fact that Philo and Josephus take pains to include women in the Sinai revelation does not imply that they viewed them as of equal standing in the face of the law. We can trace the development of the attitude to women's participation in the halakah through Second Temple literature because, despite the fact that this phase in Jewish history saw the first antinomist Jewish movement (namely Christianity), most Jewish groups, including the Jesus movement in Jesus' lifetime, shaped their identity in relation to the Jewish law. Thus, Philo, despite his allegorical reading of the Bible, took the fulfilment of the commandments very seriously. He described in great detail what they are and how (and why) they are to be followed. Josephus wrote his own version of the Mosaic laws, emphasizing the adherence to the commandments. The Qumran sect was a highly legally-minded group that defined itself over and against its opponents in its disagreements on questions of halakah. The book of *Jubilees* is a legal codex.

A large number of issues concerning women, which are quite clearly formulated in the Mishnah but which have no antecedent in the Bible, have their roots in Second Temple literature. For example, while the Mishnah includes an entire tractate devoted to women's marriage contracts—namely, Tractate *Ketubot*—a marriage contract as such is nowhere mentioned in the Bible itself. Does this mean that biblical Jews did not know of such a document, or is this only the result of the Bible's disinterest in the formulation of a legal system for women? A straightforward answer to such a question is not forthcoming, but there may be hints to it. For example, Aramaic documents from the Jewish settlement at

Elephantine in Egypt, which was contemporary with the latest events related in the Bible, include Jewish marriage contracts belonging to Jewish women.[6] These documents do not fit the halakic description of a Jewish marriage contract mentioned in the Mishnah, for they specify, for example, that a wife could initiate her own divorce, but this is obviously because the *ketubbah*, as the rabbis imagined it, had not yet come into existence. As an intermediate stage we may observe the marriage contract written by Tobias to his wife Sarah in the apocryphal book of Tobit. One translation from the Greek reads at this point in the narrative, 'And he called her mother and told her to bring a book, and he wrote an instrument of co-habitation, even that he (the father) gave her (Sarah) to him (Tobias) to wife according to the decree of the Law of Moses'[7] (Tob. 7.13). This is very different from the rabbinic *ketubbah*. It is a document between a father and a son-in-law. It is called a 'book' (βιβλίον), like the ספר כריתות of the Jewish divorce bill mentioned in the Bible (Deut. 24.1), but not a כתובה as in rabbinic literature. Yet the formulation 'according to the decree of the Law of Moses' is certainly parallel to the כדת משה ויהודאי that is mentioned in the rabbinic *ketubbah* of *y. Yeb.* 15.3, 14d, and is already attested in the documents from the Bar Kokhba period (Yadin *et al.* 2002: 126).

A similar issue is the question of divorce. The Bible mentions a bill of divorce (ספר כריתות) which a man writes for a woman, but as noted by some scholars, this law is not formulated so as to advise male Jews about how to divorce their wives. Rather, it emphasizes the unusual case of a man who divorces a woman, and the woman then goes and marries another man from whom she is subsequently also divorced. The Bible rules that, in such a case, the first husband cannot take her back (Deut. 24.1-4). Thus, the mention of the divorce document is incidental, and does not describe the document or how it normally functioned. For example, it does not imply that only a man could write such a document to a woman, and not vice versa. That this was how this biblical injunction was eventually understood by the rabbis is no indication that this is indeed how it had always functioned in Jewish society. Thus, Josephus informs us that the sister of Herod wrote a divorce bill and sent it to her husband (*Ant.* 15.259-60). Josephus is quick to add that this is against Jewish custom, and modern scholars have universally adopted his judgment, claiming that the woman had done this in her capacity as a Roman citizen, but not as a Jew. It turns out, however, that Josephus here is voicing his opinion in a debate that was raging at the time about a woman's right to divorce her husband, and which was still not definitively concluded sixty years later, when a certain Jewish woman, Shelamzion daughter of Joseph, wrote a divorce bill to her husband, and the document was preserved and discovered in the Judaean Desert.[8] Although the

6. See most recently Porten and Yardeni (1989).
7. See Charles (1913: 222).
8. See Cotton and Yardeni (1997: 67) and see also Ilan (1999: 253-62).

words of the document are quite straightforward, a standing academic debate is under way about whether this is indeed what the document means, or whether it should be interpreted differently.[9] The reason for this dispute is, of course, the preconceived notion of most scholars that rabbinic literature represented both the Judaism of its time, and the Judaism that preceded it. This notion, however, contains a fallacy which this essay aims to expose and critique. The fact that in this debate Josephus endorses the opinion of the future rabbis is a good indication that the rabbis were indeed the heirs of the Pharisees. Josephus, as is well known, was a self-declared Pharisee (*Vita* 12).

Divorce is not the only issue on which Josephus agrees with the rabbis, but on which others, whose voices are preserved in Second Temple literature, differed. Thus, although the topic is never handled by the Bible, Josephus states explicitly that women are barred from serving as witnesses in Jewish courts of law. He adds an explanation to this prohibition, which Thackeray translates, 'because of the levity (κουφότητα) and temerity (θράσος) of their sex' (*Ant.* 4.219). In other words, he states that women are too frivolous to engage in such grave activities as giving evidence in court. The rabbis too exempted women from giving evidence, and elsewhere, in another context, also concluded that women are light-headed (*b. Qid.* 80b). Yet this unison of voices between Josephus and the rabbis is interrupted by the evidence from Qumran. In the Rule of the Community (סרך העדה) we are informed that at the age of twenty, once members of the sect marry, their wives are called upon to bear witness against them in cases where they transgress the ruling of the community (1QSa 1.9-11). This text has also been variously read and disputed. Some have suggested alternative readings and some have proposed alternative interpretations.[10] However, the simple meaning of the text is that in the Qumran community, where members were constantly expected to testify against (or according to other terminology, to betray) their fellow members, women were expected to participate in the system as well. Whether understood positively, as empowering women, or negatively, as using them as instruments in a totalitarian system,[11] this text shows that the exemption of women from giving evidence was in Second Temple times anything but universal.

From the above-mentioned examples one could gain the impression that from biblical times onward women's position in society deteriorated from bad to worse. Yet the direction was not always this one. One of the issues that was hotly debated in Second Temple literature was the question of women's presence in public. The Bible does not seem to have conceptualized this issue. Women were neither forbidden to appear in public nor encouraged to do so. The

---

9. See Schremer (1998); Brody (1999); Fitzmyer (1999); also Cotton and Qimron (1998); Instone Brewer (1999).
10. See most recently Davies and Taylor (1996); Rothstein (2003).
11. See also my interpretation in Ilan (1999: 38-42).

woman of valour of Proverbs 31, for example, seems to be out and about all the time, particularly in the market place. She is compared to a merchant ship that travels far and wide to win her bread (31.14). This concept is not criticized. Yet, in Second Temple times this was a hotly debated issue. Ben Sira, whose main source of influence was Proverbs, modified this picture drastically. He maintained that a person should keep his daughter under lock and key:

> Over thy daughter keep a strict watch ... in the place where she lodges let there be no lattice, or spot overlooking the entrance round about. Let her not show her beauty to any male and among wives let her not converse (Sir. 42.11-12).

The issue is summarized more systematically by Philo:

> Market places and council halls and law-courts and gatherings and meetings where a large number of people are assembled, and open-air life with full scope for discussion and action—all these are suitable for men both in war and peace. The women are best suited to the indoor life which never strays from the house, within which the middle door is taken by the maidens as their boundary, and the outer door by those who have reached full womanhood. Organized communities are of two sorts, the greater, which we call cities, and the smaller, which we call households. Both of these have their governors; the government of the greater is assigned to men under the name of statesmanship, that of the lesser, known as household management, to women. A woman, then, should not be a busybody, meddling with matters outside her household concerns, but should seek a life of seclusion. She should not show herself off like a vagrant in the street before the eyes of other men, except when she has to go to the temple, and even then she should take pains to go not when the market is full, but when most people have gone home, and so like a free-born lady worthy of the name, with everything quiet around her, make her oblations and offer her prayers to avert the evil and gain the good (*Spec. Leg.* 3.31 [169-71]).

The ideal voiced by these two Second Temple Jewish thinkers is realized and glorified in the literary creation Judith. Although Judith is a very public heroine who goes out among men and beats them at their own game, when she is not required to act in an emergency she 'was a widow in her house three years and four months. And she made her tent on the roof of her house and put on sackcloth upon her loins and the garments of widowhood upon her, and she fasted all the days of her widowhood ...' (Jdt. 8.4-6). This woman voluntarily confines herself to exactly the sort of spaces recommended by Ben Sira and Philo. This is a pertinent opportunity to remember that the text from the rabbinic midrash Abot de Rabbi Nathan cited earlier counted among Eve's curses the fact that a woman is locked up in her house as a prisoner in jail.

Josephus, it may be noted, does not join in this clamour to confine women to their houses. In this he is not alone. The rabbis too, did not believe in confining women to the house as prisoners. However, unlike Josephus, who simply ignores the issue, the rabbis, as they are wont to do, approach it systematically. In *t. Sot.* 5.9 an interesting metaphor is used to illustrate how women should be treated with regard to freedom of movement. The metaphor describes how people respond when a fly falls into their drink. The most extreme approach is of a person who throws the whole drink away, and this is like the man who locks his wife at home (as Ben Sira and Philo suggest). The rabbis name a certain Pappus Ben Yehudah as acting so and condemn him. An extreme approach in the other direction is of a person who picks the fly out of his drink, sucks it and drinks his beverage. This, in the eyes of the rabbis, should be compared to a man whose wife goes out in the marketplace dressed indecently and with head uncovered, works in the public domain, and washes in public with other men (presumably in a mixed-sex Roman bathhouse). This action they also condemn, for they think that such a woman should be divorced without compensation. The middle ground is a person who finds a fly in his drink, removes it and consumes his drink. This is likened to a man who allows his wife to go out to the market and speak to her male and female neighbours, as well as to all her relatives. This, in the rabbis' opinion, is what most people do, and is also the proper way to deal with women and the public domain. As can be seen, this is not a feminist liberation manifesto, but it is certainly much less oppressive than what is written in Philo. Thus once again, Josephus the Pharisee and the rabbis are found to hold similar opinions on the position of women.

The issue of women's position within Jewish society seems on this score to confirm historical assertions made by scholars about the affinity between Josephus and the Pharisees, and between these and the rabbis. Another assertion made by scholars, ever since the Qumran discovery, and even more so in recent years, is that whoever the Qumranites may be (Essenes, Sadducees, neither or both),[12] they are certainly not Pharisees or rabbis, for their halakah directly contradicts that of the rabbis. By contrast with this, some of the most recent scholarship on Qumran focuses on a comparative approach between the Dead Sea Scrolls and rabbinic literature, with the aim of showing that many of the concerns embedded in the Mishnah are already a (sometimes contested) halakic issue in Second Temple times.[13]

In most cases we find the Qumranites and the rabbis on two sides of the divide. However, when it comes to the position of women, this is not always true. An important phenomenological example can here be presented. In rabbinic literature women are often lumped together with slaves, minors and other underprivileged individuals, such as the lame and the blind, as exempt from performing certain commandments.[14] In Mishnah *Qiddušin* this exemption procedure is standardized by the claim that women are obligated to perform all the negative commandments ('thou shalt not') and all positive commandments that are not dependent on time, but are exempt from all positive time-bound

---

12. For a discussion of the various possibilities, see VanderKam (1999).

13. See for other examples Yadin (2003); Fonrobert (2004). The chief scholar who follows this path is A. Shemesh, see e.g. Shemesh (2004, 2005) (Hebrew), and particularly in our context Shemesh (1998).

14. See my essay on woman as 'other' in rabbinic literature (Ilan, 2007).

commandments (*m. Qid.* 1.7). A closer look at these positive time-bound commandments shows that they mainly involve rituals, with the result that women are exempted from a significant percentage of Jewish ritual life. Thus, women are exempt from residing in the Sukkah or from putting on phylacteries (see *t. Qid.* 1.10). This categorization and exemption is a complete novelty. Nothing even remotely resembling it is found in the Bible.

Here, however, the Qumran material can be used as middle ground between the Bible and the rabbis, rather than as a counter-example to other halakic concerns. First of all, the same sort of lists are found in Qumran as in rabbinic literature. Thus, the Damascus Document reads:

> Every fool (אויל) or mentally sick or simpleton (פתי) and day-dreamer and the blind who does not see and the lame and amputated or the deaf or the small child, none of these should enter the congregation, because holy angels are present (CD 15.15-17; cf. 4Q266).

Thus, in Qumran, the presence of the holy angels within the camp explains why a large number of people who are not perfect are exempt from participation in the communal institutions of the congregation (the יחד). Women are not mentioned in this list. This is probably not an accidental omission. The list has survived in two versions of the text, one from Qumran (4Q266) and one from the Cairo Genizah (CD), and neither includes women. This probably indicates that women did participate in the public life of the congregation.[15]

However, another Qumran text suggests a different view. When describing the war camp, *The War of the Sons of Light against the Sons of Darkness* gives the following list:

> All will be included between the ages of 25 and 30, and all young children and women will not approach the camp when they go forth from Jerusalem to go to war and until they return. Neither shall any lame or blind or amputated or any man who is deformed or stricken in his flesh go out to war with them. All shall be perfect in spirit and flesh ... and any man who is impure in his private parts on the day of war will not go down with them, because holy angels are with their army (1QM 7.3-6).

The exclusion of certain groups from the war camp is explained in the same way as the exclusion from the communal institutions—the presence of holy angels. But while this did not induce the Qumranites to exclude women from the community institutions, it does explain why women are excluded from the war camp.[16] The inclusion or exclusion of women in such lists in Qumran is similar

---

15. On women in the Qumran community see now Schuller (1999); Crawford (2003).

16. Why the presence of women and angels together may be a problem is not obvious. One might speculate that women are not as holy as men, and therefore do not deserve to be in the angels' presence. However, there may be another, altogether different explanation. Perhaps it could be explained with reference to the strong attachment of the Qumranites to the story of the copulation of the fallen angels with the daughters of men (see above) as the origin of sin in the world. It seems to be the reason why, when Paul tells women in Corinth to cover their heads, he justifies his instruction by reference to the presence of angels (1 Cor. 11.10).

to their inclusion or exclusion in similar rabbinic lists (e.g. *m. Ber.* 3.3; *m. Hag.* 1.1; *m. Par.* 4.5). The lumping of women together with minors and deformed individuals is thus not a purely rabbinic invention. Although the rabbis do not explain the rejection of persons mentioned in these lists as resulting from the presence of angels, they do find this list, or others similar to it, useful.

Also, the exclusion of women from the war camp is not the only such halakah found in Qumran. Thus, a fragment from Cave 4 reads, 'A small boy and a woman shall not partake of the Pesah sacrifice' (4Q265). Here, as in rabbinic literature, women are lumped together with minors. They are also excluded from a Jewish ritual which is a positive commandment and is time-bound. In this the Qumranites resemble the rabbis conceptually. However, it may be of interest to note that, despite the rabbinic formulation that exempts women from positive, time-bound commandments, the rabbis do not exempt, but rather include, both women and minors in the celebration and consumption of the Pesah sacrifice (*m. Pes.* 8.1-3). This is probably an indication of how the two groups differed on minor (and sometimes major) points of law but held a common assumption about gender hierarchy, the partial participation of women in Jewish life, and women's affinity to both minors and to deformed and maimed individuals.

In conclusion, I think these examples suffice to show that Second Temple Jewish literature is a useful tool in the investigation of Jewish women's position on the historical-chronological continuum between the first Jewish scripture, namely, the Bible, and the second one, namely, the Mishnah and Talmud. They are an important tool for the understanding and reconstruction of Jewish women's history.

BIBLIOGRAPHY

Baynes, Leslie
    2002   'Philo, Personification and the Transformation of Grammatical Gender', *Studia Philonica Annual* 14: 31-47.

Brenner, Athalya (ed.)
    1995   *A Feminist Companion to Esther, Judith and Susanna* (FCB, 7; Sheffield: Sheffield Academic Press).

Brody, Robert
    1999   'Evidence for Divorce by Jewish Women?', *JJS* 50: 230-34.

Charles, R.H.
    1913   *The Apocrypha and Pseudepigrapha of the Old Testament*. I. *Apocrypha* (Oxford: Clarendon Press).

Chesnutt, Randall D.
    1995   *From Death to Life: Conversion in Joseph and Aseneth* (JSPSup, 16; Sheffield: Sheffield Academic Press).

Cotton, Hannah M., and Elisha Qimron
    1998   'XHev/Se ar 13 of 134 or 135 CE: A Wife's Renunciation of Claims', *JJS* 49: 108-18.

Cotton, Hannah M., and Ada Yardeni (eds.)
    1997   *Aramaic, Hebrew and Greek Documentary Texts from Nahal Hever and*

Crawford, Sidnie White
    2003   'Not According to Rule: Women, the Dead Sea Scrolls and Qumran', in Shalom M. Paul, Robert A. Kraft, Lawrence H. Schiffman and Weston W. Fields (eds.), *Emanuel: Studies in Hebrew Bible, Septuagint, and Dead Sea Scrolls in Honor of Emanuel Tov* (VTSup, 94; Leiden: E.J. Brill): 127-50.

Davies, Philip R., and Joan E. Taylor
    1996   'On the Testimony of Women in 1QSa', *DSD* 3: 223-35.

Fitzmyer, Joseph
    1995   'Tobit', in Magen Broshi *et al.* (eds.), *Qumran Cave 4. XIV. Parabiblical Texts, Part 2* (DJD, 19; Oxford: Clarendon Press): 1-76.
    1999   'The So-Called Aramaic Divorce Text from Wadi Seiyal', *Eretz Israel* 26: 16*-22*.

Flint, Peter W., and James C. VanderKam (eds.)
    1999   *The Dead Sea Scrolls After Fifty Years* (2 vols.; Leiden: E.J. Brill).

Fonrobert, Charlotte
    2004   'From Separatism to Urbanism: The Dead Sea Scrolls and the Origins of the Rabbinic "Eruv" ', *DSD* 11: 43-71.

Grabbe, Lester L. (ed.)
    1997   *Can a 'History of Israel' be Written?* (JSOTS, 245; ESHM, 1; Sheffield: Sheffield Academic Press).

Hartman, Louis F., and Alexander A. Di Lella
    1978   *The Book of Daniel* (AB, 23; Garden City, NY: Doubleday).

Hartum, A.S.
    1958   'General Introduction to the External Books', in *Ha-sefarim ha-hitsoniyim* 1 (Tel Aviv: Yavne): 5-6.

Historical Dictionary of the Hebrew Language
    1973   *The Book of Ben Sira: Text Concordance and an Analysis of the Vocabulary* (Jerusalem: Academy of the Hebrew Language) (Hebrew).

Holladay, Carl R.
    1983-96   *Fragments from Hellenistic Jewish Authors* (Texts and Translations; 4 vols.; Chico, CA: Scholars Press).

Hollander, H.W., and M. de Jonge
    1985   *The Testaments of the Twelve Patriarchs: A Commentary* (SVTP, 8; Leiden: E.J. Brill).

Ilan, Tal
    1999   *Integrating Women into Second Temple History* (TSAJ, 76; Tübingen: Mohr Siebeck).
    2006   *Silencing the Queen: The Literary Histories of Shelamzion and other Jewish Women* (TSAJ, 115; Tübingen: Mohr Siebeck).
    2007   'The Woman as "Other" in Rabbinic Literature', in D. R. Schwartz and J. Frey (eds.), *Jewish Identity in the Greco-Roman World* (Leiden: E.J. Brill): 77-92.
    forthcoming   'The Woman as "Other" in Rabbinic Literature', in D.R. Schwartz and J. Frey (eds.), *Proceedings of the Munich Colloquium on Jewish Identity 2004*.

Instone Brewer, David
    1999   'Jewish Women Divorcing their Husbands in Early Judaism: The Background to Papyrus Se'elim 13', *HTR* 92: 349-57.

Kahana, Avraham
    1937   'General Introduction to the External Books', in *Ha-sefarim ha-hitsoniyim* 1 (Tel Aviv: Mekorot): v-xvii (Hebrew).

Kee, Howard Clark.
    1983   'The Socio-Cultural Setting of Joseph and Aseneth', *NTS* 29: 394-413.

Klijn, A.F.J.
    1976   *Die syrische Baruch-Apokalypse* (Jüdische Schriften aus hellenistisch-römischer Zeit, 5; Gütersloh: Gerd Mohn).

Kraemer, Ross S.
    1998   *When Joseph Met Aseneth: A Late Antique Tale of the Biblical Patriarch and his Egyptian Wife Reconsidered* (New York: Oxford University Press).

LaCocque, André
    1990   *The Feminine Unconventional: Four Subversive Figures in Israel's Tradition* (OBT; Minneapolis: Fortress Press).

Lemche, Niels Peter
    1993   'The Old Testament: A Hellenistic Book?', *SJOT* 7: 163-93.

Levison, John R.
    1985   'Is Eve to Blame? A Contextual Analysis of Sirach 25:24', *CBQ* 47: 617-23.

Mattila, Sharon L.
    1996   'Wisdom, Sense Perception, Nature and Philo's Gender Gradient', *HTR* 89: 103-29.

Meyers, Carol
    1988   *Discovering Eve: Ancient Israelite Women in Context* (Oxford: Oxford University Press).

Milik, J.T. (ed.)
    1976   *The Books of Enoch: Aramaic Fragments of Qumran Cave 4* (Oxford: Clarendon Press).

Myers, Jacob M.
    1974   *I and II Esdras* (AB, 42; Garden City, NY: Doubleday).

Neusner, Jacob
    1980   *A History of the Mishnaic Law of Women. V. The Mishnaic System of Women* (SJLA, 33; Leiden: E.J. Brill).

Nir, Rivka
    2003   *The Destruction of Jerusalem and the Idea of Redemption in the Syriac Apocalypse of Baruch* (EJL, 20; Atlanta: Society of Biblical Literature; Leiden: E.J. Brill).

Porten, Bezalel, and Ada Yardeni (eds.)
    1989   *Textbook of Aramaic Documents from Ancient Egypt. II. Contracts* (Jerusalem: Akademon).

Rothstein, David
    2003   'Women's Testimony at Qumran: The Biblical and Second Temple Evidence', *RevQ* 21: 597-614.

Schremer, Adiel
    1998   'Divorce in Papyrus Se'elim 13 Once Again: A Reply to Tal Ilan', *HTR* 91 (1998): 193-202.

Schuller, Eileen
    1999   'Women in Qumran', in Flint and VanderKam 1999: II, 117-44.

Schwartz, Seth
    2001   *Imperialism and Jewish Society, 200 B.C.E. to 640 C.E.* (Princeton, NJ: Princeton University Press).

Shemesh, Aharon
    1998   '4Q271.3: A Key to Sectarian Matrimonial Law', *JJS* 49: 244-63.
    2004   'Things that have Required Quantities', *Tarbiz* 73: 387-405 (Hebrew).
    2005   'The Laws of Firstborn and the Cattle Tithe in Qumran and Rabbinic Halakhah', *Meghillot: Studies in the Dead Sea Scrolls* 3: 143-61 (Hebrew).

Sly, Dorothy
    1990   *Philo's Perception of Women* (BJS, 209; Atlanta: Scholars Press).

Stone, Michael E.
    1992   *A History of the Literature of Adam and Eve* (EJL, 3; Atlanta: Scholars Press).

Trenchard, Warren C.
    1983   *Ben Sira's View of Women: A Literary Analysis* (BJS, 38; Chico, CA: Scholars Press).

VanderKam, James C.
    1984   *Enoch and the Growth of an Apocalyptic Tradition* (CBQMS, 16; Washington, DC: Catholic Biblical Association of America).
    1989   *The Book of Jubilees* (CSCO; 2 vols.; Louvain: Peeters).
    1999   'Identity and History of the Community', in Flint and VanderKam 1999: 487-533.

VanderKam, James C., and J.T. Milik
    1994   'Jubilees', in Harold Attridge *et al.* (eds.), *Qumran Cave 4*. VIII. *Parabiblical Texts, Part 1* (DJD, 13; Oxford: Clarendon Press): 1-185.

Wegner, Judith Romney
    1991   'Philo's Portrayal of Women: Hebraic or Hellenic?', in Amy-Jill Levine (ed.), *'Women Like This': New Perspectives on Jewish Women in the Greco-Roman World* (EJL, 1; Atlanta: Scholars Press): 41-66.

Wills, Lawrence M.
    1995   *The Jewish Novel in the Ancient World* (Myth and Poetics; Ithaca, NY: Cornell University Press).

Yadin, Azzan
    2003   '4QMMT, Rabbi Ishmael and the Origins of Legal Midrash', *DSD* 10: 130-49.

Yadin, Yigael, *et al.* (eds.)
    2002   *The Finds from the Bar Kokhba Period in the Cave of Letters*. III. *Hebrew Aramaic and Nabatean-Aramaic Papyri* (Jerusalem: Israel Exploration Society).

Zlotnick, Helena
    2002   *Dinah's Daughters: Gender and Judaism from the Hebrew Bible to Late Antiquity* (Philadelphia: University of Pennsylvania Press).

FROM WILD MEN TO WISE AND WICKED WOMEN: AN INVESTIGATION
INTO MALE HETEROSEXUALITY IN SECOND TEMPLE INTERPRETATIONS OF
THE LADIES WISDOM AND FOLLY

Andrew Angel

In response to the issues raised by gender studies, many men have not been quick to reinvent themselves. It is probably still true to say that in Christian theology few men have bitten the bullet of outlining how men ought now to look and behave. One response has been to recommend that all Christian men become 'New Men' (McCloughry 1992; Nelson 1992, 1994). So, for example, James Nelson argues that male sexuality and spirituality are characterized by an overvaluing of earthy phallus ('sweaty, hairy, wet, throbbing animal sexuality') and solar phallus (the male desire to achieve)—the perceived hallmarks of true masculinity (Nelson 1994: 200-19). Men undervalue the flaccid penis, which is soft, smaller and altogether more vulnerable (Nelson 1992: 94-96; Nelson 1994: 199-200). Men need to embrace both phallus and penis for in embracing both lies the key to finding their true masculinity (Nelson 1994: 205-14). Thus, men may discover release from their internal conflicts, their desire to control and dominate, and so find intimacy in relationship which brings with it social, spiritual and sexual fulfilment (Nelson 1992: 79-83).

However, this project has not been without its critics. The North American poet Robert Bly wrote a now well-known critique of the 'New Man' in his book *Iron John*. He noted how many of the 'new men' attending his poetry readings were timid, lifeless and dull. Bly argues that the reason for this was rooted in their loss of masculinity. This loss results from wounds to the masculine soul taken at various different points in life. These wounds sap the energy, both sexual and divine, which is fundamental to the health of men and render them bored, frustrated and unfulfilled. The resolution of this situation is found in reclaiming the masculine soul which is done by fulfilling the three callings men have: to fight a battle; to live an adventure; and to rescue a beauty. This requires a man to face and overcome his wounds. It requires a man to find and liberate the wild man, or warrior, within his heart. The wild man is a poetic metaphor for the whole and spiritually healthy human male, who is fully in touch with his sexual energy. Robert Bly finds evidence for this mythical figure in folklore. Bly suggests that a man who has thus recovered his masculine soul, the divine energy within him, is not only a more fulfilled man but a man better suited to a post-feminist world (Bly 1990).

Bly is strongly critical of the Christian Church. He lays at its door much of the blame for the current crisis in masculinity on account of its what he calls its 'hatred of sexuality'. In denying men access to the wild man figures of folklore, the Church cut men off from finding their souls (Bly 1990: 248-49). Despite this criticism, his ideas have had a remarkable degree of influence in popular theology—notably in the work of John Eldredge (Eldredge 2001). Eldredge agrees that 'New Man' is a failed project and, drawing very heavily on the work of Bly, outlines the future for the modern Christian male in terms of becoming a wild man. His departure from Bly exists only in attempting to find a Christian theological justification for this move. Eldredge takes his lead from Longman and Reid's popularization of the work of Cross and others on the divine warrior in ancient Israel.[1] Eldredge suggests that man is made in the image of the divine warrior, and thus that the masculine soul is the soul of the warrior and the wild man. Therefore, male spirituality entails (if not consists in) the pursuit of the healing of the wounded masculine soul and the discovery of the wild man within (Eldredge 2001).

One might reasonably ask many questions of the ideas Bly and Eldredge put forward—not least, perhaps, of the use Eldredge makes of the divine warrior myth. However, I do not propose to ask or answer all such questions here. My aim is more limited. Clearly, there is a discussion about masculinity taking place within the Christian Church. This discussion involves the use of biblical studies. To the best of my knowledge, the guilds of biblical studies that exist do not appear to be taking much part in this discussion. In this paper, I wish to enter this discussion. There are many perspectives on masculinity in both biblical and extra-biblical literature. I think it worthwhile exploring these perspectives in order to see whether they contribute anything helpful to the (limited) modern theological discussion of masculinity. In this particular paper, I propose to study the interpretation of the figures of Woman Wisdom and Woman Folly from Proverbs 1–9 in three Second Temple texts: Philo's *De sacrificiis Abelis et Caini* 21-28; 4Q184; and Sir. 51.13-21. My aim in studying these texts is to explore attitudes to male heterosexuality in the writings of the Second Temple Jewish community.

Before embarking on this study, it is important to note that I take Woman Stranger (Prov. 2.16; 5.3, 20; 6.24; 7.5) and Woman Folly (Prov. 9.13-18) to operate as the opposing figure to Woman Wisdom, and thus to be identified with each other.[2] Both Woman Folly (9.13) and Woman Stranger (7.11) are described as 'boisterous', המיה. Both Folly (9.16) and Stranger (7.7) lure men who are simple (פתי) and without sense (חסר לב). The door of the house (פתח ביתה)

---

1. Cross 1973:79-194; Longman and Reid 1995; Eldredge 2001: 25.
2. Following Toy (1904: 188), McKane (1970: 365), Whybray (1994: 54-55), Murphy (1998: 281-82), Clifford (1999: 23), and Camp (1997: 92-94; 2000: 42).

of both Folly (9.14) and Stranger (5.8) is a dangerous place. Both Folly (9.15) and Stranger (7.8) lure those who pass by (עבר). Both Folly (9.16) and Stranger (7.14-20) request that a young man enter her home; and both Woman Folly (9.18) and Woman Stranger (7.24-27) lead the simple man to death and Sheol. Proverbs 1–9 seems to identify these two figures in these ways.

Proverbs 1–9

The implied reader of Proverbs 1–9 is a young man.[3] The author paints a picture of two women calling this young man. Woman Wisdom calls the young man to forms of behaviour which will bring life, although they may require self-control. Woman Folly calls the young man to a life of immediate pleasures, but does not warn him that such a life only leads to destruction. The sexuality of both Woman Wisdom and Woman Folly is depicted here. The young man is told to acquire Woman Wisdom as his lover (Prov. 4.5-9; 7.4).[4] The young man is warned to avoid the strange woman, Woman Folly, who is described as a seductress (Prov. 7.6-23).[5]

The implied reader is a young man. Young men are generally very interested in sex. Proverbs 1–9 transforms Wisdom and Folly into sexually attractive women. One, Folly, is attractive but destructive (Prov. 7.6-27). The other one, Wisdom, is attractive and capable of giving lifelong satisfying love, and making love to her will prevent one from being tempted to dally with Woman Folly (Prov. 7.4-5).

Making love and finding sexual satisfaction is an attractive prospect to a young man. It is certainly more likely to engage the imagination than learning wisdom aphorisms. The sexual imagery is designed to attract the attention of the implied reader and to engage him in the subject matter. Sexual imagery is clearly used as a pedagogical tool in Proverbs 1–9. The sexual imagery used is that which is likely to appeal to the young heterosexual male imagination, as the implied reader is a young heterosexual male. Imagery relating to male heterosexuality is used as a pedagogical tool.[6]

The main concern of the book of Proverbs is to recommend positive forms of behaviour and discourage negative ways of behaving.[7] It is therefore most

---

3. E.g. Prov. 1.8, 10, 15; 2.1; 3.1, 11, 21; 4.10, 20; 6.1, 3, 20. So Whybray (1994: 8), Clifford (1999: 6-7) and Fox (2000: 348).

4. Whybray 1994: 77-78; Murphy 1988, 1998: 27; Clifford 1999: 60-62. Although McKane (1970: 303-304) and Fox (2000: 172-78) prefer not to read this language as erotic, they admit that the argument for reading the language this way is strong. Toy (1904: 89) notes that the versions acknowledge the erotic language and translate accordingly.

5. Toy 1904: 146-57; McKane 1970: 334-41; Whybray 1994: 110-18; Murphy 1988: 43-44; Clifford 1999: 84-89; Fox 2000: 241-52.

6. Similarly, Fox (2000: 348-51).

7. Toy 1904: xi-xiv; Kidner 1964: 13-16; Whybray 1994: 4; Clifford 1999: 6-8; Fox 1996: 238-39.

unlikely that the author will use as a pedagogical tool something understood to be ethically wrong. This would confuse the reader and possibly reinforce the wrong message. Rather, the author will use pedagogical tools which reinforce the right message.

If imagery relating to male heterosexuality is used as a pedagogical tool, the author does not see the engagement of the heterosexual male imagination as something intrinsically wrong. The author clearly believes that it leads to both right and wrong actions (Prov. 5.15-23). However, his willingness to engage the male heterosexual imagination in this way suggests that he sees nothing intrinsically wrong with the male heterosexual imagination, or indeed with male heterosexuality. Indeed, the fact that he was so willing to engage with male heterosexuality as his primary pedagogical tool in the prologue to his work suggests a very positive attitude to male heterosexuality.

De sacrificiis Abelis et Caini 21-28

In *De sacrificiis Abelis et Caini* 21-28, Philo describes two women. The first of these women bears a marked resemblance to Woman Folly: she is dressed as a prostitute (Prov. 7.10; *Sacr.* 21); she entraps the young (Prov. 7.7, 13; *Sacr.* 21); she is impudent (Prov. 7.13; *Sacr.* 21); she wanders the market and streets (Prov. 7.11-12; *Sacr.* 21); she offers sexual pleasures (Prov. 7.14-20; *Sacr.* 23); she offers what is evil rather than what is good (Prov. 2.16-19; 5.1-14; 7.6-27; 9.13-18; *Sacr.* 23). The second of these women resembles Woman Wisdom in that she too cries out publicly (Prov. 1.20; *Sacr.* 26) and counsels people to seek wisdom (Prov. 1.20-33; 8.1-36; *Sacr.* 26-28). The two women of *Sacr.* 21-28 are clearly drawing on the figures of Woman Folly and Woman Wisdom in Proverbs 1–9 (Sly 1990: 15).

Although the figures are clearly drawn from Proverbs 1–9, the use to which they are put is different in *Sacr.* 21-28. The use of them remains pedagogical. However, the teaching is different. Proverbs teaches a wisdom which helps one make the most of all that is available to humanity in creation. Although it does teach the restraint of destructive emotions (e.g. Prov. 3.29-31), it also teaches the enjoyment of physical pleasures (e.g. Prov. 5.17-19). By contrast, Philo aims to teach the cultivation of the soul by the harnessing of the passions (e.g. *Leg. all.* 2.9-17, 94-108), and the denial of physical pleasures (*Op. mund.* 157-60; *Leg. all.* 3.109-10). The aim of using the figures of Woman Folly and Woman Wisdom, in *Sacr.* 21-28, is to inculcate virtue and to encourage the denial of physical pleasures as something base and evil (Sly 1990: 167-69).

Philo clearly presents Woman Folly as a sexual figure. She is dressed as a prostitute and acts with excessive licentiousness and desire (*Sacr.* 21). She offers sexual pleasures to all and sundry (*Sacr.* 23). She is highly flirtatious, aiming to excite sexual desire within her hearers (*Sacr.* 26). Philo presents her as overtly sexual. However, he has nothing positive to say about her sexuality. Rather, he describes her as overdone, cheap and possessed of 'a bastard elegance' (*Sacr*. 21).

Philo presents Woman Wisdom without reference to her sexuality. She is presented as wearing no cosmetics, bearing herself in a quiet and unobtrusive manner, being moderate in her dress and wearing only her moral virtues for jewellery (*Sacr*. 26). By contrast with Woman Folly, Philo presents Woman Wisdom almost entirely in terms of her moral character (*Sacr*. 21, 26-27). Philo clearly has no intention of his audience understanding Woman Wisdom in sexual terms.

Philo understands sexual desire and intercourse as evils (e.g. *Leg. all.* 1.39; 2.49). Indeed, he suggests that sexual desire is the origin of all evil and sin (*Op. mund.* 152). His view is quite clearly that human sexuality is bad, albeit necessary for the purpose of procreation (Loader 2004: 66-69). This view is reflected in the way in which he uses the pedagogical figures of Woman Wisdom and Woman Folly. Woman Wisdom is presented as being in no way sexual. Given his negative view of sexuality, Philo is unlikely to use a sexually attractive woman as a pedagogical aid. Therefore the sexually attractive Woman Wisdom of Proverbs 1–9 becomes the noble, fierce and unapproachable Woman Wisdom of *Sacr*. 21-28. In an equal and opposite manner, Philo transforms the sexually attractive but dangerous Woman Folly of Proverbs 1–9 into a grotesque caricature of a prostitute in *Sacr*. 21-28. In accordance with his own understanding of the nature of human sexuality, Philo rescues Woman Wisdom from her sexuality and plunges Woman Folly even more deeply into the mire of hers.

Philo is presumably writing for a male audience as philosophy was a male pursuit in the ancient world. Moreover, given that Philo has a tendency to identify woman with the irrational element in human nature,[8] it would be surprising if he expected women to read his philosophy. Therefore, he has removed the sexually attractive element from the description of Woman Wisdom so that his male audience is not sexually attracted to her. He refuses to engage the sexuality of his male audience in promotion of the good. Furthermore, he identifies sexuality with Woman Folly and decries it as vulgar and to be spurned. He actively encourages his male audience to identify their being prone to sexual attraction as evil, to reject this highly sexual figure of Woman Folly and, with her, to reject their own sexuality. Thus, Philo develops the way in which these figures are used as pedagogical aids in Proverbs 1–9 to promote his own philosophical and sexual agenda, one which clearly has the very negative view of male heterosexuality as something to be rejected.

4Q184 (or Wiles of the Wicked Woman)

Whether or not, as Vermes speculates, 4Q184 antedates the Qumran sect (Vermes 1995: 273), the fact that it has been preserved by the Qumran sect suggests that

---

8. Baer 1970: 19; Wegner 1982; Sly 1990: 215-23.

this first-century BCE text represents the views of at least some in that community.⁹ Some of the language in 4Q184 reflects that of the descriptions of Woman Folly in Proverbs 1–9. The following words and phrases can be found in both texts: 'smooth talking', חלק (Prov. 2.16; 7.5; 4Q184 1.2); 'in the middle of the night', אישון לילה (Prov. 7.9; 4Q184 1.6); and 'lies in wait', ארב (Prov. 7.12; 4Q184 1.11) (Allegro 1968: 84). Thus, the description of the Wicked Woman in 4Q184 contains linguistic echoes of Woman Folly.

The general description of the Wicked Woman is similar to Woman Folly. She descends to Sheol, or the Pit (Prov. 5.5; 4Q184 1.3, 9-10) (Strugnell 1970: 264). and she leads to the grave all who follow her (Prov. 2.18-19; 4Q184 1.10-11) (Strugnell 1970: 267). She is associated with the night and darkness (Prov. 7.9; 4Q184 1.4-7). Her adornments (Prov. 7.10; 4Q184 1.5) and couches (Prov. 7.16-17; 4Q184 1.5-6) are described. She flaunts herself in the city squares and public places (Prov. 7.12; 9.14; 4Q184 1.12). She is portrayed as an adulteress (Prov. 6.24; 7.10-19; 4Q184 1.13). She looks for an innocent man to lead astray (Prov. 7.7; 9.14-18; 4Q184 1.13-15).

Moreover, some of the vocabulary recommending the paths of wisdom reflects that of Proverbs 1–9. The following phrases are found in both texts: 'keep a commandment', נצר מצוה (Prov. 6.20; 4Q184 1.15); 'in the paths of uprightness', במעגלי ישר (Prov. 4.11; 4Q184 1.17) (Allegro 1968: 84). Thus, there is good reason to suppose that this text uses Proverbs 1–9, and more specifically, that the figure of Woman Folly was utilized in the creation of this picture of the Wicked Woman.¹⁰

However, unlike Woman Folly in Proverbs 1–9, the Wicked Woman is not primarily a representation of the adulteress. After all, as Gaster pointed out, it is hard to see how the (all-male) Qumran sectarians, isolated in the wilderness, could become prey to urban streetwalkers.¹¹ As a consequence, the Wicked Woman has been accorded a variety of allegorical interpretations: the false teachings of a rival sect (Carmignac 1965; Gazov-Ginzberg 1967), the evil power of Rome (Allegro 1964; Burgmann 1974), the demonic powers of darkness (Baumgarten 1991), evil in general (Moore 1981: 506). The text states that the Wicked Woman leads the community astray with nonsense (4Q184 1.3). She also turns righteous men from the paths of righteousness (4Q184 1.14, 16-17), makes them alter the Law (4Q184 1.15), and makes them rebel against God (4Q184 1.16). Thus, in general terms, it appears that the Wicked Woman represents the dangers of false doctrine and being led from the paths of righteousness to the paths of sin (Vermes 1995: 273; Harrington 2000: 979-80).

---

9. On the date, see Vermes (1995: 273).

10. Carmignac 1965: 373; Gazov-Ginzberg 1967: 280; Strugnell 1970: 266-67; Moore 1981: 511-17; Baumgarten 1991: 136-43; Harrington 2000: 979; Schuller 2000: 983-84.

11. Gaster 1976: 495. Similarly, Baumgarten (1991: 137).

Although she has become a metaphor for seduction into false doctrine or unrighteousness, the Wicked Woman is still presented as a sexual temptress. Her adornments (4Q184 1.5) and beds (4Q184 1.5-6) are mentioned just as are those of Woman Folly in Proverbs 1–9. She fornicates incessantly (4Q184 1.13) and is always looking out for men to lead astray (4Q184 1.13-14). However, unlike Prov. 7.5-23 (upon which the present text draws), 4Q184 scarcely recognises the excitement of the sex that the Wicked Woman has to offer. In Prov. 7.5-23, Woman Stranger says that her couch is decked out luxuriously (7.16) and it is beautifully perfumed (7.17). The sex offered will last all night and will delight both partners (7.18). The offer she makes is rather seductive and is presented as such. By contrast, the language of 4Q184 1.1-17 is starkly negative in tone. For example, the veils of the Wicked Woman are 'shadows of the twilight', her accommodation is darkness and night, her couches are 'the couches of the pit' and her adornments are 'diseases of the pit'. 4Q184 recognizes nothing positive in the sex and beauty that the Wicked Woman has to offer. All is darkness and sin. Whereas Proverbs admits that the sex of Woman Stranger offers a certain (if treacherous and ultimately destructive) delight, 4Q184 1.1-17 says nothing positive about the sex of the Wicked Woman. Proverbs admits that Woman Stranger offers pleasure, albeit temporary, but 4Q184 does not allow for any pleasure in the seductiveness of, or in being seduced by, the Wicked Woman.

As in Proverbs 1–9, the Wicked Woman is used as a pedagogical tool. She represents an evil (that of false doctrine and leaving the path of righteousness) which is to be shunned. In contrast to Proverbs 1–9, 4Q184 portrays the sex of the Wicked Woman in an entirely negative light. It is true that 4Q184 draws on Prov. 7.5-23, which has negative comments to make about sex with the Woman Stranger, rather than on a text like Prov. 5.17-20, which is much more positive about sex. However, 4Q184 does not derive its highly negative tone from its source material. This is clear because 4Q184 edits out the aspects of sex with Woman Stranger which might be construed as attractive. This editing is surely self-defeating and thus somewhat peculiar. If the community at Qumran was all male, or largely male (VanderKam 1994: 14-15, 90-91), then it is likely that the majority of them would find the allure of the seductress a reasonably powerful image. Thus, the portrayal of Woman Stranger/Folly in Proverbs 1–9 would have been pedagogically useful as the members of the community would be able to relate the allure of false doctrine to the allure of the seductress. It may seem attractive, but it is ultimately destructive. However, to portray the Wicked Woman as an object of disgust is not so pedagogically useful. Generally, men find sex attractive rather than an object of disgust. Thus, the portrayal of the sex which the Wicked Woman offers in 4Q184 suggests that the author held a very negative view of sex. Although the purpose of this text was to steer the members of the community away from false doctrine, it makes a very clear statement about the unremitting evil of the sex which is offered by the Wicked

Woman. In doing this, it betrays a very negative attitude towards the sexuality of the heterosexual male members of the Qumran community.[12]

If, as some argue, the Qumran Essenes were single celibate men who frowned upon sexual activity (Vermes 1995: 8-9; VanderKam 1994: 90-91), this would corroborate the conclusion that the author held a negative view of male heterosexuality. On the other hand, a text such as 1QS 7.12-14 may suggest that certain members of the community were prone to sexual horseplay:

> 12 Whoever walks about naked in front of his fellows, without needing to, shall be punished for six months. 13 ... And whoever takes out 'his hand' from under his clothes ... he will be punished thirty days.

If this text does suggest that there were members of the community who indulged in sexual antics, then the rulings would represent an attempt to stamp out such behaviour from the community. This would suggest that there were those at Qumran who took a very strict attitude towards male sexual expression. It is possible that 4Q184 betrays such an attitude and may represent the attempt to regulate the sexual behaviour of men at Qumran. Whether 4Q184 is read as representing such an attitude, or as suggesting that sex between a man and the Wicked Woman is an object of disgust, it is clear that 4Q184 is highly negative about male heterosexuality.

Sirach 51.13-21

Sirach was written in Hebrew by Jesus ben Sira in Palestine (ca. 190-175 BCE), and was translated by his grandson into Greek in Egypt (ca. 130-100 BCE).[13] The textual history of Sir. 51.13-21 is complex.[14] The Qumran Hebrew text (11Q5 21.11-22.1a) is clearly the closest to an original text, and the Hebrew text from the Cairo Genizah would appear to be, in large part, a later version.[15] The discussion here explores the way in which both the Qumran text and the Greek translation of Sir. 51.13-21 develop the picture of Woman Wisdom as a pedagogical tool, and what this might have to say about the understanding of male heterosexuality in the Second Temple period.

There is general agreement that Sir. 51.13-21 is a hymn to Wisdom. Likewise, although the Qumran text does not explicitly state that the author is

---

12. I make no assumption about the extent of male homosexuality in the Qumran community—I simply assume that the image of the seductress is unlikely to be an effective pedagogical tool for any male homosexuals in that community.

13. Oesterley 1912: xlv-xxiii; Snaith 1974: 1-8; Skehan 1987: 8-16; Coggins 1998: 18-20.

14. For access to the textual issues, see Hartman (1961), Delcor (1968), Skehan (1971), Rabinowitz (1971) and Skehan and Di Lella (1987: 51-62, 574-575). For major editions of the Hebrew text, see Strack (1903), Lévi (1904), Smend (1906) and Yadin (1965). For the major edition of the Greek text, see Ziegler (1965). For bibliographical details of other editions, see Skehan and Di Lella 1987: 93-94.

15. Sanders 1965: 79; Delcor 1968: 47; Skehan 1971: 387; Rabinowitz 1971: 173.

writing of Wisdom, it makes sense to read it as such. The references to finding instruction and 'my teacher' (11Q5 21.14) suggest learning from a figure with great knowledge or from Wisdom herself. The figure sought for this instruction is female, and so Wisdom would be an obvious candidate. The style of the text is reminiscent of hymns in praise of Wisdom where wisdom is presented as a bride (e.g. Wis. 8.2-16; Sir. 15.1-10), which draw on the image of Wisdom as a bride in Prov. 5.18.[16] In addition, in 11Q5 18.3-15 the Qumran text discusses the benefits that Wisdom bestows on those who are faithful to the Lord. Although this does not immediately precede 11Q5 21.11-17, it is possible that 11Q5 18.3-15 provides a context within which the female figure sought in 11Q5 21 may be read as Wisdom. Whatever the strength of that point, the fact that 11Q5 21.11-17 reflects Sir. 51.13-19 (LXX) supports the identification of this instruction-giving female figure as Wisdom, because Sir. 51.13 (LXX) explicitly identifies this figure as Wisdom.

Both as the epilogue to Sirach and as a text within a collection of psalms (11Q5), the purpose of this text is clear. It is a hymn in praise of Wisdom, extolling her for the instruction she bestows and recounting the author's desire for wisdom. However, Sanders writes of 11Q5 21.11-17 that 'a number of the words and phrases in the Hebrew are capable of more than one translation... One suspects that the *mots à double entendre* are intentional and that in those instances the two meanings were understood together' (Sanders 1965: 81). His case that this text has erotic overtones which were toned down in the Greek translation has occasioned much discussion.[17] Before visiting the text in the light of this discussion, it would be pertinent to make some general remarks about the interpretation of the text, in response to this discussion.

The fact that the primary level of meaning in the text concerns the desire of the author to learn from Wisdom does not necessarily entail that this is the only level of meaning therein. Rabinowitz argues that it is illegitimate to read double meanings into the text as it makes sense when read as a hymn to Wisdom, praising her for the benefits of knowledge which she bestows upon those who seek her (Rabinowitz 1971: 176-84). No one doubts that the text makes sense when read in that way. Nor is there any doubt that this is the primary level of meaning in this text. The question is whether the text permits reading double meanings in certain words and images which suggest a sexual relationship between the author and Wisdom.

This question cannot be decided on the basis of our own feelings of attraction or revulsion towards such a reading of the text. Thus, it is not reasonable for Rabinowitz to argue for reading שׁחק instead of שׁחק in 11Q5 21.15 on the basis that not to do so would convict Sirach of a 'lecherous aspiration'

---

16. Sanders 1965: 84; Winston 1979: 192-93; Skehan and Di Lella 1987: 264.
17. Sanders 1965: 83-84; Di Lella 1966: 93-95; Delcor 1968; Rabinowitz 1971; Muraoka 1979; Sauer 2000: 350.

(Rabinowitz 1971: 175). Sirach includes much material with which many would want to take issue today (e.g. Sir. 42.9-14). However, the fact that this material is not pleasant in the sight of the reader does not render the material inauthentic. Similarly, it is unreasonable to decide the authenticity of a reading of the Hebrew on the basis of whether the reader finds that reading attractive. It is better decided—if at all possible—on the basis of the evidence of the text itself.

In interpreting this text, it is important to bear in mind that it is a hymn in praise of Wisdom. Wisdom is a female figure, presented to some extent in Proverbs 1–9 as a sexually attractive figure. Young men ought to seek her for a bride. The precedent for using sexual metaphors for seeking Wisdom exists. The question is whether Sirach develops this metaphor or not.

The argument set out below for reading the motif of seeking Wisdom in this way is cumulative. If there were just one word capable of bearing a sexual double meaning, then this might be written off as coincidence. However, as a number of words are capable of bearing such a meaning, it seems more likely to be a deliberate ploy on the part of the author. The Greek translator includes words with sexual connotations in the LXX text as well. Given the presence of such words in the earliest extant Hebrew text, it is easier to believe that the translator is trying to convey the sense of double meaning of the Hebrew original than that the presence of such double meanings is coincidence.

The double meanings identifiable in the Qumran text are as follows:

(a) Muraoka notes that in the Mishnah, the sages are said to compare women's sexual maturation with the three-stage growth of figs (Muraoka 1979: 172):

> The Sages spoke of (the physical development of) a woman in figurative speech: an unripe fig, a fig in its early ripening stage and a ripe fig. She is like an unripe fig while she is yet a child; a fig in its early ripening stage when she is in the age of her maidenhood... (*m. Nid.* 5.7).

He suggests that this constitutes a parallel to the description in 11Q5 21.12 of the blossoms dropping and grapes ripening (Muraoka 1979: 172). The picture of the blossoms dropping as the grapes ripen on the vine in 11Q5 21.12 is an image of the ripening of fruit, just as is the picture of the fig ripening in *m. Nid.* 5.7. As the ripening of the fig in *m. Nid.* 5.7 refers to the sexual maturation of a woman, it is plausible to interpret the ripening of the grapes in 11Q5 21.12 in the same way. Although the comparison in *m. Nid.* 5.7 is with a fig and in 11Q5 21.12 with grapes, there may still be some merit in the parallel. In 11Q5 21.12 the grapes gladden the heart of ben Sira. In the previous line (11Q5 21.11) Wisdom came to ben Sira in her beauty, as a result of which ben Sira pays her constant attention (11Q5 21.12). Thus, it is possible that the image of ripening grapes continues from the previous line the idea of ben Sira being sexually attracted to Wisdom.

(b) The primary meaning of לְקַח (11Q5 21.14) must be teaching, and ben Sira refers to the teaching he receives from Wisdom. However, it is clear from Prov. 7.21 that לְקַח can also mean 'seductive speech' (Sanders 1965: 82; Muraoka 1979: 170). Clearly, however, the seductive speech of Wisdom is both attractive and good—unlike that of Woman Stranger in Prov. 7.21. Hence, although the primary meaning of לְקַח in 11Q5 21.14 is 'instruction', this does not exclude the possibility of a double meaning with a sexual connotation.

(c) It seems best to assume the root שחק for ואשחקה (11Q5 21.15) and so translate 'I had fun'. This has a sexual connotation.[18] Rabinowitz suggests reading שׁחק, arguing that the phrase ought to be translated 'I constantly trod her (path)' (Rabinowitz 1971: 175). However, שחק connotes crushing and eroding. Even in Sir. 6.36, it refers to feet wearing down a doorstep rather than walking.[19] If this meaning of שׁחק were taken, the translation would either result in a somewhat violent image of crushing Wisdom, which would seem out of place here, or in wearing her down which, contrary to Rabinowitz's intention, as a metaphor could accommodate a sexual connotation.

(d) It is quite plausible that טוב (11Q5 21.15) be read as 'pleasure' as well as good.[20] The primary meaning of this word is surely good, as Rabinowitz argues, and being zealous for this good must describe the eagerness with which ben Sira seeks wisdom (Rabinowitz 1971: 178). However, given that the preceding statement refers to sexual enjoyment, it is difficult not to read a second layer of meaning here by which ben Sira compares his zeal for wisdom to his desire for sexual pleasure.

(e) Similarly, 'I set my soul ablaze for her', חריתי נפשי (11Q5 21.15-16) refers at one level to the depth of desire that ben Sira has for wisdom. Nevertheless, the metaphor of setting one's soul ablaze easily accommodates a romantic or sexual connotation. Again, it is difficult not to read this phrase as bearing such a double meaning given the context. Ben Sira is confessing to holding a candle for Wisdom.

---

18. Sanders 1965: 82. Rabinowitz (1971: 178) agrees that such a reading would produce such a translation and meaning.
19. HALOT 1464.
20. HALOT 370-72.

(f) Muraoka suggests that the phrase וברומיה לוא אשלה is best translated 'in the moments of her exaltation, I will not let up', the moments of her exaltation being a reference to orgasm (Muraoka 1979: 172). Whilst it is certainly possible that this refers to ben Sira's never-ending labour to reach the heights of understanding that Wisdom offers (Rabinowitz 1971: 179), the double meaning is certainly possible here.

(g) Muraoka comments that the meaning of מערמיה (11Q5 21.17) is uncertain. It is possible that it refers to the mysterious doctrines of Wisdom.²¹ Indeed, it is very likely that this is the primary meaning of the term in this hymn to Wisdom. However, מערם can refer to physical nakedness, as 2 Chr. 28.15 bears witness.²² Thus, in talking of the mysterious doctrines of Wisdom, ben Sira uses chooses a term that might also picture her physical nakedness. This image of a young man looking upon the physical nakedness of a woman is surely a sexually charged metaphor (Sanders 1965: 81-83).

Thus, if it is accepted that coincidence is not the best explanation for the multiple possible double meanings in this text, all of which suggest a sexual relationship between the author and Wisdom, then it is legitimate to read 11Q5 21.11-17 as a hymn to Wisdom which has erotic overtones. The Greek text of Sir. 51.13-21 supports such a reading:

(a) Ziegler's edition of the LXX of Sirach reads καὶ τὰ ἀγνοήματα αὐτῆς ἐπενόησα ('and I noticed her sins of ignorance') for Sir. 51.19d (Ziegler 1965: 366). Ziegler notes a variant which reads ἀγνεύματα ('chastities') instead of ἀγνοήματα ('sins of ignorance') in v. 19d. This variant would render v. 19d 'I noticed her chastities', rather than 'I noticed her sins of ignorance'. As a translation, the variant makes more sense than the reading adopted by Ziegler's edition because it makes little sense to attribute sins of ignorance to Wisdom. The earliest extant Hebrew (11Q5 21.17) attests an original reading in which the author perceived the nakednesses of Wisdom, and it seems that ἐπενόησα translates אתבונן and τὰ ἀγνεύματα αὐτῆς translates מערמיה from that text. There is evidence here either that the original Greek translation read ἀγνεύματα or, though probably less likely, an early copyist of the LXX text who knew the Hebrew (as preserved by 11Q5 21.17) turned editor and corrected the translation. Either way, Sir. 51.19d (LXX) suggests that Wisdom is understood as a sexual figure.

---

21. Muraoka 1979: 172. Similarly, Rabinowitz 1971: 180.
22. HALOT 616.

(b) Deutsch notes that ben Sira finds Wisdom in a state of levitical purity, ἐν καθαρισμῷ (Sir. 51.20 [LXX]). This is the state in which she is now ready to have sexual intercourse after her period of uncleanness (Deutsch 1982: 406). This adds to the erotic imagery of the text.

(c) Sir. 51.21 (LXX) states that ἡ κοιλία μου ἐταράχθη to seek out Wisdom. The term κοιλία may refer to reproductive organs[23] and the ταράσσω means 'stir up' or 'unsettle'.[24] Thus, ben Sira claims that his loins were being stirred up to seek out Wisdom. There is a clear sexual connotation to such a reading (Muraoka 1979: 172-74).

Thus, there is sufficient evidence to warrant the conclusion that the Greek translator wished to convey the sense that ben Sira pictures himself as Wisdom's lover in Sir. 51.13-21 (LXX). The fact that the translator does this supports the view that the Greek draws on a Hebrew original which also painted this picture.

Given the culture in which ben Sira wrote, and the way in which he writes about women, it is most likely that he writes for a male audience (Skehan and Di Lella 1987: 90-92). In Sir. 51.13-21, he writes a hymn about his love of Wisdom in which he describes the female figure of Wisdom in erotic language. This hymn seems to be designed to engage the imagination of a heterosexual male. He clearly desires other men to seek Wisdom (Sir. 51.23-26). The purpose of engaging the imagination of heterosexual men in this manner is to encourage them to seek wisdom and live according to her dictates. Therefore, the erotic imagery is pedagogical. Ben Sira has taken the mildly erotic description of seeking Woman Wisdom from Proverbs 1–9 and has developed it in this hymn.

The evidence of 11Q5 21.11-17 and Sir. 51.13-21 (LXX) suggests that ben Sira was happy to engage the imagination of the heterosexual male and to explore erotic imagery. He is happy to use sexual imagery to describe his spirituality and to motivate other men to engage themselves in developing their own spirituality. This denotes a high view of male heterosexuality—quite in contrast with those of both *Sacr.* 21-28 and 4Q184. However, given the reputation of ben Sira for his negative attitude towards women and his treatment of them as disposable possessions,[25] it is very interesting that his relationship with Wisdom is not all one-way traffic. It would be true to say that Wisdom has become an object of his sexual desire and there is much in the text to support such a view. However, in his world of sexual metaphor, Wisdom acts too. She comes to him (11Q5 21.11), albeit when he is searching her out. She speaks to him

---

23. BAGD 437.
24. BAGD 805.
25. Skehan and Di Lella 1987: 90-92. See especially Sir. 7.19-26, 25.13–26.18, 42.9-14.

seductively (11Q5 21.14), and, in a way, he submits to her in giving her his honour (11Q5 21.14-15). Much as the sexual imagery speaks clearly of a man making love to a woman, it also speaks of a woman making love to a man. It is true that this comes from a male author and thus from his world of fantasy, but in this fantasy world, Wisdom is not so much an object of his desire as a lover in a mutual quest for sexual pleasure.

Conclusion

My aim in this brief study has been to explore attitudes to male heterosexuality in the writings of the Second Temple Jewish community. The three texts studied all develop the imagery and the use of the figures of Woman Wisdom and/or Woman Folly of Proverbs 1–9. In *Sacr.* 21-28, Philo desexualized Woman Wisdom and oversexed Woman Folly in order to promote his message that one should seek wisdom and flee physical and emotional sensations, including male heterosexuality. 4Q184 exaggerated the picture of Woman Folly as adulteress and harbinger of death, in order to deter Qumran sectarians from following the doctrines of other groups. In doing so, it demonstrated a very negative attitude towards male heterosexuality. Ben Sira, in the Hebrew text of Sir. 51.13-21, played up the sexual nature of Woman Wisdom in a highly erotic manner, in order to engage the imagination of his male readers. He demonstrated a very positive attitude towards male heterosexuality, and painted a picture in which Wisdom is the sexual partner of the man who seeks truth rather than the object of his lust.

The picture that this very brief survey gives of attitudes to heterosexual male sexuality in Judaism in the period 200 BCE to 200 CE is interesting. Although it is difficult to tie texts to groups of people, the fact that these views are found in Philo, Sirach and at Qumran suggests two things: that different groups within the Judaism of this period had points of view on male heterosexuality; and that their views were widely differing. There is limited evidence of discussion and disagreement on the topic, as shown by the Qumran material examined above. The Qumran text 4Q184 is undoubtedly negative towards heterosexual male sexuality. However, quite the most erotic rendering of Sir. 51.13-21 also comes from Qumran. Therefore, there must have been a variety of views on the topic within that community. It is clear from this study that within Judaism of this period there was some discussion of male heterosexuality—and this discussion may be of interest to the modern reader. In view of the tendency of the modern theological discussion to link male spirituality and sexuality, it is interesting that that we see a similar link in the ancient discussion we have studied. It might be profitable to ask further questions of the ancient discussion, not simply about what other attitudes there might be found in other texts (such as *Joseph and Aseneth*, the *Testaments of the Twelve Patriarchs* and the books of the NT) but also questions of why different people and groups held the viewpoints on male heterosexuality that they did. Perhaps such study might help wild men become wise, rather than wicked, men.

BIBLIOGRAPHY

Allegro, John M.
    1964   'The Wiles of the Wicked Woman', *PEQ* 96: 53-55.
    1968   *Qumran Cave 4, 1 (4Q158-4Q186)* (DJD, 5; Oxford: Clarendon Press).

Baer, Richard A.
    1970   *Philo's Use of the Categories Male and Female* (ALGHJ, 3; Leiden: E.J. Brill).

Baumgarten, Joseph M.
    1991   'On the Nature of the Seductress in 4Q184', *RevQ* 15:133-43.

Bly, Robert
    1990   *Iron John: A Book about Men* (Rockport, MA: Element).

Burgman, Hans
    1974   'The Wicked Woman: Der Makkabäer Simon?', *RevQ* 8:323-59.

Camp, Claudia V.
    1997   'Woman Wisdom and the Strange Woman: Where is Wisdom to be Found?', in Timothy K. Beal and David M. Gunn (eds.), *Reading Bibles, Writing Bodies: Identity and the Book* (Biblical Limits; London: Routledge): 85-112.
    2000   *Wise, Strange and Holy: The Strange Woman and the Making of the Bible* (JSOTSup, 320; GCT, 9; Sheffield: Sheffield Academic Press).

Carmignac, Jean
    1965   'Poème allégorique sur la secte rivale', *RevQ* 5: 361-74.

Clifford, Richard J.
    1999   *Proverbs* (OTL; Louisville, KY: Westminster/John Knox Press).

Coggins, Richard J.
    1998   *Sirach* (Guides to Apocrypha and Pseudepigrapha; Sheffield: Sheffield Academic Press).

Cross, Frank Moore
    1973   *Canaanite Myth and Hebrew Epic. Essays in the History of the Religion of Israel* (Cambridge, MA: Harvard University Press).

Delcor, Matthias
    1968   'Le texte hébreu du cantique de Siracide LI,13 et ss. et les anciennes versions', *Textus* 6:27-47.

Deutsch, Celia
    1982   'The Sirach 51 Acrostic: Confession and Exhortation', *ZAW* 94: 400-409.

Di Lella, Alexander A.
    1966   Review of *The Psalms Scroll of Qumran Cave 11*, by J.A. Sanders, in *CBQ* 28: 92-95.

Eldredge, John
    2001   *Wild at Heart* (Nashville: Nelson).

Fox, Michael V.
    1996   'The Social Location of the Book of Proverbs', in Michael V. Fox, *et al.* (eds.), *Texts, Temples, and Traditions: A Tribute to Menahem Haran* (Winona Lake, IN: Eisenbrauns): 227-39.
    2000   *Proverbs 1–9* (AB, 18a; New York: Doubleday).

Gaster, Theodor H.
: 1976 *The Dead Sea Scriptures, in English Translation* (Garden City, NY: Anchor Books, 3rd edn, revised and enlarged).

Gazov-Ginsberg, Anatoly M.
: 1967 'Double-Meaning in a Qumran Work: The Wiles of the Wicked Woman', *RevQ* 6: 279-85.

Harrington, Daniel J.
: 2000 'Wisdom Texts', in Schiffman and VanderKam 2000: II, 976-80.

Hartman, Louis F.
: 1961 'Sirach in Hebrew and in Greek', *CBQ* 23: 443-51.

Kidner, Derek
: 1964 *The Proverbs: An Introduction and Commentary* (TOTC; Leicester: IVP).

Lévi, I.
: 1904 *The Hebrew Text of the Book of Ecclesiasticus* (Semitic Study Series, 3; Leiden: E.J. Brill).

Loader, William
: 2004 *The Septuagint, Sexuality and the New Testament: Case Studies on the Impact of the LXX in Philo and the New Testament* (Grand Rapids: Eerdmans).

Longman, Tremper, and Daniel G. Reid
: 1995 *God is a Warrior* (Studies in Old Testament Biblical Theology; Grand Rapids: Zondervan).

McCloughry, Roy K.
: 1992 *Men and Masculinity: From Power to Love* (London: Hodder and Stoughton).

McKane, William
: 1970 *Proverbs* (OTL; London: SCM Press).

Moore, Rick D.
: 1981 'Personification of the Seduction of Evil: The Wiles of the Wicked Woman', *RevQ* 10: 505-19.

Muraoka, Takamitsu
: 1979 'Sir. 51:13-20: An Erotic Hymn to Wisdom?', *JSJ* 10:166-78.

Murphy Roland E.
: 1988 'Wisdom and Eros in Proverbs 1–9', *CBQ* 50: 600-603.
: 1998 *Proverbs* (WBC, 22; Nashville: Thomas Nelson).

Nelson, James B.
: 1992 *The Intimate Connection: Male Sexuality, Male Spirituality* (London: SPCK).
: 1994 'Embracing Masculinity', in James B. Nelson and Sandra P. Longfellow (eds.), *Sexuality and the Sacred: Sources for Theological Reflection* (London: Mowbray): 195-215.

Oesterley, W.O.E.
: 1912 *The Wisdom of Jesus the Son of Sirach; or Ecclesiasticus; in the Revised Version with Introduction and Notes* (Cambridge Bible for Schools and Colleges; Cambridge. Cambridge University Press).

Rabinowitz, Isaac
: 1971 'The Qumran Hebrew Original of Ben Sira's Concluding Acrostic on Wisdom', *HUCA* 42: 173-84.

Sanders, J.A.
: 1965 *The Psalms Scroll of Qumrân Cave 11 (11QPsa)* (DJD, 4; Oxford: Clarendon Press).

Sauer, Georg
    2000   *Jesus Sirach (Ben Sira) übersetzt und erklärt* (Göttingen: Vandenhoeck & Ruprecht).
Schiffman, Lawrence H., and James C. VanderKam (eds.)
    2000   *Encyclopedia of the Dead Sea Scrolls* (2 vols.; Oxford: Oxford University Press)
Schuller, Eileen M., and Cecilia Wassen
    2000   'Women: Daily Life', in Schiffman and VanderKam 2000: II, 981-84.
Skehan, Patrick W.
    1971   'The Acrostic Poem in Sirach 51:13-30', *HTR* 64: 387-400.
Skehan, Patrick W., and Alexander A. DiLella
    1987   *The Wisdom of Ben Sira* (AB, 39; New York: Doubleday).
Sly, Dorothy
    1990   *Philo's Perception of Women* (BJS, 209; Atlanta: Scholars Press).
Smend, Rudolph
    1906   *Die Weisheit des Jesus Sirach* (Berlin: Georg Reimer).
Snaith, John G.
    1974   *Ecclesiasticus, or the Wisdom of Jesus Son of Sirach* (CBC; Cambridge: Cambridge University Press).
Strack, Hermann L.
    1903   *Die Sprüche Jesus', des Sohnes Sirachs* (Leipzig: Böhme).
Strugnell, John
    1970   'Notes en marge du volume V des "Discoveries in the Judean Desert of Jordan" ', *RevQ* 7:163-276.
Toy, C.H.
    1904   *A Critical and Exegetical Commentary on the Book of Proverbs* (ICC; Edinburgh: T. & T. Clark).
VanderKam, James C.
    1994   *The Dead Sea Scrolls Today* (London: SPCK).
Vermes, Geza
    1995   *The Dead Sea Scrolls in English* (Sheffield: Sheffield Academic Press, rev. and extended 4th edn).
Wegner, Judith Romney
    1982   'The Image of Woman in Philo', in Kent Harold Richards (ed.), *Society of Biblical Literature 1982 Seminar Papers* (Chico: Scholars Press, 1982): 551-63.
Whybray, R.N.
    1994   *Proverbs* (NCB; London: Marshall Pickering; Grand Rapids: Eerdmans).
Winston, David
    1979   *The Wisdom of Solomon* (AB, 43; Garden City, NY: Doubleday).
Yadin, Yigael
    1965   *The Ben Sira Scroll from Masada* (Jerusalem: Israel Exploration Society).
Ziegler, Joseph (ed.)
    1965   *Sapientia Iesu Filii Sirach* (Septuaginta 12.2; Göttingen: Vandenhoeck & Ruprecht).

Genizah Marriage Contracts: Contrasting Biblical Law and Halakhah with Mediaeval Practice

Rebecca Jefferson

1. Introduction

The Cairo Genizah is a collection of roughly one quarter of a million manuscripts amassed over a thousand years in a room above the women's gallery of the Ben Ezra synagogue in Fustat. Mostly derived from the tenth to the thirteenth centuries, its contents—from the sacred to the secular, the momentous to the mundane—have transformed the study of mediaeval Jewish history. With regard to the history of women, the Genizah preserves thousands of documents that relate to their everyday lives including letters, court records, documents of betrothal, and marriage contracts (*ketubbot*). A number of excellent critical editions of these documents have been produced; still lacking, however, is a comprehensive study of the lives of women in the period based on the manuscript evidence, as well as individual studies that focus on questions of gender and status. In order to stimulate further interest, this paper will summarize what Genizah marriage contracts have revealed about women's status when comparing mediaeval practice to biblical and rabbinic law.

Three distinct styles of contracting a marriage are discernible in the documents emanating from the Cairo Genizah. These styles may be termed Babylonian, Palestinian and Karaite according to the tradition of Judaism in which they originated; marriage contracts with a fusion of two or more of these styles are also found. Babylonian-style contracts were the most conservative of the three; rigidly formulaic in structure, they were more symbolic than practical and eventually came to represent the 'standard' *ketubbah*. Karaite and Babylonian contracts shared many common features, but Karaite contracts resembled functioning legal documents, containing elements such as the mutual obligation clause unknown in the Babylonian tradition. Palestinian-style contracts were more detailed and more fluid than their Babylonian and Karaite counterparts; in fact, no one Palestinian contract was exactly like another, even when the scribe was the same.[1]

---

1. Friedman (1980–81) has published 67 Palestinian-style marriage documents from the Cairo Genizah. The largest number (approximately 37) were composed in the eleventh century and about 16 were written in Tyre.

However, common formulas and patterns can be detected that were either unique to the Palestinian tradition (the divorce clause and the inclusion of special provisions), or were shared by both the Palestinian and Karaite communities (clauses of volition, mutual obligations, and extensive dowries). Jewish law did not require these elements to be written into the marriage contract: they were either innovations based on earlier traditions or local custom, or they were superfluous as the principles they outlined already existed in statutory law.[2] Their appearance in Palestinian and Karaite-style *ketubbot* not only highlights the comprehensive method of writing legal documents in that period, it also suggests that the practice of contracting of a marriage was more inclusive, and that the woman was accorded a more equal status, than was otherwise supposed. In order to demonstrate this, we will consider in turn each of these now-extinct *ketubbah* clauses.

2. *Volition*

In the opening section of a typical Palestinian-style marriage contract one often finds a clause of volition comprising a statement by the groom, in either the first or third person, that he is marrying the bride willingly and has not been coerced.[3] Thirty-one of the sixty-seven *ketubbot* published by Friedman contain this clause, including a formulary from an eleventh-century Palestinian prayer-book:

> There came this master X, the groom, b. master X, and he declared, intentionally, willingly, voluntarily, and of his own choice; and he is not coerced, not vexed, not distressed, not enticed, and not intoxicated, rather with complete faculties and with full senses (that) he desires to marry this X daughter of master X.[4]

The volition clause also appears in Karaite marriage contracts, although structured differently: 'And I am not coerced, not mistaken, not in error and under no compulsion, but with full resolve and willingly I have married…'[5] The statement by the Karaite groom that he is 'not in error' suggests that Karaite brides demanded even greater protection from the unilateral, and potentially capricious, nature of the Jewish divorce laws than their Palestinian or Babylonian counterparts.

---

2. Their absence in Babylonian contracts may have been due to superstition (see Friedman [1969: 30]). Mention of the wife's burial rights, for example, might have seemed an inauspicious start for a marriage. In conjunction with clauses relating to death, Karaite *ketubbot* contain the phrase 'God forbid'.

3. The same language of volition is extant in contemporary Arabic legal documents; for example, the contract of a tax farmer reads, 'He called people to be his witnesses, while acting voluntarily, in accordance with his will, not forced, coerced or constrained' (Khan 1993: No. 63, l. 8).

4. Friedman 1980–81: II, No. 8, Side a ll. 3-10.

5. Olszowy-Schlanger 1998: No. 39, l. 5.

Olszowy-Schlanger suggests that the absence of a volition clause in Babylonian-style marriage contracts may be due to the fact that some Talmudic sources (e.g. *B. Bat.* 48b) and later commentators like Maimonides were willing to validate marriages contracted out of compulsion. Conversely, she continues, the Karaites believed that a marriage was only valid when both parties acted out of free will, and so with this in mind they probably adopted the volition formula from non-marriage legal deeds. The Palestinian tradition may also have adopted the volition clause independently, or it may have been influenced by Karaite tradition (Olszowy-Schlanger 1998: 179-80). Friedman, however, rejects the idea of Karaite influence on the Palestinian *ketubbah*, arguing that the influence is the other way around and that much of what exists in Palestinian-style contracts stems from earlier traditions already existing in sources such as the Palestinian Talmud and a poorly preserved *ketubbah* from Antinoopolis in the fifth century CE (Friedman 2002: 175-76). In addition, Friedman demonstrates the difficulty of interpreting *B. Bat.* 48b given the variant readings across its sources. The notion of 'free will' was no doubt elemental in Jewish marriage law, he asserts, and the addition of a volition clause simply demonstrated that Palestinian marriage contracts were like any other Jewish legal document, that is, 'primarily a deed issued by the groom in favor of the bride and particularly specifying his obligations'.[6]

In Palestinian *ketubbot* it is usually only the groom's volition that is specified, although a rare example of the bride's volition appears in the marriage contract of a ransomed captive woman: 'And this bride listened to him (accepted his proposal) and willingly consented to be married to him...'[7] Karaite marriage contracts, however, regularly employ the phrases 'she accepted' and 'she wished' in a section after the details of the groom's financial obligations that is devoted to the bride's acceptance. An eleventh-century Karaite marriage formulary provides an example of how the bride's wishes should be recorded:

> And such-and-such daughter of [so-and-so, the] bride heard the words of this so-and-so son of so-and-so, the groom, and wanted, with [full] resolve, ... without coercion, to be married to him, to be his help, his wife and companion in purity, holiness and awe...[8]

In sum, the addition of a volition clause was probably superfluous as rabbinic law may have recognized marriages contracted out of compulsion or, conversely, because the notion of free will was a given. Yet, not only do we encounter the question of coercion discussed by the Jewish sages, we also

---

6. Friedman 1980–81: I, 134. This idea is also supported by the appearance on the Palestinian-style *ketubbot* of other seemingly superfluous clauses, like the husband's obligation to ransom his wife, that were already provided for in statutory law (*m. Ket.* 4.9).
7. Friedman 1980–81: II, No. 27, l. 7.
8. Olszowy-Schlanger 1998: No. 53, verso ll. 8-11.

find particular types of duress listed such as distress and enticement. Thus, at the very least, such marriage contracts afforded the woman safeguards against the sudden dissolution of her marriage and the loss of financial protection based on false claims of compulsion, entrapment or even a simple mistake.

3. *Mutuality*

Both Palestinian and Karaite marriage contracts incorporated a 'mutual' clause consisting of the husband's proposal clause (based on Exod. 21.10) and the bride's acceptance clause that mirrors it.[9] The aforementioned eleventh-century Palestinian formulary provides an ideal example:

> And he undertook to esteem, honor, nourish, provide for, and clothe her, in the manner of Jewish men who esteem, honor, nourish, provide for, and clothe their wives faithfully. Similarly, this X, daughter of master X, accepted and undertook to esteem, honor, attend and serve her husband in purity, in the manner of respectable women, the daughters of Israel, who esteem, honor, attend and serve their husbands in purity and cleanness.[10]

The section devoted to the Karaite wife's acceptance is even more extensive:

> And this bride Rivqa accepted the words of our beloved and dear El'azar, the groom, and wished to be married to him, to be his wife and companion in purity, holiness and awe, to obey, esteem, respect and help him, and to do in his house all that the pure daughters of Israel do in the house of their husbands, and to behave towards him in truth, justice, love, compassion, honesty and faith ...[11]

Here, too, scholars are in disagreement over the direction of influence. Olszowy-Schlanger proposes that contemporary Arabic contracts provided a model for the Karaites which, in turn, influenced Palestinian usage (Olszowy-Schlanger 1998: 268). Friedman again cites the fifth-century *ketubbah* from Antinoopolis as a Palestinian precedent (Friedman 2002: 175-76). Yet, in terms of the question of status, it is the very existence of such a clause that is most interesting, especially when the woman's semi-active role is compared to the near-silent female of the Babylonian-style *ketubbot*:

> 'Be my wife, [... And I will ...y]ou, in the manner of decent Jewish men, who serve, nourish, provide for, and honor [their wifes faithfully.' And this Lu'lu'a,] the [vir]gin, the bride, daughter of (our) m(aster and) l(ord) Shemarya [accepted his proposal] and became his wife.[12]

---

9. An Islamic marriage contract from the Cairo Genizah also reflects an arrangement of mutuality: 'The husband accepted that with a valid acceptance and each guaranteed to convey to the other what was required' (Khan 1993: No. 33, ll. 6x–8x).

10. Friedman 1980–81: II, No. 8, Side a ll. 11-15–Side b ll. 1-8.

11. Olszowy-Schlanger 1998: No. 26, ll. 17-19.

12. Friedman 1980–81: II, No. 21, ll. 18-20.

Other indications of mutuality are found in occasional expressions of marital love. An example of this appears in a fragmentary Palestinian-style contract from eleventh-century Egypt: '[…] their husbands in purity and cleanness, according to the law, in l[ove …]'.[13] A more frequently occurring quotation (based on Mal. 2.14) in Palestinian-style marriage contracts suggests a sense of companionship between husband and wife: '… to [m]arry this Mubā[raka(?) the bride,] the [virg]in, daughter of m(aster) Nathan, (may his) e(nd be) g(ood), b. Yeshuʻa [… to be] my companion and my wife in covenant'.[14] Karaite *ketubbot*, on the other hand, make regular reference to love, affection and companionship. Indeed, Olszowy-Schlanger writes that Karaite 'wifehood' was regularly defined in terms inspired from the Bible: 'his wife and his alliance' (Mal. 2.14) or 'his help' (Gen. 2.18) (Olszowy-Schlanger 1998: 207).

Reciprocal language also appears in the concluding clauses of twelve Palestinian-style marriage contracts: 'And with this understanding, the two sides concluded and consented, not being coerced nor compelled; and they told the scribe to write and the witnesses to testify.'[15] Nevertheless, despite such acknowledgments of the bride's wishes, perfect equality did not exist: the groom's formula is often recorded in first-person speech while the bride's is always reported in the third person. Moreover, the woman was ultimately obliged to obey her husband and, however much her language might mirror his, she was still under his dominion.

4. *Dowry*

It was not required that the contents of the bride's dowry be written into the marriage contract. Yet, thirty-five known Palestinian *ketubbot* and twenty-three Karaite *ketubbot* contain extensive, detailed lists of belongings on which, it seems, no item was too cheap or insignificant to be mentioned:

> … three mattresses and 18 cushions and a dress … 20 [?] din. / In addition a belt and 8 boxes of *khalanj* wood, a box … / a jug, a big bucket, two small cheap buckets, a chandelier … for wax … / and another one small, a small rose water bottle, a whitened container …[16]

According to biblical law (based on Num. 27.8), the woman did not normally inherit from her father's estate, but by the talmudic period, it had become common to regard the dowry as a 'practical substitute for succession' (Epstein 1927: 90-91). A dowry was usually worth a multiple of the value of the groom's marriage

---

13. Friedman 1980–81: II, No. 47, l. 1.
14. Friedman 1980–81: II, No. 20, ll. 5-6.
15. Friedman 1980–81: II, No. 26, ll. 17-19.
16. Olszowy-Schlanger 1998: No. 38, ll. 3-6.

payments; a common ratio was ten times as much, although figures were sometimes inflated to reflect well on the bride (Goitein 1967–93: IV, 186). Once provided, a woman's dowry was her husband's responsibility, but it remained under the wife's exclusive ownership and control throughout the marriage. Indeed, Palestinian-style contracts often contain the phrase 'And they are for her and for her son after her' at the end of the dowry list.[17] A few Palestinian contracts also state that should the wife predecease her husband and die childless, the dowry would be split in two and half would be returned to 'the house of her fathers'. In Karaite contracts, however, the whole dowry is to be returned to her paternal family:

> '... they will be under his jurisdiction, and in his possession ... and he will not change anything from them without the knowledge of his wife, this Ghāliya ... if, God forbid, this Ghāliya, the bride, leaves [this world without a child from this Thābit] ben Jacob, all these belongings, except for [what is worn out] will return [to her heirs from her paternal family]'.[18]

Karaite Jews were numbered among the upper echelons of the society that produced the Genizah documents, and this is reflected in the amounts of some of the marriage payments and dowries. In eight Karaite marriage contracts the groom's marriage payments total one hundred or more dinars, and seven Karaite dowries are worth over one hundred dinars (two are valued at more than a thousand dinars).[19] These were huge sums (even if inflated), given that the average monthly income was two dinars (Goitein 1967–93: I, 359). It is not surprising, therefore, that the bride's father (who often acted as her agent) would wish to have these items clearly delineated. Together with the groom's marriage payments, the dowry offered an insurance against financial destitution in widowhood and divorce; it may also have provided a disincentive to precipitous divorce action.[20]

Thus, in negotiating the couple's future together, every aspect of the bride's welfare was taken into account. Indeed, so detailed and comprehensive were these deeds that some brides stored their *ketubbah* with family or friends for safekeeping (Goitein 1967–93: III, 113-14). Again, the attention to detail in this section of Genizah marriage contracts underlines the practical and equitable nature of Jewish marriage in that society. Indeed, the rabbinic principle that 'any stipulation made with regard to financial matters is valid' is thoroughly applied here (Goitein 1967–93: II, 328).

17. See Friedman (1980-81: II, No. 2), for example.
18. Olszowy-Schlanger 1998: No. 37, ll. 26-31.
19. See the tables compiled by Olszowy-Schlanger (1998: 204, 238).
20. In 41 Palestinian contracts the groom's marriage gift was split into an advanced and a delayed payment, a practice that was probably influenced by local customs restricting the husband's unilateral right to divorce. See Rapoport (2000: 31-32).

5. *Divorce*

Contrary to standard practice, twelve Palestinian-style contracts contain a divorce clause.[21] Four of these, from Tyre, preserve evidence of a unilateral divorce formulation:

> ... and there remain incumbent upon him ten perfect, weighted dinars... She has no right to claim of them one *peruta* as long as he is alive and she is under his jurisdiction and he fulfills her three needs. But if he hates without any misconduct (on her part) and does not fulfill her three needs, he shall pay them to her, viz. the balance of her *mohar*, of twelve dinars, and release her with a bill of divorce.[22]

The unilateral divorce clause is positioned after the groom's financial obligations, perhaps to emphasize the penalty paid by the husband for a gratuitous divorce and thus to provide a further deterrent.

Jewish law only recognizes the right of the husband to initiate divorce (*m. Yeb.* 14.1). Yet a woman could 'rebel' and get the courts to compel the husband to divorce her if she relinquished her claim on her *ketubbah* payments. Such a practice is hinted at in the Jerusalem Talmud (*Ket.* v. 30b) and was later enacted by the Babylonian Saboraim who, according to the testimony of R. Meiri, based themselves on the Talmud when allowing a widespread custom to become general practice; it was overruled, however, by later authorities (Friedman 1969: 33-35).

Nevertheless, the ability of the wife to initiate divorce proceedings was prevalent in the Palestinian communities of the tenth to twelfth centuries. Eight manuscripts from Tyre and Egypt retain evidence of a mutual divorce clause. A similar practice also existed in the predominant Muslim society and was referred to as a 'ransom-divorce'.[23] Two manuscripts from the Cairo Genizah exhibit most of the wording of the mutual divorce clause; five contain incomplete evidence, and just one (probably from the tenth century) has a full version:

> If this Sa'īd, the groom, hates this Malīḥa, does not desire her, and wants to separate from her, he shall pay her all that is written and specified in this marriage contract completely. And if this Malīḥa hates this Sa'īd, her husband, and desires to leave his home, she shall lose her *ketubba* money, and she shall not take anything except that which she brought in from the house of her fathers alone; and she shall go out by the authorization of the court and with the consent of our masters, the sages.[24]

---

21. This is not without precedent. a divorce clause is found in a fifth-century BCE marriage contract from the Jewish military colony in Elephantine. See Jackson (2004) for a discussion of this document and the development of the wife's right to initiate divorce.

22. Friedman 1980–81: II, No. 11, ll. 15-20.

23. Most divorce cases in mediaeval Islamic society were the result of a consensual separation brought about by the wife forfeiting all or part of her financial claims (Rapoport 2005: 69-70).

24. Friedman 1980–81: II, No. 3, ll. 4-7.

Curiously, one of the fragmentary contracts contains the phrase 'gratuitous hatred' (derived from the unilateral divorce law) in the bride's half of the clause. This suggests that, in some cases, the bride could initiate a divorce and not lose her marriage payments if she could prove some misconduct on her husband's part.[25]

Three out of the eight documents known to contain the mutual divorce clause provide clear information about the bride's economic status. In two cases the bride owns a substantial dowry; in the third case, she was promised a large marriage gift, which may suggest that mutual divorce was limited to the affluent classes.[26] Accordingly, both sides would have required assurances against financial loss. Certainly, a woman would have needed to have independent means in order to forfeit her claim on the marriage payments that provided for her future security.

But the mutual divorce clause also reveals something of the woman's status in its language. Friedman noticed that these documents replaced the standard biblical phrase for divorce, which literally means 'drive out', with an Aramaic reference to 'partnership': 'If this Natha[n, the groom, hates] [this] Rachel, his wife, and does not desire her partnership—a gratuitous hatred, he shall pay her for all that is wr[itten and specified in this] marriage [contract], completely'.[27] The term 'partnership', Friedman believes, is indicative of a sense of equality underlying the marriage deed.[28]

6. Special Provisions

After recording the dowry, many ketubbot of the Palestinian tradition add stipulations about matters already addressed in Jewish law. For example, eight Palestinian-style contracts (again, mostly from Tyre) contain clauses relating to inheritance, burial or ransom. In addition, special circumstances are taken into account; for example, one unique but damaged eleventh-century manuscript preserves part of a proviso about the wife's mental health: 'And he stipulated for her: "If you go mad, [...] [...] your *ketubba* money..."'.[29] Another singular contract concerns the transfer of property from the bride's mother: 'And Turfa, the bride's mother, performed a *[qi]nyan* of herself, with an implement suitable for this (affirming) that she gave the third of the house'.[30]

---

25. Friedman 1980–81: II, No. 6, l. 14.
26. See Friedman 1980–81: II, Nos 1 and 3 and No. 2 respectively.
27. Friedman 1980–81: II, No. 2, ll. 31-34.
28. Friedman 1980–81: I, 330.
29. Friedman 1980–81: II, No. 2, ll. 37-38.
30. Friedman 1980–81: II, No. 38, l. 12

A number of contracts from the Genizah address the issue of 'mixed' marriages between Karaites and Rabbanites. In these clauses, the separate ritual practices of both sides were taken into account. An example is the marriage contract of a Karaite woman who is entering her third marriage:

> ... he shall not profane against his aforementioned wife [the festivals of the Lord] according to the sighting of the Moon, and he shall not light the Sabbath candles against her, and not force her in her food and drink ... ... And this Rayyisa accepted in favour of her aforementioned husband that she shall not profane against him the festivals of our brethren the Rabbanites all the time she is with him.[31]

With regard to which clauses were chosen for inclusion, no one Palestinian *ketubbah* was exactly like another. Thus, in this aspect of variability, the contracts are relatively equitable: the two parties and their individual circumstances are considered and a unique partnership is formed out of their specific negotiations.

7. Conclusions

A close examination of the marriage contracts from the Cairo Genizah reveals the common practice of including contractual clauses already existing in statutory law. Four factors may have motivated this practice. The first and primary consideration was economic: by including such clauses, the terms of the marriage contract provided financial protection for the bride in the event of widowhood or divorce. In the case of the dowry, the items listed there constituted an inheritance, and it is natural to assume that the paternal family wished to protect its assets. All parties concerned (the father providing the provisions, the husband assuming responsibility for them, and the wife reclaiming them) would no doubt feel reassured by their careful itemization.

A second impulse, not unrelated to the first, may have been an unconscious desire to provide further impediments to divorce. The addition of superfluous clauses like volition, the positioning of the divorce clauses, and the detailed provisions on the dowry may have reminded the parties of the requirements and penalties for initiating a divorce. Thirdly, it appears that Genizah society fully embraced R. Simeon b. Gamaliel's proposal (*m. Ket.* 6.4) that 'in all things they should follow local custom'. As we have seen, the clauses described herein were found in non-marriage documents as well as in contemporary Arabic legal deeds; some probably stemmed from earlier Palestinian traditions perhaps revived under the influence of the surrounding culture or, given the predominance of Tyrian contracts, were due to local or individual scribal practice.

---

31. Olszowy-Schlanger 1998: No. 56, ll. 32-35.

Finally, a sense of partnership must have been a motivating factor. By incorporating the contractual style of non-marriage deeds, the parties emphasized the bilateral nature of the agreement at hand. Furthermore, the addition of clauses unknown or only partially known in Jewish law, like the divorce clause, suggests that medieval Jewish women had far more equality in practice than a plain reading of the law would suggest. This relative equality of status is also evident in the language of the contracts, particularly in the actual use of the term 'partnership'.

In summary, the marriage contracts from the Cairo Genizah embodied the essence of rabbinic law which allowed for any agreement to be made between a husband and wife as long as it was in 'proper legal form and not contrary to Biblical law or public weal' (Epstein 1927: 269). In embracing this idea, the men and women of the mediaeval Mediterranean world established an elaborate but even-handed approach to realizing their future married lives together.

Friedman no.	Date (century 1)	Place of origin	Volition	Mutual clause	Dowry	Divorce clause	Special provisions specified
1	11	Egypt	√	√	774	√	√
2	11	Tyre	√	√	40+	√	√
3	10				456⅓	√	√
4	11			√		√	√
5					?	√	√
6	10/11	Egypt	√	√		√	√
7	11	Aleppo		√			√
11	11	Tyre	√	√	16+	√	
58		Tyre?			17+	√	
59	11/12	Tyre	√	√	?	√	
60	11	Tyre	√	√		√	
66						√	√

Fig. 1: *Table of Palestinian-style marriage contracts containing a divorce clause; based on Friedman 1980–81*

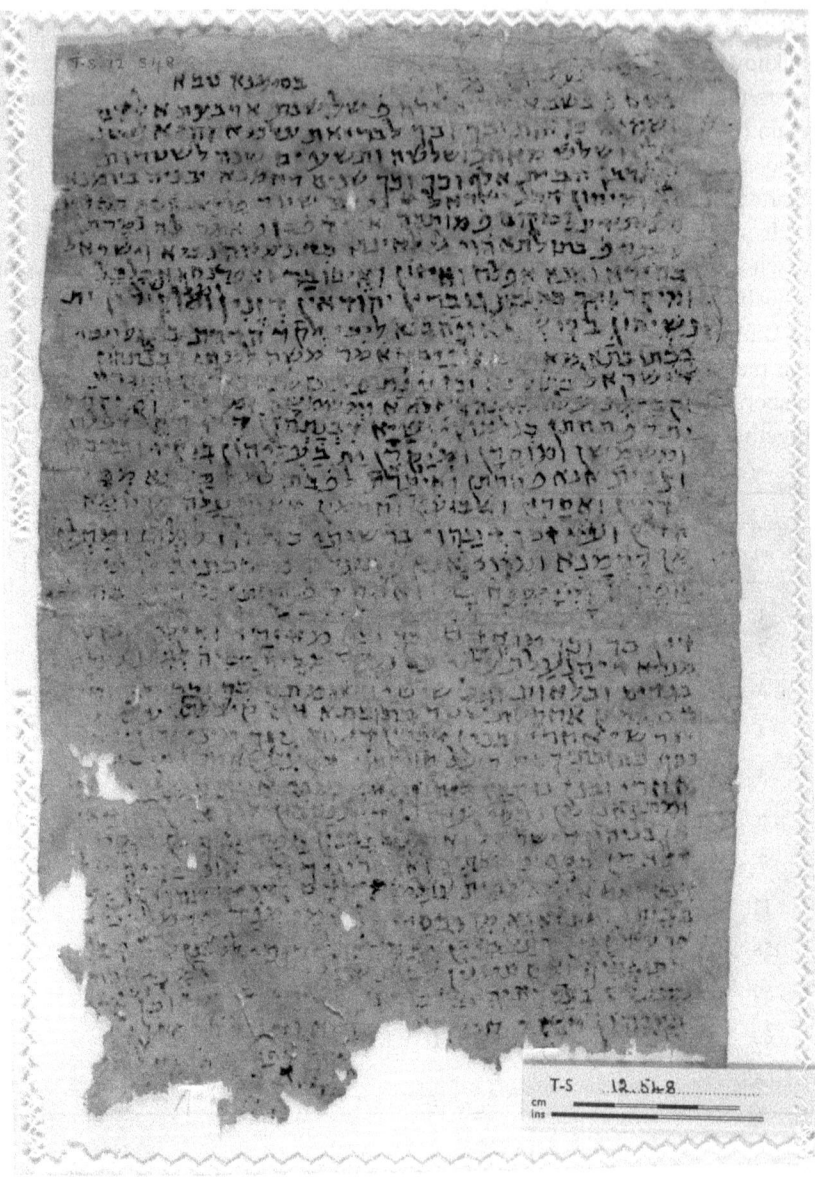

Fig. 2: *A marriage contract formulary 1081/2 containing half of the mutual divorce clause (CUL T-S 12.548). Reproduced by kind permission of the Syndics of Cambridge University Library.*

BIBLIOGRAPHY

Epstein, Louis M.
    1927   *The Jewish Marriage Contract: A Study in the Status of the Woman in Jewish Law* (New York: Jewish Theological Seminary of America).

Friedman, Mordechai Akiva
    1969   'Termination of the Marriage upon the Wife's Request: A Palestinian Ketubba Stipulation', *PAAJR* 37: 29-55.
    1980–81   *Jewish Marriage in Palestine: A Cairo Geniza Study* (2 vols.; Tel Aviv: Tel Aviv University, Chaim Rosenberg School of Jewish Studies; New York: Jewish Theological Seminary of America).
    2002   'Marital Age, Violence, and Mutuality', in Stephan C. Reif (ed.), *The Cambridge Genizah Collections: Their Contents and Significance* (Cambridge: Cambridge University Press): 160-77.

Goitein, Shelomoh D.
    1967–93   *A Mediterranean Society: The Jewish Communities of the Arab World as Portrayed in the Documents of the Cairo Geniza* (6 vols.; Berkeley: University of California Press).

Jackson, Bernard S.
    2004   'How Jewish is Jewish Family Law?', *JJS* 55: 201-29.

Khan, Geoffrey
    1993   *Arabic Legal and Administrative Documents in the Cambridge Genizah Collections* (Cambridge: Cambridge University Press).

Olszowy-Schlanger, Judith
    1998   *Karaite Marriage Documents from the Cairo Geniza: Legal Tradition and Community Life in Mediaeval Egypt and Palestine* (Leiden: E.J. Brill).

Rapoport, Yossef
    2005   *Marriage, Money and Divorce in Medieval Islamic Society* (Cambridge Studies in Islamic Civilization; Cambridge: Cambridge University Press).

Indexes

Index of References

Old Testament

Genesis		25.19-28	12	20–23	21
1–50	5, 49	25.22-23	53	20.10	24
1	31	29.24	46	21.2-6	39
1.27-28	30	29.29	46	21.2	42
1.28	25	29.35	53	21.4	40, 41, 44
2–3	6	30	6	21.5-6	40, 42
2	129	30.3-4	47	21.7-11	40, 41, 42,
2.16-17	12	30.3	46, 48, 49		43, 44
2.18	131, 166	30.9	47, 48	21.7	43
2.23	30	30.14-16	49	21.8	43
3	129, 130	30.20	48	21.9	43
3.2-3	12	32.23	47	21.10	28, 44, 49,
3.6	13	35.22	48		165
3.16	11, 130,	35.23-26	48	22.17 [H]	134
	133	38	5, 6	22.18 [H]	21
6	129, 133	39	48	22.19 [E]	21
6.1-4	133	46.8-19	48	25.20	60
15–17	107	46.19-24	48	29	70
15	107	48.3-19	48	29.4-6	67
16.1–18.15	6	49.3-4	48	29.4	70
16.1	46			32.12	58
16.2	46, 47, 48,	*Exodus*		37.9	60
	49	12.19	24	40.12-13	67
16.5-6	47	14.16-17	107	40.12	70
17	107	15.1-21	106	40.30-32	71
18	56, 117	15.1	106, 108		
18.1	117	15.8-9	107	*Leviticus*	
18.2	117	15.20-21	53	8.6-9	67
18.6	117	15.20	112	8.6	67, 71
18.7-8	117	15.21	106	11–15	71
18.9-10	117	19	69, 70	11.25	67, 72
21	6	19.10-11	69	11.28	67, 72
21.10	48, 50	19.11	67	11.40	67, 72
21.12	47	19.14	67	12	20, 21, 67,
25.6	48	19.15	69, 134,		73, 75, 77
25.19–27.40	6		135	12.1-5	130

12.2	73, 75	15.28-30	75	18.29	24, 25
12.4-5	73	15.28	76	18.30	22
12.4	76	15.30	76	19.1	22
12.6-8	73	15.31-33	73	19.20-22	42
12.8	76	16.4	67, 71	20	21, 25
13–14	72	16.24	67, 68, 71	20.1-5	25
13.6	67, 72	16.26	67, 71	20.6	25
13.28-37	72	16.28	67, 71	20.10-21	25
13.29	72	16.29	24	20.22	25
13.34	67, 72, 77	17	71	22.6	67
13.38-39	72	17.8-9	25	25	42
13.38	72	17.12-13	24	25.39-46	41
13.40-44	72	17.15-16	67, 72, 77	25.40	41
14	72	18	20, 21, 22, 23, 24, 25, 27, 28, 29, 31, 32, 35	25.41	41
14.7	77			25.44-46	45
14.8	67, 72			26	24, 25
14.9	67, 72			26.16-17	24
14.11	77	18.1-5	22, 24	26.18-20	24
14.14	77	18.1	22	26.21-22	24
14.47	67	18.2	23	26.23-26	24
15	21, 67, 69, 70, 73, 75, 76, 77, 78	18.3	23	26.33	25
		18.4	23		
		18.5	26	*Numbers*	
15.1-2	73	18.6-18	22, 26, 34	5	20, 21, 72
15.2-15	73	18.6	26, 29, 31	5.1-4	72
15.5	67, 70, 72	18.7-8	32	5.3	72
15.6	67, 72	18.7	32	5.6	72
15.7-12	74, 75	18.8	30	5.11-31	20, 77
15.7	67, 72	18.9	32	6	71
15.8	67, 72	18.10	32	8	70
15.10	67, 72	18.11	32	8.6-7	70
15.11	67, 72, 75	18.12	32	8.8-13	70
15.12	75	18.13	32	8.14	70
15.13	67, 72, 74	18.14	32	19	67, 71, 72
15.12-15	75	18.15	30, 32	19.7	67
15.14	76	18.16	30, 32	19.8	67, 71, 77
15.16-18	34, 73	18.17	32	19.10	67, 71, 77
15.16	67, 72, 74	18.18	33	19.19	67, 72
15.18	67, 72, 74, 78, 79	18.19-23	22	19.20	72
		18.19	34	19.21	67, 71
15.19-24	73	18.20-23	34	20.24	61
15.19-23	79	18.20	28	26.5	48
15.19	74	18.22	28	27.8	166
15.21	67, 72	18.23	26	27.14	61
15.22	67, 72	18. 24-30	22, 24	30	20, 21
15.24	34, 35, 74, 78, 79	18.25	25		
		18.26-28	25	*Deuteronomy*	
15.25-30	73	18.26	24	1.26	61
15.26-27	79	18.27	24	1.43	61
15.27	67, 72	18.28	25	7.1-5	113

Deuteronomy (cont.)		5.2-9	115	10.15	118		
7.2-5	116	5.2	113	10.16	119		
9.23	61	5.3	113	10.22-27	114		
15	42	5.4	113	10.22-26	119		
15.1	42	5.6	113	10.27	117		
15.12	42	5.8	118	10.28	116		
15.17	42	5.9	114	10.42	107		
20–21	115, 116	5.10-12	114	10.43	118		
20	116	5.10	118	11.4	118		
20.16-18	113, 116	5.13-14	107	11.11	116		
21.10-14	40, 44	6.1	116	11.15	115		
21.11	45	6.2-5	113	11.20	107		
21.13	45	6.3	113	11.23	115		
21.14	46	6.5	107	22.13-20	113		
22.13-21	20	6.6-11	113	23	108, 115		
22.29	46	6.7	113	23.2	106		
22.30 [E]	21	6.9	113	23.4	115		
23.1 [H]	21	6.13	113	23.6	115		
24.1-4	136	6.17	116	23.10	115		
24.1	136	6.20	107	23.14	115		
25.5-10	20	6.21	116, 118	24	108		
27.12-13	47	6.25	111	24.1-26	106		
27.20-23	21	6.26	114	24.1	106, 107		
31.12	135	6.27	117	24.2-15	113		
		7.1	116	24.3	115		
Joshua		7.5	118	24.4	115		
1-12	106, 108	7.11-13	116	24.6	115		
1.6	115	7.25-27	116	24.7	115		
1.8	113	7.25-26	114	24.8	115		
1.13-15	115	7.26	117	24.9	115		
1.14	110, 118	8.3	113	24.11	115		
1.18	61	8.11	113				
2	107, 110	8.19	116	*Judges*			
2.1	110, 116	8.25-26	118	4	107		
2.3-6	118	8.26	114, 116	4.17-21	113		
2.9-11	108, 110, 113	8.28	117	4.18	118		
		8.29	117	4.22	118		
2.14	111	8.30-35	106, 107	5	53, 107		
2.17-21	111	8.32-35	114	5.1-31	106		
3.8	113	8.35	106, 110, 118	5.1	108		
3.9-13	113			11.1-7	50		
3.13	107	9–12	119	11.34	106		
4.2-7	113	9.6-27	118	19	5		
4.7	114, 117	9.6	118				
4.13	113	10.6	118	*Ruth*			
4.14	117	10.7	113	2.19-20	53		
4.20-22	114	10.12-14	107	3.9	28		
4.23-24	117	10.12-13	107	4.17	93		
5.2-10	107	10.14	107				

Index of References

1 Samuel
1–2	53
17.48-54	107
18.6	106, 119
18.7	107
28.3	134

2 Samuel
1.19	107

1 Kings
8.7	60
13.21	61
13.26	61
20.35	91

1 Chronicles
2.34-35	48
5.1	48

2 Chronicles
15.12-15	107
28.15	156

Nehemiah
5	41
5.2	42
5.5	42

Job
5.27	60
28.3	60
28.27	60

Psalms
6.11	58
9.4	58
9.14	61
25.18	61
27.12	58
28.1	61
28.3-4	58
30.1	58
30.4	61
31.8	61
31.9	58
69.2-3	61
69.15-16	61
78.54-55	108
80.8-11	108
88.5-6	61
88.18	61
105.44-45	108
119.153	61
135.10-12	108
139.1	60
139.23	60
143.6	56
143.7	61

Proverbs
1–9	146, 147, 148, 149, 150, 151, 154, 157, 158
1.8	147
1.10	147
1.15	147
1.20-33	148
1.20	148
2.1	147
2.4	60
2.16-19	148
2.16	146, 150
2.18-19	150
3.1	147
3.11	147
3.21	147
3.29-31	148
4.5-9	147
4.10	147
4.11	150
4.20	147
5.1-14	148
5.3	146
5.5	150
5.8	147
5.15-23	147
5.17-20	151
5.17-19	148
5.18	153
5.20	146
6.1	147
6.3	147
6.20	147, 150
6.24	146, 150
7.4-5	147
7.4	147
7.5-23	151
7.5	146, 150
7.6-27	147, 148
7.6-23	147
7.7	146, 148, 150
7.8	147
7.9	150
7.10-19	150
7.10	148, 150
7.11-12	148
7.11	146
7.12	150
7.13	148
7.14-20	147, 148
7.16-17	150
7.16	151
7.17	151
7.18	151
7.21	155
7.24-27	147
8.1-36	148
9.13-18	146, 148
9.13	146
9.14-18	150
9.14	147, 150
9.15	147
9.16	146, 147
9.18	147
20.27	60
31	138
31.14	138

Isaiah
1.15	56
47.3	27
50.1	41

Jeremiah
4.31	56
9.19	91
22.20-22	61
30.14	61
34	41
34.9	42
34.14	42

Lamentations
1	63
1.2	59

Lamentations (cont.)		23.10	27	*Galatians*	
1.9	54, 56, 57, 58, 61	23.18	27	3.28	5
		23.22	61		
1.11-22	54	23.28	27	PSEUDEPIGRAPHA	
1.11	56, 57, 61	23.29	27	*1 Enoch*	
1.16	59			7.1	133
1.18-22	56	*Hosea*		8.1	133
1.18-20	57	2	28		
1.18-19	56, 62	2.9-10 [E]	28	*Jubilees*	
1.18	56, 57, 61	2.9 [E]	28	3	130
1.19	61	2.10 [E]	28	3.8-14	130
1.20	56, 57, 61, 63	2.11-12 [H]	28	3.24	130
		2.11 [H]	28	4.15	133
1.21-22	58	2.12 [H]	28	4.22	133
1.21	57, 58			5.1-2	133
1.22	56, 57	*Malachi*		5.6-11	133
2.4-5	58	2.14	166		
2.11	59			*Letter of Aristeas*	
2.18	59	APOCRYPHA		250	132
2.20-22	54, 56, 57	*Tobit*			
2.20	62	7.13	136	QUMRAN	
2.21	57, 61			*1QM*	
3	55, 56, 59, 63	*Judith*		7.3-6	140
		8.4-6	138		
3.1	57			*1QS*	
3.40-66	56	*Wisdom of Solomon*		7.12-14	152
3.40-44	60	8.2-16	153		
3.42-43	57			*1QSa*	
3.42	56, 57	*Wisdom of Ben Sira*		1.9-11	137
3.43-54	57	6.36	155		
3.43	57	7.19-26	157	*4Q184*	
3.46	57	15.1-10	153	1.1-17	151
3.48-51	59	25.13–26.18	157	1.2	150
3.48	61	25.24	129	1.3	150
3.49-50	58	42.9-14	154, 157	1.4-7	150
3.52-54	61	42.11-12	138	1.5-6	150, 151
3.52	57	51.13-21	146, 152, 156, 157, 158	1.5	150, 151
3.56	61			1.6	150
3.59-66	58			1.9-10	150
3.59	58	51.13-19	153	1.10-11	150
3.60	57	51.13	153	1.11	150
		51.19	156	1.12	150
Ezekiel		51.20	157	1.13-15	150
16.8	27	51.21	157	1.13-14	151
16.33	61	51.23-26	157	1.13	150, 151
16.36-37	27			1.14	150
16.36	61	NEW TESTAMENT		1.15	150
23	27	*1 Corinthians*		1.16-17	150
23.5	61	11.10	140	1.16	150
23.9	61			1.17	150

Index of References

4Q265
4Q265 141

11Q5
18.3-15 153
21 153
21.11–22.1 152
21.11-17 153, 156, 157
21.11 154, 157
21.12 154
21.14-15 158
21.14 153, 155, 158
21.15-16 155
21.15 153, 155
21.17 156

CD
15.15-17 140

MISHNAH
Ber.
3.3 141

Hag.
1.1 141

Ket.
4.9 164
6.4 170

Nid.
5.7 154

Par.
4.5 141

Pes.
8.1-3 141

Qid.
1.7 140

Šab.
2.6 133

Yeb.
14.1 168

Yom.
3.3 69

TALMUDS
b. B. Bat.
48b 164

b. Hag
3a 135

b. Qid.
80b 137

b. San
67b 134

y. Ket.
5.30b 168

y. San.
7.19 134
7.25d 134

y. Yeb.
15.3 136
15.14d 136

TOSEFTA
Qid.
1.10 140

Sot.
5.9 138

MIDRASHIM
Genesis Rabbah
17.8 133

Mekilta de Rabbi Ishmael
Yitro, Bahodesh
3 135

Mekilta de Rabbi Simeon b. Johai
22.17 134

PHILO
Dec.
32 134

Leg. all.
1.39 149
2.9-17 148
2.49 149
2.94-108 148
3.109-10 148

Op. mund.
151-52 131
151 131
152 131, 149
156 131
157-60 148
165 131

Sacr.
21–28 146, 148, 149, 157, 158
21 148, 149
23 148
26–28 148
26–27 149
26 148, 149

Spec. leg.
1.201 131
3.169-71 138

JOSEPHUS
Antiquities
1.49 130
3.78 134
4.219 137
12.11-118 129
15.259-60 136

Against Apion
2.52-54 129

Life
12 137

OTHER ANCIENT JEWISH WORKS
Abot de Rabbi Nathan
1.1 133

OTHER ANCIENT SOURCES
Code of Hammurabi
146-47	47
154	21
155	21
156	21
157	21
158	21
170-71	47

Hittite Laws
187	21
188	21
189	22
190	21, 22
191	22
195	22
199	21
200	21

Laws of Lipit-Ishtar
25-26	47

Middle Assyrian Laws
Tablet A	21

INDEX OF AUTHORS

Ackerman, S. 94
Aichele, G. 5
Allegro, J.M. 150
Alt, A. 84
Anderson, C. 20
Anzaldúa, G. 3
Assmann, J. 110
Avalos, H. 91
Avigad, N. 44

Bach, A. 20, 113
Bachofen, J.J. 87
Baer, R.A. 149
Bal, M. 113, 118
Balentine, S.E. 56
Baumgarten, J.M. 150
Baynes, L. 131
Be'er, I. 20
Beauvoir, S. de 4, 7
Bell, C. 68
Bem, S.L. 30
Berlin, A. 55, 59, 60, 61, 63
Bigger, S.F. 30, 32, 33, 34
Bird, P. 54, 84, 88, 111
Blank, S.H. 56
Bly, R. 145, 146
Bodenhorn, B. 94
Bourdieu, P. 112
Bowen, N.R. 91
Braun, J. 106
Brenner, A. 30, 31, 91, 106, 127
Brettler, M.Z. 53, 54
Brody, R. 137
Brown, C.A. 107
Brueggemann, W. 8, 9
Brumfiel, E.M. 89, 96
Budd, P. 24
Budde, K. 43
Burgmann, H. 150
Bush, F.W. 28

Buss, M. 97
Butler, J. 6, 7, 9, 29

Camp, C.V. 91, 146
Cardellini, I. 41
Carmignac, J. 150
Carter, C.E. 84, 91
Chapman, C.R. 115, 119
Charles, R.H. 126, 136
Chavel, S. 41
Chesnutt, R.D. 127, 128
Chirichigno, G.C. 42
Cixous, H. 11, 13, 14
Clifford, R.J. 146, 147
Clines, D.J.A. 114
Coggins, R.J. 152
Cohen, S.J.D. 76, 114
Cohn, C. 115
Connerton, P. 112
Cotton, H.M. 136, 137
Coulanges, N.F. de 87
Craven, T. 110
Crawford, S.W. 140
Cross, F.M. 146
Crumley, C.L. 88, 89, 95, 96, 97
Crüsemann, F. 41
Cushman, B.W. 94

Daly, M. 3
David, M. 42, 43
Davies, P.R. 137
Davis, N.Z. 109
Delcor, M. 152, 153
Dessel, J.P. 84
Deutsch, C. 157
Dever, W.G. 54, 84
Di Lella, A.A. 126, 152, 153, 157
Dobbs-Allsopp, F.W. 54, 59
Driver, S.R. 43

Earle, T. 89
Ehrenreich, R.M. 95
Eilberg-Schwarz, H. 110, 114
Eldredge, J. 146
Ellens, D.L. 73, 74, 75
Epstein, L.M. 166, 171
Esler, P.F. 84, 99
Exum, J.C. 108, 110

Fausto-Sterling, A. 31
Fewell, D.N. 26, 117
Fitzmyer, J. 128, 137
Fleishmann, J. 43, 44, 45
Fonrobert, C. 139
Fontaine, C.R. 91
Foucault, M. 11
Fox, M.V. 147
Freedman, H. 107
Fried, M. 89, 97
Friedman, M.A. 162, 163, 164, 165, 166, 167, 168, 169, 171
Frymer-Kensky, T. 20, 62, 76, 88
Fuchs, E. 88, 89

Gane, R. 68
Gaster, T.H. 150
Gazov-Ginzberg, A.M. 150
Gero, J.M. 95
Gerstenberger, E.S. 22, 23
Geyer-Ryan, H. 109
Gilchrist, R. 87
Gilders, W.K. 68
Gitin, S. 84
Goitein, S.D. 91, 167
Goldingay, J. 114
Goldstein, J.S. 115, 116
Gorman, F.H. 32
Gottwald, N.K. 84, 89, 93, 97
Grabbe, L.L. 126
Greenberg, M. 56
Gross, R.M. 87
Gunn, D.M. 26, 117

Harrington, D.J. 150
Harris, J.G. 107
Hartley, J.E. 23, 29, 32
Hartman, L.F. 126, 152
Hartum, A.S. 126
Havea, J. 20

Hawk, L.D. 114
Heim, K.M. 55
Hendel, R. 109, 114
Hirsch, M. 109, 110
Holladay, C.R. 129
Hollander, H.W. 127
Houtman, C. 47
Hudson, M. 41

Ilan, T. 134, 136, 137, 139
Instone Brewer, D. 137
Irigaray, L. 7, 8, 10, 11, 13, 14

Jackson, B.S. 39, 40, 41, 42, 43, 44, 45, 48, 49, 50, 107, 168
Jenson, P.P. 32
Johnson, A.W. 89
Jonge, M. de 127
Joosten, J. 23, 24, 26
Joyce, R.A. 94

Kahana, A. 126
Kaiser, B.B. 55
Kee, H.C. 128
Keller, C. 4
Kempinski, A. 107
Kessler, M. 42
Khan, G. 163, 165
Kidner, D. 147
King, E.M. 96
King, L.W. 47
King, P.J. 88, 90
Kirk, A. 109
Klijn, A.F.J. 126, 127
Knohl, I. 53
Kraemer, R.S. 110, 127, 128
Kramer, S.N. 59
Kray, S. 87
Kristeva, J. 10, 12, 13
Kruger, P.A. 28

LaBianca, Ø.S. 98
LaCocque, A. 127
Lamphere, L. 90
Lanahan, W.F. 54
Larranaga, C. 110
Lemche, N.P. 126
Leonardo, M. di 90
Lerner, G. 87

Index of Authors

Lévi, I. 152
Levine, B.A. 23, 24, 29, 30, 34
Levine, E. 43, 44
Levinson, B.M. 20
Levison, J.R. 129, 130
Levy, J.E. 95, 96
Leydesdorff, S. 109
Lipka, H.B. 24
Lipton, D.L. 48
Loader, W. 149
Longman, T. 146
Lorde, A. 3

Maccoby, H. 68
Maher, V. 93
March, K.S. 92, 93
Matthews, V.H. 20
Mattila, S.L. 131
Mayes, A.D.H. 84
McCloughry, R.K. 145
McCulloch, W.S. 95
McKane, W. 146, 147
McNutt, P.M. 84, 89, 90
Meacham, T. 76
Mendelsohn, I. 41, 91
Mendenhall, G.E. 84, 89
Meyers, C. 54, 84, 85, 90, 91, 92, 93, 94,
    97, 106, 109, 110, 111, 112, 129
Milgrom, J. 23, 24, 32, 66, 67, 68, 72, 75
Milik, J.T. 127, 129
Miller, C.W. 57
Miller, R.D. 97
Minsky, M. 95
Mintz, A. 55, 56
Mitchell, G. 114
Mohrmann, D.C. 24, 30
Moore, M.S. 107
Moore, R.D. 150
Muraoka, T. 153, 154, 155, 156, 157
Murphy, R.E. 146, 147
Myers, J.M. 126

Nelson, J.B. 145
Nelson, R.D. 114
Nelson, S.M. 98
Neubauer, J. 109
Neufeld, E. 43, 45
Neusner, J. 129
Newman, J.H. 56

Newsom, C. 4
Nielsen, K. 28
Nir, R. 127
Noth, M. 84

O'Connor, K.M. 55
Oesterley, W.O.E. 152
Olszowy-Schlanger, J. 163, 164, 165, 166,
    167, 170
Olyan, S.M. 28

Papert, S. 95
Passerini, L. 109
Pedersen, J. 84
Philip, T.S. 20
Phillips, A. 21
Pirson, R. 48, 49
Plaskow, J. 69, 98, 114, 134
Poethig, E.B. 106
Polzin, R. 113
Porten, B. 136
Potter, D.R. 96
Pressler, C. 20, 42

Qimron, E. 137
Quinn, N. 90

Rabinowitz, I. 152, 153, 155, 156
Rapoport, Y. 167, 168
Rattray, S. 30
Reid, D.G. 145
Renkema, J. 60
Ringe, S.H. 4, 88
Rogers, R.J. 96
Rogers, S.C. 93
Rogerson, J.W. 88
Rooke, D.W. 21
Roth, M.T. 21, 43, 47
Rothstein, D. 137
Rowbotham, S. 87
Rowlett, L.L. 108
Ruane, N. 35
Ruether, R.R. 5, 99

Saller, R.P. 87
Sanders, J.A. 152, 153, 155, 156
Sarna, N.M. 44
Sauer, G. 153
Sawyer, D.F. 5, 6

Scattolin, C.M. 95
Schäfer-Lichtenberger, C. 86
Schearing, L. 20
Schenker, A. 33
Schloen, J.D. 86, 88
Schor, N. 7
Schremer, A. 137
Schuller, E.M. 140, 150
Schüssler Fiorenza, E. 4
Schwartz, S. 129
Seeman, D. 117, 118, 119
Seibert, I. 106
Service, E. 89
Shemesh, A. 139
Sheppard, G.T. 59
Sivan, H. 20
Skehan, P.W. 152, 153, 157
Sly, D. 131, 148, 149
Small, D.B. 96
Smend, R. 152
Smith, M.S. 63
Smith, V. 109, 110
Smith, W.R. 84, 87, 88
Snaith, J.G. 152
Solvang, E.K. 94
Spencer, H. 84
Stade, B. 87
Stager, L.E. 88, 90
Stanton, E.C. 2, 4
Starn, R. 109
Stein, G.J. 89
Steinberg, N. 84
Stone, L. 33
Stone, M.E. 132
Strack, H.L. 152
Strathern, A.J. 112
Strugnell, J. 150
Sweely, T.L. 93

Taqqu, R.L. 92, 93
Taylor, J.E. 137
Thompson, P. 109
Tosato, A. 45
Toy, C.H. 146, 147
Trenchard, W.C. 130
Trexler, R.C. 115

Trible, P. 4, 5, 108

Van Seters, J. 45
VanderKam, J.C. 127, 129, 133, 139, 151, 152
Vaux, R. de 88
Vermes, G. 149, 150, 152

Wailes, B. 96
Walker, A. 3
Washington, H.C. 114, 115, 116
Wassen, C. 21
Wassersfall, R.R. 80
Watkins, T.F. 41
Weber, M. 84, 86
Weed, E. 7
Wegner, J.R. 21, 66, 70, 74, 76, 77, 131, 149
Weinfeld, M. 41, 42
Wellhausen, J. 84, 88
Wenham, G.J. 73, 74
Werline, R.A. 56
West, C. 109, 110
Westbrook, R. 42, 44, 45, 46, 47
Westermann, C. 60
Wharton, A.S. 30
White, J.C. 96
Whybray, R.N. 146, 147
Whyte, M.K. 94
Wills, L.M. 127
Winston, D. 153
Wright, D.P. 68, 70, 75
Wright, J.E. 84

Yadin, A. 139
Yadin, Y. 136, 152
Yardeni, A. 136
Yee, G.A. 113
Younger, K.L. 119

Zagarell, A. 96, 98
Zevit, Z. 98
Ziegler, J. 152, 156
Zimmerman, D.H. 109, 110
Zlotnick, H. 127
Zonabend, F. 93

www.ingramcontent.com/pod-product-compliance
Lightning Source LLC
Chambersburg PA
CBHW071421160426
43195CB00013B/1768